Race, Gender, and Punishment

Critical Issues in Crime and Society
Raymond J. Michalowski, Series Editor

Critical Issues in Crime and Society is oriented toward critical analysis of contemporary problems in crime and justice. The series is open to a broad range of topics including specific types of crime, wrongful behavior by economically or politically powerful actors, controversies over justice system practices, and issues related to the intersection of identity, crime, and justice. It is committed to offering thoughtful works that will be accessible to scholars and professional criminologists, general readers, and students.

Mary Bosworth and Jeanne Flavin, eds., *Race, Gender, and Punishment: From Colonialism to the War on Terror*

Raymond J. Michalowski and Ronald C. Kramer, eds., *State-Corporate Crime: Wrongdoing at the Intersection of Business and Government*

Susan L. Miller, *Victims as Offenders: The Paradox of Women's Violence in Relationships*

Susan F. Sharp, *Hidden Victims: The Effects of the Death Penalty on Families of the Accused*

Robert H. Tillman and Michael L. Indergaard, *Pump and Dump: The Rancid Rules of the New Economy*

Mariana Valverde, *Law and Order: Images, Meanings, Myths*

Michael Welch, *Scapegoats of September 11th: Hate Crimes and State Crimes in the War on Terror*

Race, Gender, and Punishment

FROM COLONIALISM TO THE WAR ON TERROR

MARY BOSWORTH
JEANNE FLAVIN
EDITORS

RUTGERS UNIVERSITY PRESS
New Brunswick, New Jersey, and London

LIBRARY OF CONGRESS CATALOGING-IN-PUBLICATION DATA

Race, gender, and punishment: from colonialism to the war on terror/edited by
Mary Bosworth and Jeanne Flavin.
    p. cm. — (Critical issues in crime and society)
    Includes bibliographical references and index.
    ISBN-13: 978-0-8135-3903-4 (hardcover: alk. paper)
    ISBN-13: 978-0-8135-3904-1 (pbk.: alk. paper)
    1. Discrimination in criminal justice administration—United States—History.
2. Punishment—United States—History.   3. United States—Race relations—History. I. Bosworth, Mary. II. Flavin, Jeanne, 1965– III. Series.
    HV9950. R333   2007
    364.608'0973—DC22   2006010513

A British Cataloging-in-Publication record for this book is available from
the British Library

This collection copyright © 2007 by Rutgers, The State University

Individual chapters copyright © 2007 in the names of their authors

Manufactured in the United States of America

Mary: For my parents
Jeanne: For Pierre

Contents

ACKNOWLEDGMENTS

THIS BOOK HAS BEEN A LONG TIME IN THE MAKING, and it is testimony to the patience of the contributors and to their shared belief in the importance of this topic that it is finally complete. We would like to thank each author for their original contribution and the time and care they have taken in writing and revising their manuscripts. Considering the historical, theoretical, and policy implications of the intersections of race, gender, and punishment in the United States is a demanding challenge, and one to which the authors in this collection have responded gamely. We hope that this book will inspire its readers not only to think deeply about the problems of contemporary and historical America, but to think differently. A persistent theme across the chapters is the need to break free from disciplinary boundaries and topics, to reimagine the task of the criminologist. Only in this way may it be possible to redress some of the inequalities that so characterize U.S. society and the nation's system of punishment. We hope this book contributes to this task.

We have enjoyed working with Rutgers University Press, particularly editor Adi Hovav and series editor Ray Michalowski, who have supported the project from the outset. Thanks also goes to editorial assistant Beth Kressel, copyeditor Paula Friedman, and production editor Nicole Manganaro. We would also like to thank Claire Renzetti for her longstanding interest in this book, and Stephanie Bush-Baskette for her involvement in the early stages of this collection. Artist Chuck Waldo designed the striking cover, solely on the basis of email messages about the content of the book; we also thank Seth Ferranti and Diane Schulte for putting us in touch with Chuck. We could not have finished this project without the competent and good-humored editorial and administrative assistance of Amy Desautels, Rosa Giglio, Paula Genova, Julie DiMatteo and Natalie Cordero of Fordham University's department of sociology and anthropology.

Mary would like to thank Professor Denis Galligan for providing intellectual sanctuary at the University of Oxford Centre for Socio-Legal Studies, and a welcome respite from the vicissitudes of life in America. For her part, much of the editing occurred while a visiting fellow at Wolfson College, Oxford, and at the University of Oxford Centre for Socio-Legal Studies in

2004/2005, while the final touches were done following her appointment to the Katzenbach Research Fellowship at the same institution. Mary would also like to thank Anthony, who was, as usual, supportive of and interested in her project, despite being absent in the United States for at least part of it. Her daughter Ella also provided much-needed distraction and love, as did her parents, with whom she was all too briefly reunited during their joint sabbatical in Oxford.

Jeanne is grateful to the Bosworth-Gerbino family; time spent with Mary, Anthony, and Ella served as a wonderful antidote to some of the more tedious aspects of editing this volume.

Fordham University gave Jeanne well-timed course relief and a grant to cover some editorial expenses. Jeanne is also keenly grateful to many of her colleagues in the Fordham's department of sociology and anthropology, but especially to Dr. Mary Powers, whose sane voice and imminent reason helped Jeanne to see her way clear when administrative duties began to take their toll. Similarly, Jeanne owes a great debt to her friends, especially Miki Akimoto, Hugo Benavides, and Ed Gallagher, whose fine minds are matched only by their sense of the absurd, and their unfailing confidence and support.

Mary would like to dedicate this collection to her parents, in recognition of their emotional and intellectual support as well as their good humor and love, without all of which she would be quite at sea. Jeanne dedicates the book to Pierre Diaz, who taught her not to be afraid to write like she cares.

Race, Gender, and Punishment

INTRODUCTION

Race, Control, and Punishment

FROM COLONIALISM TO THE GLOBAL WAR ON CRIME

Mary Bosworth and Jeanne Flavin

A TROUBLING RELATIONSHIP exists among race, social control, and punishment. This relationship manifests itself in myriad ways, from the demographic characteristics of penal populations to race differentials in sentencing. It also appears in forms harder to measure, such as institutional racism in police departments, or, more difficult still, public fears and assumptions about minorities.

Typically, criminologists interested in race begin by enumerating the disproportionate representation of minorities in the criminal justice system. "One out of three young black men is in prison or on probation or parole," we are told, or "There are more young black men in prison than in college." Less often, the rapidly growing number of Hispanics under the control of the criminal justice system or the devastating impact of the war on drugs on black women and Latinas is mentioned. In attempting to explain these phenomena, researchers try to determine whether police target minorities, whether judges are more punitive when dealing with people of color, or whether prison or probation officers vary their treatment depending on the race or ethnicity of the men and women they supervise.

The widespread overrepresentation of minorities in penal systems that occurs around the world is nowhere more evident than in the United States. Since 1989, the number of black people incarcerated has surpassed that of whites, even though black men and women constitute only around 13 percent of the general population. According to the most recent figures available, in midyear 2004, 43 percent of the 1.9 million men in state or federal prisons or in jail were counted as black, 36 percent as white, and 19 percent as Hispanic. In women's institutions, 45 percent of the 183,400 inhabitants were listed as white, 37 percent as black, and 16 percent as Hispanic (Harrison and Beck 2005).

Statistics such as these provide vital empirical information about race and gender in the criminal justice system. Without them, the nature and scope of the overrepresentation of minorities in all segments of the justice process would remain unknown and unacknowledged. Approaching the relationship among race, punishment, and social control in this fashion, however, often unintentionally reifies essentialist assumptions about race. Terms such as "black" and "white" become static and self-evident, despite the fact that ideas about the nature of difference are socially constructed and historically situated. In the process, scholars tend to treat gender and race disparities in punishment and criminal processing as distinct from other forms of social control operating elsewhere in society. Yet the same forces that render young black men vulnerable to supposedly random police stop-and-searches, namely racial profiling, also help determine a whole range of other social relations including who is allowed to enter the country, which women are encouraged or discouraged from reproducing, and how indigenous or foreign cultural expression is valued.

Using the existence of the disproportionate numbers of minority men and women in the nation's prisons and jails as a starting point, the chapters in this book examine distinct historical periods and communities. By considering the influence of four sociohistorical processes—colonialism, slavery, immigration, and globalization—the authors point to the structural and cultural factors shaping public sentiment and criminal justice policy. In doing so, they reveal how ideas and practices of punishment both depend on and uphold a whole series of wider social practices and beliefs. The prison and other forms of official social control, in other words, not only require particular (if unspoken) ideas about race to exist, but also legitimate them.

In examining the legacy of colonialism and slavery, we can see, for example, continuities in ideas about indigenous and African American populations that reveal the prison to be merely one of many systems of social control structuring people's lives. Similarly, inspections of recent legislation about immigration suggest that the present levels of fear and suspicion of foreigners are not entirely new, but are as much a part of the United States as are the Statue of Liberty and Ellis Island. Finally, by looking beyond the borders of the United States, we can learn how the forces of globalization are both exporting U.S. ideas about punishment and drawing specific populations into the nation's prisons and detention centers.

COLONIALISM

Colonialism refers to the extension of a nation's sovereignty over territory and people both within and outside its own boundaries, as well as the beliefs used to legitimate this domination. Colonialism not only has economic consequences, insofar as it makes it easier to dominate another group of people's resources and labor, but it has cultural consequences as well. In particular, the sense of cultural or racial superiority that accompanies colonialism makes it easier to justify the mistreatment or discrimination of the colonized.

Criminologists have, for the most part, paid little attention to colonialism as a set of practices and ideas. Although of course some have examined the crime, punishment, or policing of groups such as Native Americans and Latinos, rarely have they done so in light of an historical and ideological appreciation of the forces of colonialism (but see Ross 1998). Given the existence and influence in other disciplines of postcolonial studies, such silence over the ideological component of this form of inequality is curious (for two classic studies, see: Bhabha 1994; Said 1993).

Colonialism, like each of the factors that underpin this collection, operates both structurally, through particular institutions, and ideologically, through culture and the construction of the imaginary. The seizing of land from Native Americans, Mexicans, and others had to be justified, as did these peoples' subsequent misery and maltreatment. Views of the innate superiority of the settlers, whether based on religion, science, or simply raw economic greed, had to be constantly shored up and legitimated. The criminal justice system, then as now, played a pertinent role in this exercise, as it was used to mark out, shame, and punish those designated as unworthy. It did not operate alone, however; instead, laws and punitive practices were often backed up or integrated within other institutions and practices, like wars, the treaties that followed wars, religious instruction, and merchants' practices. Ideas of race and gender proved particularly crucial in shoring up these configurations of power (Donaldson 1992; Lewis and Mills 2003).

The goal of the first section of the book is not to identify one sole cause of the historical and contemporary treatment of colonized peoples in and beyond the United States, but rather to point to how certain ideas of cultural superiority infiltrated criminal justice practice both in the past and present, and continue to shape penal practices and beliefs today. Chapter 1, "Situating Colonialism, Race, and Punishment," provides a theoretical discussion and historical overview of colonialism in the Americas. Focusing attention on the ways indigenous cultural practices were often criminalized, Geeta Chowdhry and Mark Beeman suggest that the construction of "crime" overlapped with perceptions of race, class, and gender relations to sustain and legitimize colonial power relations. In turn, they point to the ongoing impact of these historical relations on ideas and practices of punishment today.

Chapter 2, "Ordering the Other: Reading Alaskan Native Culture Past and Present," demonstrates how culture and the freedom to express traditions and beliefs are crucial to strategies both of domination and of resistance. Using nineteenth-century narratives from a settler woman and from a retired general, Cyndi Banks examines Euro-American depictions of Alaskan Natives during the early colonial period, how cultural differentiation was practiced, and how Alaskan Natives have preserved their cultures through adaptation and resistance. In chapter 3, "Colonialism and Its Impact on Mexicans' Experiences of Punishment in the United States," Martin Urbina and Leslie Smith draw upon the example of Mexico to show how the lingering effects of colonialism influence criminal justice policy today. Historically, white Americans have vilified the populations they colonized; Mexicans, like Native Americans, were thought undeserving of the land they occupied. Today, Mexicans in the United States are similarly maligned. Frequently represented in the media as illegal immigrants or gang members, they are subject to heavy police scrutiny and are incarcerated in disproportionate numbers.

SLAVERY

Slavery is a criminal activity that is outlawed by United Nations (UN) conventions, though it continues in some form across a number of societies. It involves total domination, usually to secure the labor of an individual or a group. Control is enforced by actual or threatened violence and by other forms of coercion. Historically, slave states in the United States were based on chattel slavery, in which individual women and men were the legal property of others.

Since the 1980s, it has become reasonably commonplace in the U.S. academy to recognize the contemporary effects of the system of chattel slavery. Historians, sociologists, literary theorists, and even criminologists (Myers 1998; Walker 2003) have provided manifold evidence of the contemporaneous and current devastation wreaked by the "peculiar institution." Even so, it remains worth stating that racial disparities in the twenty-first century owe their form and nature, in part, to an institution over three hundred years old.

The significance of slavery, like that of colonialism, lies not only in its barbarous practices, but also in the ideas that it generated. Based commonly on a mixture of pseudoscience and religion, although generally underpinned by an unchecked desire for economic gain, slavery established insidious cultural constructions of racial inferiority that have yet to disappear. Stock figures such as the mammy, the male sexual predator, and the promiscuous, lascivious black woman permeated U.S. culture, and remain evident today (Collins 1990). It is in fact the very banality and everyday nature of these constructions that makes them hardest to pin down as the causes of structural inequalities that so shape black and white relations today. It is perhaps for this reason that criminologists concerned with race, though focusing on the treatment and experiences of African Americans, have tended to favor quantitative explanations over cultural ones. The three chapters in the second section strive to alter this tendency by tracing the impact of slavery on contemporary views about race, gender, and punishment.

In chapter 4, "Multiple Jeopardy: The Impact of Race, Gender, and Slavery on the Punishment of Women in Antebellum America," Vernetta Young and Sharon Spencer document how sex and race, as well as status and class, influenced what crimes were punished and the form official sanctions took. In particular, they point out the ways in which the "cult of true womanhood" which protected many white women effectively excluded all black women. As a result, black women were not able to lay claim to any of the benefits of their gender, but were instead condemned because of their race.

The fifth chapter, "We Must Protect Our Southern Women": On Whiteness, Masculinities, and Lynching," provides support for structured action theory and its emphasis on the situational salience of gender, race, class, age, and sexuality in the commission of crime and in responses to it. In this chapter, James Messerschmidt articulates the relationship among large-scale social change, racial masculinities, and lynching during Reconstruction and its immediate aftermath (1865–1900) in the U.S. South. Through the practice of mob lynching, white supremacist men constructed a specific type of "pure" and "good" white masculinity that was juxtaposed against "impure" and "evil" black masculinity. Mob lynchings permitted white supremacist men to attain status, reputation, and self-respect while disclaiming an African American man's right to citizenry, freedom, or self-determination.

Throughout the world, practices amounting to a form of slavery continue to exist (e.g., trafficking in persons, servile marriage, sweatshop labor rings, forced labor, and debt bondage: the exploitation of domestic and migrant labor). In the United States, we also see the vestiges of slavery in the modern-day social control of black women. Such issues are dealt with in chapter 6, "Slavery's Legacy in Contemporary Attempts to Regulate Black Women's Reproduction." Here, Jeanne Flavin demonstrates how slavery's legacy of paternalism and stereotyping continues to exert its influence through the regulation of black women's ability to conceive, bear, and raise children. By stigmatizing and controlling the behaviors of a subordinate group, paternalistic practices permit us to justify the punitive treatment of a black woman "for her own good." Similarly, stereotypes about black women's unreliability and immorality make it easier to justify separating mothers from their children through incarceration and other forms of involuntary separation.

IMMIGRATION

Immigration refers to the act of moving to or settling in another country or region, either temporarily or permanently. Legal immigrants to the United States (as contrasted with visitors or travelers) come to join family members, to work, or, in a fraction of cases, as refugees. On March 1, 2003, the Homeland Security Act of 2002 abolished the Immigration and Naturalization Service and moved its responsibilities to three agencies within the Department of

Homeland Security: the U.S. Citizenship and Immigration Services (USCIS), Immigration and Customs Enforcement (ICE), and Customs and Border Patrol (CBP). CBP deals specifically with border-related activities and generally detains people for short periods of time; ICE, by contrast, has become the second largest federal investigative agency, and picks up all enforcement activities that fall beyond the purview of CBP; ICE also is the agency charged with deporting undocumented people within the United States. The service aspects of the INS were left fairly intact, with the transfer of responsibility for processing immigration-related services like green cards, asylum, and naturalization to USCIS. The immigration-enforcement part of INS, however, was merged with U.S. Customs, the responsibilities divided between ICE and CBP. This has led to no small degree of confusion and competition over "turf." These changes in the INS and in immigration legislation in the United States over the past decade have made clear what has long been the case: that citizenship and punishment are intricately linked. Particularly since September 11, 2001, but also well before that date, foreigners have been peculiarly subject to surveillance, control, and detention.

Unlike colonialism and slavery—both practices founded on thinly disguised violence and brutality—immigration potentially benefits those who immigrate as well as the nation that hosts them. Many immigrants settle happily and succeed in their host country and so the relationship between immigration and punishment is somewhat complicated to identify. The United States has always been notably receptive to foreign-born populations willing to work. To that extent, economics was for many years the primary motivator for immigration policy. Simple financial and mercantile need, however, was never the sole factor in determining who was welcome and who was not. Instead, certain populations were completely excluded, were accepted in small numbers, or had their actions and rights strictly controlled. Immigration, was, in other words, an effective means of dividing and defining the population of workers. More than that, however, similar ideas of U.S. cultural superiority to those characterizing colonialism have always impacted newly arrived foreigners, as has also the racist binary of slavery for those considered not white.

Following the upheaval and mass immigration that occurred during and after the Second World War, immigration policies in the United States have become increasingly shaped by cultural concerns. Who will assimilate? Who is trustworthy? Who is a risk? Where possible, the United States, like so many other countries, has sought to exclude unwanted foreigners before they arrive; interceptions on the high seas, border refusal, airline return have all been and remain common practice. At the same time, however, for those individuals who either managed to infiltrate the border or who, once allowed in, were found to be problematic, the prison has become the inevitable site of confinement.

In chapter 7, "Immigration, Social Control, and Punishment in the Industrial Era," Kitty Calavita sets the discussion against an historical backdrop of immigration and social control in the United States. Focusing on the interconnections between the labor market and immigration policy, Calavita reveals how opinions of the merits of foreigners closely follow economic factors. When jobs are plentiful, borders are open; when they are not, borders close. To justify changes in policy, the public and the government often invoke particular visions of race and ethnicity. Thus, Chinese immigrants were initially prized for their supposed capacity for back-breaking labor; when there was no longer a need for them, scaremongering about their cultural differences and inadequacies was rife.

The next two chapters in this section address aspects of the United States government's response to immigrants after September 11, 2001, and continue the discussion of how punishment and citizenship have become intricately linked. In chapter 8, "Identity, Citizenship, and Punishment," Mary Bosworth considers the current role of the prison and detention center in shaping and safeguarding America's borders. Bosworth observes that the prison and detention center seems to have acquired new vibrancy and enhanced legitimacy, in effect becoming the "new borderlands" where identity has become a measure of security, and anyone diverging from the norm is viewed as a potential threat.

In chapter 9, "Immigration Lockdown before and after 9/11: Ethnic Constructions and their Consequences," Michael Welch asserts that, since the mid-1990s, the United States has been engaged in a moral panic with regard to illegal immigrants that has led to the criminalization of certain ethnic minorities. The law enforcement sweeps and mass detentions in the wake of September 11, 2001, are not new phenomena, but rather reflect a continuation and expansion of earlier punitive tactics. Welch examines the consequences of constructing certain minorities as "criminals." In particular, he presents some of the practical problems associated with the INS/ICE's heavy reliance on detention as a key mechanism of social control.

Globalization

Globalization has been called "the new colonialism." Generally speaking, globalization refers to the period after the collapse of the Berlin Wall and the thawing of the Cold War in 1989. Like the term "colonialism," "globalization" refers not only to the processes of economic and cultural expansionism, but also to the ideas that justify these processes and ways of thinking about them (Stiglitz 2003; Winant 2004). Technological, military, and political developments of the past two decades have created a world in which we are no longer as constrained by national borders (Bauman 2000). Industries have moved offshore in search of cheaper labor and bigger markets, while, as the sole remaining "superpower," the United States has exported its particular brand of military might and neoconservative politics.

In many respects, globalization ties together all the previous issues of colonialism, slavery, and immigration. Driven by factors from each, and exacerbating the inequalities of all, it characterizes the current state, as well as the domestic and foreign policies of, the world. One of the key issues that globalization renders most clear is the paradox of agency. For, as with immigration, there are some positive effects of globalization: opening markets, spreading economic wealth, and so on, may not be intrinsically problematic. New industries provide employment, particularly for women in many developing countries. The difficulty seems to lie in the power of each nation and its people to determine the shape and nature of the economic relations being thrust upon them. Sweatshops on the border with Mexico not only are economically oppressive, but have exacerbated race and gender inequalities, resulting in increased violence against the predominantly female workforce, and in allegations of a new form of slavery. Likewise, demands made by the World Bank when determining loans to developing countries often seem out of step with those nations' priorities and needs.

Although scholars typically associate globalization with purely economic concerns, contributors to this section show both how the United States is exporting its methods of punishment globally, and also how economic factors associated with global capital render specific populations at risk for punishment within and outside the borders of the United States. Lisa Sanchez introduces the final section in chapter 10, "The Carceral Contract: From Domestic to Global Governance," by documenting similarities between the treatment of gang members on U.S. streets and that of those deemed to be terrorists. According to Sanchez, current rhetoric about the war on terror is reinscribing and bolstering constructions of race and identity that have long existed in the United States. In doing so, the fear and anger about external threats is turned back to deal with internal, locally grown problems of civil disorder and gang affiliation. In the end, it is again young men of color who suffer the consequences.

In chapter 11, "Latina Imprisonment and the War on Drugs," Juanita Díaz-Cotto places the war on drugs in an international context to reveal how women of color are being swept behind bars in Europe, the Americas, and the United States. Building on her groundbreaking earlier work on Puerto Rican prisoners in New York State, Díaz-Cotto shows how ideas of gender and race are intersecting in the implementation of policies that were ostensibly designed to punish high-level drug offenders, to the detriment of Latinas not only in the United States but in Mexico, Bolivia, and elsewhere. Most Latinas play only marginal roles in the drug trade; once incarcerated, these women are further punished by being held in institutions with little or no programming or assistance.

Continuing in this vein, Vivien Miller analyzes attempts to export U.S.-style supermax prisons. Chapter 12, "Tough Men, Tough Prisons, Tough

Times: The Globalization of Supermaximum Secure Prisons," begins with a discussion of the development of the supermax before turning to examine its contemporary form in a global context. Comparing what is known about institutions in the state of Florida and in the U.S. naval base at Guantánamo Bay, Cuba, Miller argues that the supermax not only tends to depend on and uphold certain ideas about race, but also legitimates a particular vision of masculinity.

CONCLUSION

Just as we have learned that punishment is an expression of historically contingent sensibilities (Garland 1990), ideas of race, of difference, of "Other," and of belonging play into our strategies of how to respond to crime. As the contributors to this collection demonstrate, to appreciate how ideas of difference underpin punitive sentiments and practices, we need to expand our gaze from the usual criminal justice agencies to include more diffuse forms of social control. We also need to be aware of the historical and global context of contemporary policies. There is growing recognition among scholars and the larger public that our corrections system could not survive in its current form in the absence of widely shared racialized assumptions about who is criminal and deserves to be punished. The question of how racial prejudices and discrimination depend on our correctional system is thornier and ultimately far more unsettling. As a result, it has been largely left unexplored. If the symbiotic, self-propagating, and ultimately damaging relationship between race and punishment is to be broken, then we must gain a deeper understanding of it. To do so requires that we take a hard look at the conditions that permit this relationship not only to survive, but to thrive. The collection of essays that follows is a first step at such an examination.

WORKS CITED

Bauman, Zygmunt. 2000. *Globalization.* New York: Columbia University Press.

Bhabha, Homi. 1994. *The location of culture.* New York: Routledge.

Collins, Patricia Hill. 1990. *Black feminist thought.* New York: Routledge.

Donaldson, Lisa. 1992. *Decolonizing feminisms: Race, gender, and empire building.* Chapel Hill: University of North Carolina Press.

Garland, David. 1990. *Punishment and modern society.* Oxford: Clarendon Press.

Harrison, Paige M., and Allen J. Beck. 2005. *Prison and jail inmates at midyear 2004.* Bureau of Justice Statistics Bulletin. Washington, DC: U.S. Department of Justice. NCJ 208801.

Harrison, Paige M., and Jennifer Karberg. 2004. *Prison and jail inmates at midyear 2003.* Bureau of Justice Statistics Bulletin. Washington, DC: U.S. Department of Justice. NCJ 203947.

Lewis, Reina, and Sara Mills. 2003. *Postcolonial feminist theory: A reader.* New York: Routledge.

Myers, Martha. 1998. *Race, labor, and punishment in the New South*. Columbis: Ohio State University Press.

Ross, Luana. 1998. *Inventing the savage: The social construction of Native American criminality*. Austin: University of Texas Press.

Said, Edward. 1993. *Culture and imperialism*. New York: Knopf.

Stiglitz, Joseph E. 2003. *Globalization and its discontents*. New York: W. W. Norton & Company.

Walker, Alice. 2003. *The color purple*. New York: Harvest Books.

Winant, Howard. 2004. *The new politics of race: Globalism, difference, justice*. Minneapolis: University of Minnesota Press.

PART ONE

Colonialism

CHAPTER 1

Situating Colonialism, Race, and Punishment

Geeta Chowdhry and Mark Beeman

THE EPOCH OF IMPERIALISM, and its offshoot, European colonialism, have had a profound effect on the modern world. Global material inequalities and cultural hierarchies, the social construction of race, gender and class, and systems of crime and punishment have been shaped in meaningful ways by imperialism and European colonization. Although European colonialism focused mainly on territorial expansion and material accumulation, the durability of conquest rested in large part on imperial constructions of culture in which the social constructions of race and the inscribing of a world racial order provided legitimacy to the imperial enterprise and convinced otherwise "decent men and women to accept the notion that distant territories and their native people *should* be subjugated" (Said 1994, 10). This chapter provides an overview of colonialism by discussing the nature and scope of imperialism and its links with European colonialism. We suggest that imperialism needs to be understood not only in its relation to the accumulation of capital, but also in its cultural and ideological manifestations. In addition, by focusing, in the last section of this chapter, on the experience of African Americans in the United States, we interrogate the role that colonialism has played in the social construction of race as well as a racialized global hierarchy and a system of punishment that criminalizes difference.

The manner in which the colonial experience manifested itself depended in large part on the colonizer and the colonized. Therefore, generalizations about the experience are often regarded as undesirable since they inscribe history in essentialist and homogenizing terms. The study of colonialism as "a singular monolithic structure" that relies on a "fixed, essentializing identity" for all locations and subjects is critiqued by numerous postmodern and postfoundational scholars instrumental in the revival of colonial studies in the 1980s (Desai 2001; see also Cooper and Stoler 1997). However, Desai (2001, 11) has suggested that postfoundationalist accounts of colonialisms, unlike the antifoundationalist ones, are "interested not so much in debunking foundations but rather in historicizing their emergence." Like the postfoundationalists, we suggest that broad historical and cultural patterns of the imperialist project are identifiable and can be complemented by a more historicized and nuanced analysis of imperialism in a particular location. Thus, though the early part of this chapter situates imperialism, colonialism, and empire in history and focuses on the foundational role of race in the cultural constructions of empire, the latter part examines the manifestation of empire, race, and punishment in colonial America.

SITUATING IMPERIALISM, COLONIALISM, AND EMPIRE

According to Edward Said, the term imperialism denotes "the practice, theory and the attitudes of a dominating metropolitan center ruling a distant territory," while colonialism symbolizes the "implanting of settlements on distant territory," and empire is a "relationship," the control of the political sovereignty of one state by another (Said 1994, 9). Imperialism and colonialism are thus the instruments through which empire is achieved.

European imperialism was comprised of two overlapping waves (Fieldhouse 1965). The first wave, referred to by some scholars as the era of "high" or "classical" imperialism, originated in the fifteenth century with the development of the shipping industry, so that small sailing ships could travel long distances carrying both crew and cargo. During this time, also called the period of mercantile capitalism, Spain and Portugal controlled much of South America and Asia. Although explorers prior to Columbus had landed on American shores, it was the 1492 "discovery" of America by him that initiated the colonization of most of the Americas by Spain. Vasco de Gama of Portugal meanwhile had found a successful route to Asia. In 1493, a Papal Bull recognizing the colonial adventures of Spain and Portugal allocated the trade in metals from South America to Spain and the trade in sugar, spices, slaves, and ivory from Asia and Africa to Portugal (Chilcote 1999, 3).

Soon aware of the abundance of profits incurred in lands "far away," Britain, France, and the Netherlands used their military power to maneuver trade advantages as well. In many instances, this competition for colonies led to naval skirmishes between traders. According to Kiernan, for example, the early Europeans "were pirates, traders, grabbers and settlers by turn" (Kiernan 1969, 24). Ferguson (2003) has also suggested that the early years of mercantile capitalism in Britain meant piracy on the high seas. As British "buccaneers" sought to be competitive in the search for precious metals, such as gold and silver, with Portugal and Spain, many resorted to raiding the ships of Spaniards. Cognizant of the wealth secured from piracy, Queen Elizabeth I, like other European monarchs, blessed the piracy expeditions with state patronage. In addition, the European nation-states chartered and financed commercial trading companies and collaborated with European merchants to secure exclusive economic rights in the Americas. Realizing that political control guaranteed exclusive rights to resources, labor, and markets, and thus tremendous profits, European nations conquered these lands and established political rule over them. By the end of the sixteenth century, Portugal and Spain had colonized most of Central and South America, Britain and France had colonies in North America and the Caribbean, and the Netherlands had some colonies in South America and the Caribbean.

Harry Magdoff (1969; 1978) has suggested that the period from 1400 to 1870, or what we have called the first wave of colonization, can be understood as having three distinct phases. The first phase of mercantile capitalism lasted from 1400s to the mid-1600s, with Europe establishing control over the resources (land, labor, and minerals) of the colonized areas. The second phase, from 1650 to 1770, was the era in which the search for commodities, including human commodities or slaves, played a critical role. The third phase of classical imperialism lasted from 1770 to around 1870; this period included the independence of North and South America, with the British colonists of what became the United States declaring independence in 1776, followed by the colonists of most of South and Central America in the 1800s. The independence of the Americas, and in particular of the United States of America, did not result in the decolonization of the African American, however. Rather, the process of colonization, as discussed in the latter part of this chapter, determined African Americans' life chances for much of the postcolonial period.[1]

The second wave of imperialism and colonization, also referred to as the "new imperialism," lasted from about 1870 through the end of World War II. Its targets were Asia and Africa. During this period, Europe shifted from mercantile capitalism, in which capital accumulation was accomplished through trade, to industrial capitalism. The search for raw materials and new markets, essential ingredients in the growth of industrial capitalism in Europe, played a critical role in the second wave of imperialism (see for example Brewer 1989; Hilferding 1910; Hobson 1894, 1902; Lenin 1939; Luxembourg 1913). The "great African land rush" or the struggle for raw materials and markets, led to a scramble for new colonies in Africa, resulting in an arbitrary division of the continent at the Berlin Conference of 1884–1885. By 1914, seven European nations—France, Britain, Germany, Portugal, Spain, Belgium, and Italy—had colonized all of Africa and controlled its wealth and its people.

The colonization of Asia, including the Middle East, also occurred in the late nineteenth and early twentieth century, and much of Asia was also divided between the competing imperial powers. For example, India was "the jewel in the crown" of the British Empire, while Indochina (Laos, Cambodia, and

Vietnam) became a French colony, and the Philippines a dependency of the United States. Japan, Thailand, and China were never occupied, although China was divided into spheres of influence by competing imperial powers and Hong Kong was ceded to Britain as a result of the Treaty of Nanking, signed in 1848. Following the disintegration of the Ottoman Empire and the discovery of oil, the Middle East came under the influence of European powers, particularly the British and the French.

Anticolonial movements and nationalist struggles for independence in Asia and Africa began after World War II, with India gaining independence in 1947 and much of Africa following suit in the 1960s. However, it is argued by some scholars that, despite the formal independence of countries in Africa and Asia, a neocolonial dependency on former colonial powers and international financial institutions as well as trade regimes still exists (see for example Amin 1974; Baran 1957; Frank 1967).[2]

THE "SUCCESS" OF COLONIZATION

The "success" of colonization rested on several key factors. Based on the work of Niall Ferguson (2003) and others, we suggest that the British Empire was built (1) by a "public-private partnership" where the crown created the political and economic conditions necessary for colonial ventures, leaving it up to "private individuals to take the risks—and put up the money," (2) on the global movement of people through both forced as well as willing migration and settlement, and (3) through the development of a coercive legal apparatus as well as extra-legal mechanisms in which force and punishment played major roles.

Numerous scholars agree that modern imperialism has strong links to the development of capitalism as a mode of production. The role played by private capital in the periods of both mercantile and industrial capitalism was central to the colonial enterprise (see for example Hilferding 1910; Hobson 1894, 1902; Lenin 1939; Luxembourg 1913).[3] Marxist and non-Marxist scholars have suggested that colonial territories, which provided new markets and the production of agricultural and human commodities, became the suppliers for Western consumption of goods and Western industrialization. Indeed, most scholars agree that a European economic crisis, fueled by underconsumption, was averted by colonization.[4] The dynamics of the public-private partnership under colonization can be understood by examining the production and trade in cash crops. For example, the growth of a cash crop such as sugar was encouraged by the British on their plantations in Jamaica.[5] Henry Morgan, a British citizen who had acquired his wealth through piracy on the high seas, invested in land in Jamaica, where he grew sugarcane using slaves for labor. The sugar was exported to Britain. The British imposed high tariffs on the imports of sugar and earned considerable revenue for the state. In return, the political control established by the British over Jamaica guaranteed exclusive control over the growth of sugar and the trade in sugar to individual British merchants like Henry Morgan and to British chartered companies (Ferguson 2003). Thus the private-public partnership formed under colonialism became the basis for the tremendous wealth of individuals, companies, and the colonial state. Similarly, the trade in other cash crops such as tea, coffee, cacao, groundnuts, and spices also created and sustained culinary developments in Europe, with great opportunities for the accumulation of capital by Europeans. As John Stuart Mill posited:

> These [outlying possessions of ours] are hardly to be looked upon as countries, . . . but more properly as outlying agricultural or manufacturing estates belonging to a larger community. Our West Indian colonies, for example, cannot be regarded as countries with a productive capital of their own . . . [but are rather] the place where England finds it convenient to carry on the production of sugar, coffee and a few other tropical commodities. (Quoted in Said 1994, 59)

Both forced and willing migration and settlement were essential to the colonial project. As Ferguson (2003, 53) points out, "Between the early 1600s and the 1950s, more than 20 million people left the British Isles to begin new lives across the seas. No other country in the world came close to exporting so many of its inhabitants." Many went to the Americas, others to Africa, and yet others were sent to serve penal sentences in Australia. These individuals created "settler" colonies in North America, Australia, and South Africa. In 1587 the first British settlement, on Roanoke Island, was established in North America. Like its second counterpart several years later, it did not survive. Thus the landing of the pilgrims on November 9, 1620, is marked as foundational to the "settling" of North America. The concept of "terra nullius," or no-man's-land, was used to suggest that North America, like Australia, was not previously occupied and was thus available for the taking. The dispossession of Native Americans in North America and aborigines in Australia was accomplished by "settlers" through deceit, disease, and force, in effect decimating the culture, livelihood, and health of Native inhabitants (Kiernan 1969, 229; see also Banks, this volume).

The movement of indentured labor from Europe to the Americas, as well as from Asia to Europe, the Americas, and Africa, and within Asia itself, was a significant part of the colonial project and is central to understanding race relations and ethnic politics in many postcolonial societies. "Between a half and two-thirds of all Europeans who migrated to North America between 1650 and 1780 did so under contracts of indentured servitude" (Ferguson 2003, 69). Forced migration and settlement exemplified by the slave trade, "whose toil laid the foundations of the modern world," occurred mainly from

Africa to the Americas (Kiernan 1969, 201). The demographic map of the modern world was thus altered through population movements that occurred as a result of colonization.

Finally, the development of a coercive legal and extra-legal apparatus was central to the creation of fear and maintenance of order in colonized territories. Power was central to the colonial project. Whether the Europeans saw themselves as part of a *mission civilisatrice* or as safeguarding their possessions in a "wild" landscape amongst "savage" inhabitants, power was intrinsic to the colonizing structure. In turn, such power was ensured through colonial edicts and policies that protected colonial interests against those of the colonized, through the criminalization of cultural practices and through brute force. "It was Britain's mission, said the writer of a book on the North-west frontier who styled himself 'a man of peace' by preference, 'to spread amongst these savages the power of that great civilizer, the Sword'" (Kiernan 1969, 312). The cultural production of a racialized and hierarchical colonial discourse did much to normalize these excesses in the minds of otherwise decent individuals across Europe, and to convince them "that certain territories and people *require* and beseech domination" (Said 1994, 9).

COLONIAL DISCOURSE AND RACE

Although coercion, force, and material exploitation were an essential part of colonization, the more subtle cultural production of an inferior, dehumanized, and "racialized colonial subject" was "critical to the efficacy of colonization" (Chowdhry and Nair 2002, 17). The cultural construction of a dehumanized colonial subject by the colonizers centered around the objectification of the "natives," what Aimé Césaire had in mind when he said "my turn to state an equation: Colonization = 'thingification'" (Césaire 1972, 21).

Colonial discourse achieved "thingification" of the colonized through a discourse on race. Our intention in highlighting the foundational role of race in colonial discourse is not to suggest a Manichean "prefigured formula" in which a white colonizer acts as "a sovereign hierarchical operator" perfectly managing all interactions and events (Desai 2001, 18–22). Indeed, the colonial narrative on race was often mediated by other ideas about gender, class, religion, etc. and, like colonization itself, was often contradictory and contested (see Stoler 1995; Cooper and Stoler 1997; McClintock 1995). However, we suggest that it would be a mistake to underestimate the consistency, power, and reach of colonization and the colonial cultural constructions of race.

Although prejudice based on race and ethnicity can be traced to antiquity, modern racism has its origins in the colonial encounter. Anthropological and scientific discourses on race in the eighteenth and nineteenth century constructed race as a hierarchical and biological category to explain global differences in physiognomy and culture and to provide the raison d'être for colonization. Thus, while modern accounts of race were socially constructed in the eighteenth and nineteenth century, the "scientific" rationale for race that posited that "people at the bottom are intrinsically inferior material (poor brains, bad genes or whatever)" naturalized it as a biological category (Gould 1981, 31). Gould, who has analyzed the dialectical relationship between a colonial culture and science, including American polygeny, craniometry, the measuring of bodies and intelligence, and the science of recapitulation, suggests that the eighteenth- and nineteenth-century views on race had a profound influence on the development of some branches of science. Much of the scientific work on intelligence, craniometry, etc. reproduced the racist biases of society and imbued them with an air of objectivity (Gould 1981).

Imperialist expansion was supported by an ideology in which cultural production, in its broadest sense, played a critical role. Although colonial discourses on race are embedded in particular histories and geographical locations, there is much that is common among them. Many colonialists represented the colonized as inferior, as savages (see also Banks, and Urbina and Smith, this volume). Subscribing to social Darwinism, settlers suggested that the natives were inferior to the "master race" and that "primitive races" would inevitably (and perhaps desirably) be wiped out by the more "civilized" European ones (Brantlinger 1995). Although some anthropologists, such as James Pritchard, were concerned about the "Extinction of Primitive Races," they nevertheless felt that colonization exemplified the march of progress that would enable savages to become civilized (see Brantlinger 1995, 45). Indeed, civilization and domination of nature became the rationalization for the British to forcibly take lands from indigenous peoples of North America. Under the guidelines of the Doctrine of Discovery and the Right of Conquest, European ownership of colonial territory was limited to uninhabited land, land acquired by consent of the indigenous population, or land acquired as compensation for "just wars." Indigenous resistance to either colonial trading rights or Christian proselytizing was viewed as justification for war. The British, however, not satisfied with these limitations on land acquisition, established the Norman Yoke, which allowed settlers to dispossess Native Americans of land that was not being "developed" (Churchill 2003). Hence the legal requirement of consent was avoided.

Colonialists also portrayed the colonized as childlike. Influenced by evolutionism, the idea of recapitulation, in which human groups are ranked higher or lower, was used in a biologically deterministic way to compare all "inferior groups—races, sexes, and classes— . . . with the children of white males" (Gould 1981, 114). According to Gould, E. D. Cope, an American paleontologist, ranked four groups in the following manner, with Europeans the highest: "nonwhite races, all women, southern as opposed to northern European whites, and lower classes within superior races" (Gould 1981, 114).

In this classification, nonwhite races were closest to being childlike and thus less developed as adults, more emotional and not capable of rational thought. Similarly, an American anthropologist, D. G. Briton claimed that "the adult who retained the most fetal, infantile or simian trait, is unquestionably inferior . . . Measured by these criteria, the European or white race stands at the head of the list, the African or Negro at its foot" (quoted in Gould 1981, 116).

These themes of the sometimes threatening savage, sometimes childlike racial Other, are evident in the experience, for example, of African Americans during both the colonial and postcolonial periods. The relations of African Americans vis-à-vis whites have been characterized as paternalistic during the slave period, with the childlike slave needing the guidance of the paternalistic white master, and competitive after abolition, with the free African American a hostile threat to white values and white superiority (van den Berghe 1967; Wilson 1980; see also Flavin, this volume). Although the two forms have been presented as tied to the distinct economic structures under which they existed, in reality the dominant group could hold both views simultaneously and mete out punishment accordingly.

COLONIZATION, RACE, AND INVOLUNTARY
SERVITUDE IN COLONIAL AMERICA

The argument can be made that the most revealing feature of relations between the dominant group and people of African descent, both in the continental British colonies and subsequently in the United States for most of its history, is the subjugation of the latter to involuntary servitude. The social construction of race became inexorably tied to political rights, crime, punishment, and confinement. Set in the colonial experience, the interaction of these constructions continued to evolve to meet the economic and social demands of the dominant caste, creatively extended by both legal and extra-legal mechanisms. Thus involuntary servitude, this colonization of the African American, continued beyond independence, beyond emancipation, by both law and custom.

Originally, Africans, like many Europeans, came to British continental America as indentured servants, not slaves. Like their European counterparts, they worked off their indentured service and were set free. The first Africans came to Virginia in 1620, and by 1630 records indicate some had become property holders and employed indentured servants themselves. But the process of race-based discrimination was soon underway. In 1640, three indentured servants (two white and one African) escaped from their master. Upon their capture, all were whipped. In addition, the whites served one year to their master beyond their original service plus three years service to the colony. The African, however, was sentenced to serve his master for the remainder of his life (Finkelman 1985). In other words, slavery seems to have evolved, in part, as a punishment reserved for Africans originally indentured. English indentured servants, presumably protected by English rights and the Christianity they shared with their masters, avoided such punishment. From the 1640s through the 1660s, with the principle of lifelong involuntary servitude established for Africans in colonial America, individual colonies began enacting legislation declaring "negroes" sent to the colonies, and their offspring, slaves for life. In short, slavery in British colonial America became a "punishment" for being black.

The economic advantages of slavery seemed to override questions about its legality. Colonial law was grounded in English law, but English law questioned the premise that the king's subjects could be enslaved. The Magna Carta seemed to establish the principal of due process. By 1772, the question of slavery was decided in the court case of *Somerset v. Stewart*. James Somerset was a slave who had traveled from the colonies to England with his master. While there, Somerset escaped, but was later captured and held to be returned to his master as a slave. His legal representatives argued he should not be returned to his master, on the grounds that slavery was contrary to the British Constitution. Lord Mansfield, presiding over the case, ruled "I cannot say this case is allowed or approved by the law of England; and therefore the black must be discharged" (*Somerset v. Stewart*, 1772, 19).

Despite the apparent contradiction of slavery with the British Constitution, the American colonial elite had secured an important source of labor and were not inconvenienced by the ruling across the Atlantic.[6] Indeed, they enacted legislation guaranteeing not only a perpetual population of slaves, but also punishments unique to slave status. "An Act for the Better Ordering and Governing of Negroes and Slaves, South Carolina 1712," was a comprehensive code that other colonies used to model their own codes (Rothenberg 2001). It stated that "negroes, mulattos, mustizoes or Indians" who had previously been enslaved would remain slaves, as would their children. Mobility was confined to the plantation unless the slave was escorted or had a "ticket" issued by the master or mistress specifying the name of the slave and his business off the plantation. Failure to have a ticket would result in the slave being whipped, plus "any white person" could "beat, maim, assault or kill a "negro or slave . . . who shall refuse to shew his ticket" (An Act for the Better Ordering and Governing of Negroes and Slaves, South Carolina 1712, 2001, 442). Unusually harsh and inhumane punishments were created for even minor offenses. For the slave's first offense for petty larceny (stealing or destroying goods valued at less than twelve pence), the punishment was "to be publicly and severely whipped, not exceeding forty lashes . . . second offense, shall either have one of his ears cut off, or be branded on the head with a hot iron . . . for his third offense, shall have his nose slit . . . a fourth time . . . shall be adjudged to suffer death, or other punishment, as the said justice shall think fitting" (An Act for the Better Ordering and Governing of Negroes and Slaves, South Carolina 1712, 2001, 445; see also Young and Spencer, this volume).

More serious crimes often called for death in a manner left to the judge's discretion. Justices of the peace and judges were most likely to be used when slaves were accused of criminal behavior beyond their master's plantations. In reality, most transgressions on the plantations were punished by the discretion of the master or the overseer. Out of sight of any regulatory body, punishments could be particularly cruel, whether an offense had been committed or not. Some slaves were whipped so badly they could not move for days, while others were beaten to death (Genovese 1974). Iron collars, small cells with barely enough room for one adult, and burning slaves alive were used for a variety of offenses. Castration had been openly used to punish slaves for running away, insurrection, and rape, and was privately used to punish slave men who showed interest in the same enslaved women coveted by their masters (Genovese 1974).

The issue of sexual relations between slaves and whites created a dilemma for the British throughout the American colonies, but found its most extreme reaction in the continental colonies. In areas where the European-to-slave population ratio was small, miscegenation was readily accepted. This was true not only for the Spanish and Portuguese settlements, but also for the British in the Caribbean. Accepting miscegenation and recognizing offspring of mixed heritage, the Spanish acknowledged divisions such as mulatto, sambo, qaudroon, mestize, etc., while the British in the island colonies granted superior status to subjects of mixed descent vis-à-vis the African population. It was not seen as proper to force "mulattos" to do field labor, and in Jamaica, by 1733, the designation "mulatto" was dropped after three generations of mixed heritage, leaving those subjects the same rights as whites (Winthrop 1987). The population make-up encouraged British male settlers to seek non-European women for sexual relationships, and the privileges of property ownership and citizenship could be granted to their offspring. On the island colonies there was no prohibition on extramarital miscegenation as such, and with one exception no prohibition on interracial marriage (Winthrop 1987).

The situation in continental America was much different. Indigenous people had been killed off or transferred away from population centers; people of African descent were a minority of the population; and the British settlers and their offspring made up the majority. Here, the British immigrants attempted to recreate the racial-cultural community left behind in Britain, and the people imported from Africa were deemed inferior, necessary for hard labor but generally inadequate for the rights bestowed on the British members of the colonial community. A population with mixed heritage was perceived as a threat to a clearly delineated barrier between free subjects and slaves. Although the "mulatto" was recognized as a social reality, the legal status of the mulatto was the same as that of the "negro." The colonial elite came to a consensus that any discernable African heritage, even the most minor or remote, gave one the status of being black. The rule of hypodescent ensured that a mixed population would be placed with Africans in one lower caste, thus preventing both Africans and their descendants from escaping lifelong involuntary servitude.

The antimiscegenation policies employed were not always consistent, but were always directed at the same goal—separation of the races. Thus a perceived economic necessity joined ideological obsession. The most obvious threat to the system was a loss of separate racial identities, and the most obvious response was to prohibit sexual relations across racially designated categories. Originally, local leaders seemed to be of the view that immediate punishment or even penance would address the problem. In Virginia in 1630 a white man who admitted his transgression in church was "soundly whipped" for "lying with a negro," and in 1640 a white male and African woman who together had a child were punished, her by whipping, him by doing "penance in church according to the laws of England" (Wadlington 1987, 602). But penalties soon grew much harsher, especially when white women were involved. Maryland enacted legislation in 1664 that a white woman who married a slave would be punished by serving the slave's master for the duration of the slave's life, and that children born to them would be slaves (Bell 1992). Although consistent with white patriarchal privilege, this legislation did not accomplish its intent. Given the shortage of slave labor, slave owners were known to encourage marriages between their own slaves and white female servants, using the new legislation to extended the services of the wife and procure lifelong services of the children. Realizing that the legislation was inadvertently encouraging rather than discouraging interracial unions, in 1681 Maryland enacted legislation that masters who encouraged the unions of their slaves with white women servants would be fined ten thousand pounds in tobacco, the married servant would be set free, and all children of that union would also be free (Bell 1992). This legislation, once again, encouraged interracial marriages, but this time the incentive was for white female servants who hoped to terminate their indentured service. In 1692, new legislation forbade all interracial marriage and sexual relations, with punishments of seven years service for free black men or white women whose unions resulted in children, with the children to remain servants until thirty-one years of age (Bell 1992).

This condemnation of unions between the white female and the African American male established a pattern which was to last until the U.S. Supreme Court struck down the ban on interracial marriage in 1967. The white plantation owner, on the other hand, had sexual access to enslaved women. Racism combined with white male supremacy encouraged white female–African

American male relationships to be viewed in the context of rape, often resulting in the castration or death of the male. Rape laws were, however, meant to
protect white women only. Enslaved African American women could not
legally be *raped*, since their rape was not designated as a crime (Genovese
1974; see Young and Spencer, this volume). The enslaved woman had no legal
control over her sexual intimacy or sexual reproduction. The authority of her
master determined with whom she was allowed to engage in sexual relations.
A former slave observed that the white males controlling the society who had
insisted on an antimiscegenation code were the first to violate it (Genovese
1974). Hence, though African American male/white female relations were
viewed as a serious crime, white male–African American female relations,
while not expected to be flaunted publicly, were treated as the plantation
owner's property rights (see also Messerschmidt, this volume).

INDEPENDENCE, CONTINUED
COLONIZATION, AND PUNISHMENT

Colonization of African Americans did not end with the independence of
the United States from Britain. Although independence granted new freedoms to whites, the majority of African Americans remained enslaved for
nearly another century. While the celebrated language of equality in the
Constitution made slavery more difficult to rationalize, African Americans
remained Constitutionally less than equal, as designated by the three-fifths
compromise. Driven by economic motivation and the colonial ideology of
white supremacy, plantation-economy states, in particular, fiercely held onto
involuntary servitude to provide their labor needs. In effect, legalized involuntary servitude ensured that the plantation remained essentially the same as
during the colonial era, with punishment by and large under the control of
the plantation owner.

Nevertheless, in addition to the "all men created equal" theme of the
Constitution, a host of other factors placed slave owners increasingly on the
defensive. Following independence, states not dependent on slave labor either
eliminated slavery in their state constitutions or began enacting legislation for
the gradual abolition of slavery. Pressure mounted to abolish the slave trade,
which both England and the United States legally prohibited by 1807. Country after country in the Americas either abolished slavery or enacted legislation for gradual emancipation in the nineteenth century. All British colonies
had abolished slavery by 1838, all French and Danish colonies ten years later,
and all Dutch colonies by 1863 (Sanderson 1998). Still, in the United States
the southern elite not only held onto their right to own slaves, they forged a
strategy to increase their political power by extending slavery into other areas
of the country. The only method that seemed able to dismantle the lifelong
involuntary servitude system in the South was war.

The defeat of the Confederacy in the Civil War and the enactment of the Thirteenth, Fourteenth, and Fifteenth Amendments to the Constitution appeared to have finally resolved the issue of race-based involuntary servitude. Yet, although the colonial legacy of slavery had been legally addressed, colonial ideology remained fixed, and the southern elite explored creative ways to reintroduce race-based involuntary servitude. One method drew directly from the colonial tradition. The system of apprenticeships, used from the beginning of mass European migration to the colonies, was resurrected as a means to confine African American children to the plantations from which they had recently been liberated. For example, the Mississippi Black Codes enacted in November 1865 contained apprentice statues that required justices of the peace and sheriffs to give the names of all African American "orphans" or children whose parents could not adequately provide for them to the county judge. The judge's responsibility was to bind the children to a competent adult with *preference given to their former owners* (rather than, say, to their own relatives). The apprenticeship would bind the child to the authority of the master until the age of twenty-one for males, eighteen for females. The assistant commissioner of the Freedmen's Bureau reported that, on the request of any citizen, justices of the peace and sheriffs would place children into the apprentice program regardless of the ability of their parents to provide for them (Nieman 1987). This program destroyed the integrity of the African American family as a unit and effectively re-enslaved the African American child.

The Black Codes also were designed to prevent African Americans from leaving plantations, by using the criminal justice system to restrict adult mobility and to reintroduce involuntary servitude. Recalling that the Thirteenth Amendment to the Constitution stated "neither slavery nor involuntary servitude, except for punishment of a crime, shall exist within the U.S. or any place subject to their jurisdiction," southern states made "vagrancy" a crime immediately after the Civil War. In essence, it made unemployment, for African Americans, a crime. Such laws were passed in a number of states in 1866, in some cases not even attempting to disguise their racist intent. Mississippi law stated "freedmen, free Negroes, and mulattos" without employment or business were vagrants and subject to imprisonment, fines, or, at the court's discretion, serving the penalty bonded to an employer. Georgia law specified the vagrant could be sentenced to the public works or bound out to a private employer. Other former Confederate states passed similar laws, designed to force African Americans to either sign yearly labor contracts (presumably with their former owners) or be bound to their former owners through vagrancy penalties. Florida law specified that even those who had signed labor contracts could still be punished as "vagrants" if during the course of the contract they exhibited "idleness" or "disrespect" toward their employers (DuBois 2001).

Debt peonage was also employed, sometimes in conjunction with criminal fines, other times simply through an advance given to the contracted employee who knew that, without work, a vagrancy charge could be made. Although debt peonage had been made illegal in 1867, the Department of Justice found the practice still widespread forty years later (Cohen 1987). When it was challenged in court, lawyers and judges sympathetic to plantation owners argued that, although bonding the laborer based on indebtedness might not be legally binding, the act of leaving service without paying off a debt constituted "fraud" on the worker's part. (Daniel 1987, 65). For fraud, the offender could be fined, jailed, and bonded to the employer, who paid off the legal fees. Hence the laborer was technically bonded to the plantation for the criminal penalty associated with fraud, rather than for the original debt owed.

The use of crime and punishment to place African Americans in involuntary servitude altered the southern prison system from a predominately white prison population prior to emancipation, to a predominately African American prison population after the Civil War. Postwar penal institutions were segregated, with whites only sentenced to prison for the most serious crimes. African Americans filled these prisons, predominately charged with less serious crimes (Oshinsky 1997). Southern county jails also served as mechanisms to provide labor for various projects, again rounding up African Americans for minor offenses. Records from 1932 show that 97 percent of Georgia's county convict population was African American (Cohen 1987).

Convict leasing laws had been enacted by nearly every southern state by the 1880s, and states slowly discovered this to be a profitable enterprise. The state simply leased prisoners through a contractor for work on plantations, mines, railroads, swamp clearance, etc. The system was set up so that convict labor could easily be acquired when needed. In addition to establishing criminal penalties for minor offenses, thus creating a large county jail population, some states would change petty crimes into felonies to help fill their prison labor needs; for example, stealing a farm animal worth ten dollars was changed to a felony in Mississippi (Oshinsky 1997). Unlike slavery, where the owners had considerable investment in their slaves, in the convict leasing system, the investment by the employers was minimal. If a worker became ill or died, the state simply supplied a healthy replacement. The less spent on feeding and sheltering workers, the more profits were made. Consequently, the convict leasing system had a shameful mortality record. In 1884–1885, 27 percent of the Tennessee's convict lease workers died, and, from 1877–1886, 45 percent of South Carolina convicts leased to the Augusta Railroad project died (Cohen 1987). In Parchman Penitentiary in Mississippi, not one convict in the leasing program survived a ten-year sentence (Oshinsky 1997).

In the segregated southern prisons, the most dangerous and unhealthy leasing assignments were generally reserved for African American prisoners.

For example, in Mississippi, whites were housed in the prison, while African Americans went out on convict leasing chain gangs. In Parchman in 1882, 17 percent of the African American prisoner population died, as compared to 2 percent of the white prison population (Oshinsky 1997).[7] Convict lease prisoners were chained together and were punished by whippings, beatings, hanging by the thumbs with whipcords, confinement to air-tight boxes, and funneling water down the throat (Womack 1998). Eventually, public distaste for convict leasing resulted in the programs being dismantled, but forced labor remained. Prisons shifted from the convict lease system to their own prison work projects or state-run public work projects.

Overwhelmingly, the forced labor systems of the south relied on African American workers, with the prison labor being a predominately male system. However, although African American women commonly worked outside the home, there were times where labor shortages resulted in the southern criminal justice system specifically targeting African American women to meet labor needs. During the two world wars, under the auspices of "fight or work" programs, southern states began applying their vagrancy laws to African American women. Some had gainfully employed husbands, and they, like most white women, worked unpaid taking care of their home and children. Others, like many white women, were living off of the military pay checks sent home while their husbands served overseas. Despite working full time in their homes, African American women were told to get jobs or be charged with vagrancy violations and sentenced to work. There is no record of enforcing the same penalties on white women in similar circumstances (White 2000).

CONCLUSION

We have explored some of the linkages among colonization, the social construction of race, and the construction of a system of punishment based on racialized difference. In colonial America, as elsewhere, European colonization, which was based on a successful public-private partnership, created a structural and ideological framework in which people of color were constructed as racially inferior. This ideological framework provided the cultural and moral justification for the colonial appropriation of both land and labor and for constructing a race-based system of punishment.

Land acquisition was, in large part, construed as a project of civilization and development, with British law subscribing to the principle that ownership rights went to those who intended to cultivate the land. Hence much of the uncultivated or "wilderness" land occupied by Native Americans was turned over to European settlers. Cultivation on a large scale was labor intensive during the colonial era. The unwillingness of European immigrants to work for low wages on plantations resulted in plantation owners relying on forced labor, with racism providing the justification for enslaving people of African descent. The inferior status of the colonized meant that the legal system created penalties for people of color for behaving in manners that would have been considered legal had they been white. In many instances, this system was supplemented by extra-legal force as well.

Although the dehumanization of colonial subjects and involuntary servitude found its basis in colonial rule, in the United States the colonial legacy remained a powerful force in extending a race-based system of punishment in the penal code. Race-based punishments remained entrenched and unaffected by independence and the drafting of the U.S. Constitution. Race-based slavery, a colonial project, stayed legally intact for nearly a century past independence. With the legal abolition of slavery after the Civil War, new forms of race-based forced labor were established, commonly justified as punishments for criminal violations. The Black Codes, apprenticeships, debt peonage, convict leasing, and even "fight or work" programs ushered race-based forced labor into the modern era.

NOTES

1. Some scholars use the idea "internal colonialism" to explain the current situation of Native Americans and Chicanos(as)/Latinos(as) in the United States. Internal colonialism suggests that the situation of some populations within a nation-state is akin to a colonized state. The appropriation of indigenous land and resources, the use of indigenous labor in ways distinct from "mainstream labor," the differential political and civil rights bestowed on indigenous populations, and their cultural colonization leads to the creation of an internal colony. The economic development and political and cultural identity of the "colonizers" thus derives from the colonization of these groups.

2. Many scholars from the dependency school suggest that the formal independence of previously colonized countries of Africa, Asia, South America, and the Caribbean has not meant the end of exploitation. Even though formal colonization has ended, neocolonization continues through multinational corporations, trade, and other mechanisms, such as structural adjustment programs etc. For example, Andre Gunder Frank has argued that a net outflow of resources occurs from the Third World, leading to the "development of underdevelopment." Samir Amin suggests that peripheral capitalism cannot develop in the same ways as core capitalism because of unequal exchange, repatriation of profits to the core countries, and other reasons.

3. For an excellent overview of the Marxist literature on imperialism, see Brewer (1989).

4. The British non-Marxist scholar Hobson (1902) and the Russian Marxist Lenin (1939) suggested that the profit motive for the growth of capitalism had engendered certain economic crisis in Europe. The argument goes somewhat like this. Mergers, acquisitions, and downsizing by corporations in search for more profits led to increasing unemployment and poverty as well as decline in consumption in Europe. This consumption decline led to a decrease in profit margins and to further downsizing. The spiral of decline in consumption and downsizing led Europe to an economic crisis. Marx had predicted that the deepening of the economic crisis would lead to the proletariat developing class consciousness, becoming a "class-for-itself," and leading the proletariat revolution in England. We all know that this prediction did not materialize. Lenin suggested that mercantile capitalism and the subsequent

colonization of Africa, Asia, and the Americas averted the economic crisis in Europe by finding new markets for European goods and new commodities for Europe. The expansion of capitalism thus occurred through colonization, and the colonies became the "raw materials" for the economic, political, and cultural expansion of Europe.

5. The French grew sugar in Haiti and Guadeloupe. The British had tea plantations in India, Kenya, and Sri Lanka (previously known as Ceylon). The French encouraged the growth of groundnuts (peanuts) in West Africa, particularly Senegal. The desire for chocolate led to the development of extensive cacao farming in West Africa. Cotton, grown in Egypt, India, and the southern plantations of colonial America, provided the inputs for the textile mills in Lancashire. Thus colonization led to immense changes in the agricultural landscape of these countries. The implications of colonization for the famines and food shortages that were to follow in many of these countries are immense.

6. From 1700 to 1769, more Africans were brought into the thirteen colonies than were all European immigrants combined, during the same period (Fogleman 2002).

7. As a comparison, a survey of prisons in four northern states for 1881–1885 found the mortality rate to be approximately 1 percent (Cohen 1985).

WORKS CITED

Amin, Samir. 1974. *Accumulation on a world scale*. New York: Monthly Review Press.

An Act for the Better Ordering and Governing of Negroes and Slaves, South Carolina, 1712. 2001. In *Race, class, and gender in the United States*, ed. Paula Rothenberg. New York: Worth Publishers.

Baran, Paul. 1957. *The political economy of growth*. New York: Monthly Review Press.

Bell, Derrick. 1992. *Race, racism, and American law*. 3rd edition. Boston: Little, Brown and Company.

Brantlinger, Patrick. 1995. Dying races: Rationalizing genocide in the nineteenth century. In *The decolonization of imagination: Culture, knowledge and power*, ed. Jan Nederveen Pieterse and Bhikhu Parekh. 1995. London and New Jersey: Zed Press.

Brewer, Anthony. 1989. *Marxist theories of imperialism: A critical survey*. New York: Routledge.

Césaire, Aimé. 1972. *Discourse on colonialism*. Trans. Joan Pinkham. New York and London: Monthly Review Press.

Chilcote, Ronald, ed. 1999. *The political economy of imperialism: Critical appraisals*. Boston, Dordrecht/London: Kluwer Academic Publishers.

Chowdhry, Geeta, and Sheila Nair. 2002. *Power, postcolonialism, and international relations: Reading race, gender, and class*. London: Routledge.

Churchill, Ward. 2003. *Perversions of justice: Indigenous peoples and Angloamerican law*. San Francisco, CA: City Lights.

Cohen, William. 1987. Negro involuntary servitude in the South, 1865–1940: A preliminary analysis. In *Race relations and the law in American history*, ed. Kermit Hall. New York: Garland Publishing.

Cooper, Frederick, and Ann Laura Stoler, eds. 1997. *Tensions of empire: Colonial cultures in a bourgeois world*. Berkeley and Los Angeles: University of California Press.

Daniel, Pete. 1987. Up from slavery and down to peonage: The Alonzo Bailey case. In *Race relations and the law*.

Desai, Gaurav. 2001. *Subject to colonialism: African self-fashioning and the colonial library*. Durham, NC: Duke University Press.

DuBois, W. E. B. 2001. The Black Codes. In *Race, class, and gender*.

Ferguson, Niall. 2003. *Empire: How Britain made the modern world*. London: Penguin Books.

Fieldhouse, D. K. 1965. *The colonial empires: A comparative survey from the eighteenth century.* New York: Delacorte Press.

Finkelman, Paul. 1985. *Slavery in the courtroom: An annotated bibliography of American cases.* Washington: U.S. Library of Congress.

Fogelman, Aaron. 2002. Migrations to the thirteen British North American colonies, 1700–1775: New estimates. In *Annual editions: Race and ethnic relations 2002/2003,* 12th edition, ed. John Kromkowski. Guilford, CT: McGraw-Hill/Dushkin.

Frank, Andre Gunder. 1967. *Capitalism and underdevelopment in Latin America: Historical studies of Chile and Brazil.* New York: Monthly Review Press.

Genovese, Eugene. 1974. *Roll, Jordan, roll: The world the slaves made.* New York: Pantheon Books.

Gould, Stephen J. 1981. *The mismeasure of man.* New York, London: W. W. Norton and Company.

Hilferding, Rudolf. 1910. *Finance capital: A study in the latest phase in capitalist development.* London: Routledge and Keegan Paul, 1981.

Hobson, John Atkinson. 1894. *The evolution of modern capitalism.* London: Walter Scott Publishing, repr. 1906.

———. 1902. *Imperialism: A study.* Ann Arbor: University of Michigan Press, repr. 1965.

Hochschild, Adam 1998. *King Leopold's ghost. A story of greed, terror, and heroism in Colonial Africa.* Boston, New York: Houghton Mifflin.

Kiernan, Victor. 1969. *The lords of human kind: Black man, yellow man, and white man in an age of empire.* Boston, Toronto: Little Brown Company.

Lenin, Vladimir Ilyich. 1939. *Imperialism: The highest stage of capitalism.* New York: International Publishers.

Luxemburg, Rosa. 1913. *The accumulation of capital.* London: Routledge and Keegan Paul, repr.1951.

Magdoff, Harry.1969. *The age of imperialism: The economics of U.S. foreign policy.* New York: Monthly Review Press.

———. 1978. *The age of imperialism: From the colonial age to the present.* New York: Monthly Review Press.

McClintock, Anne. 1995. *Imperial Leather. Race, Gender, and Sexuality in the Colonial Contest.* New York, London: Routledge.

Nieman, Donald. 1987. The Freedmen's Bureau and the Mississippi Black Code. In *Race relations and the law.*

Oshinsky, David. 1997. *Worse than slavery: Parchman Farm and the ordeal of Jim Crow justice.* New York: Free Press.

Rothenberg, Paula, ed. 2001. *Race, class, and gender in the United States.* New York: Worth Publishers.

Said, Edward W. 1994. *Culture and imperialism.* New York: Vintage Books.

Sanderson, Stephen. 1998. *Macrosociology: An introduction to human societies.* 4th edition. New York: Longman.

Somerset v. Stewart 1772. In *Equal protection and the African American Constitutional experience,* ed. Robert Green. Westport: Greenwood Press.

Stoler, Ann Laura. 1995. *Race and the education of desire.* Durham: Duke University Press.

van den Berghe, Pierre. 1967. *Race and racism.* New York: John Wiley and Sons.

Wadlington, Walter. 1987. The loving case: Virginia's antimiscegenation statute in historical perspective. In *Race relations and the law.*

White, Walter. 2000. Compulsory Work Laws (1919). In *Equal protection and the African American.*

Wilson, William. 1980. *The declining significance of race*. Chicago: University of Chicago Press.

Winthrop, Jordan. 1987. American chiaroscuro: The status and definition of mulattoes in the British Colonies. In *Race relations and the law*.

Womack, Marlene. 1998. Leasing of prisoners was one of Florida's dark secrets. In the Panama City, FL, *News Herald*. March 29. http://www.newsherald.com/archive/local/wm032998.htm (accessed on May 25, 2005).

CHAPTER 2

Ordering the Other

READING ALASKAN NATIVE CULTURE
PAST AND PRESENT

Cyndi Banks

ON MARCH 30, 1867, a Treaty of Cession was concluded
between the United States and the Emperor of All the Russias; for $7.2 million,
the emperor ceded to the United States the area of land now known as Alaska.[1]
The land mass, which Russia had ruled since 1741, included in its 586,412
square miles a number of what the treaty referred to as "uncivilized native
tribes," who were to be subject to the laws and regulations of the United States.
Unlike the other inhabitants, Russians and Creoles (who were of mixed native
and Russian ancestry), the Alaskan Natives were not to receive United States
citizenship (Lautaret 1989, 2–3). Sources suggest that though at first the Tlingit
thought about driving the Americans away, they were discouraged from doing
so by the chief of the Chilkat, "who pointed out that the Americans had many
cannon" (Congressional papers cited in Krause 1956, 266).

The formal U.S. acquisition of Alaska and the indigenous reaction to its
purchase ushered in a new era of colonialism in America that may be fruit-
fully examined to understand the social control and punishment of indigenous
people today. The colonizers disrupted and displaced Alaskan Native cultures to
create order out of perceived chaos, to reinforce white hegemony, and to further
the colonial project in Alaska. Past (and present) forms of oppression imposed on
the native peoples of Alaska sought to render their cultures marginal, subordinate, and insignificant. Strategies included: waging war on them, decimating
their populations by infecting them with Euro-American diseases, exchanging
their goods for liquor, and encouraging a culture of alcohol abuse. Indigenous
languages were forbidden in missionary and public schools, while many Alaskan
Native children were forcibly placed in schools with the aim of "Christianizing"
and assimilating them into the dominant culture. In the face of these challenges,
local cultures sometimes resisted. They also adapted and changed.

Documents from this period of history demonstrate how culture and the freedom to express traditions and beliefs are crucial to strategies both of domination and of resistance. In particular, Euro-American representations of the Alaskan Native and records of the past reveal how the natives of Alaska and their cultures were ordered and controlled by American colonizers. Together, they disclose how the colonizers distanced themselves from the natives and adopted practices that reinforced cultural difference, Euro-American cultural superiority, and a sense of Alaskan Natives as "the Other."

This chapter explores Euro-American representations of Alaskan Natives in the early colonial period as they appear in an autobiographical narrative of a surgeon's wife "on the frontier" and in an account of a general who thought himself "perfectly in command" of the natives. These texts add texture and context to the official records, while also revealing significant gender divisions among the colonizers. Such accounts are then related to the long-term effects of colonization on the cultures of Alaskan Natives. This comparison helps to explain how Alaskan Natives have persevered through adaptation and resistance. This chapter ends by mapping continuities in the treatment and response of Alaskan Natives in the criminal justice system today.

THE COLONIAL GAZE

In a book called *An Army Doctor's Wife on the Frontier* (1962), historian Abe Laufe published a series of nineteenth-century letters written by one Mrs. McCorkle Fitzgerald about her experiences of life in Alaska. Fitzgerald was the wife of a military surgeon who was posted to Sitka (located in southeast Alaska on the west side of Baranof Island) between August 1874 and April 1876. In describing her experiences on the frontier, she paints a picture of the Alaskan Native as the Other, based in equal parts on fear and apprehension about them and on fascination with their cultural alterity. Her narrative aptly illustrates Bryan Turner's view (Turner 1994, 37) that "we understand other cultures by slotting them into a pre-existing code or discourse which renders their oddity intelligible . . . by drawing on various forms of accounting which highlight differences in characteristics between 'us' and 'them' . . . A table of positive and negative attributes is thus established by which alien cultures can be read off and summations arrived at."

Fitzgerald's description of natives appears in a series of letters she wrote to her mother. In them, she describes Sitka as a "dirty little town around the army post habited by Russians and the Indian village off to one side" (Laufe 42). Natives are denied access to the army post until after nine each morning and they must leave by three that same day. According to Fitzgerald, the natives are "the most horrible, disgusting, dirty hideous set with painted faces and rings through noses and chins" (42).

Fitzgerald's interactions with the Tlingit of Sitka occur primarily through commerce. She recounts, "[t]hey are traders" and "come to your backdoors every day with things to sell: venison, birds, fish, berries etc" (43). Demonstrating that the Tlingits show a clear response to white needs and a white economy, Fitzgerald reports the availability of carved wooden salad spoons and forks for sale. Native foods and artifacts could also be found in the town stores where many Euro-Americans preferred to purchase—rather than to trade for them, because, according to Fitzgerald, "trading with the natives yourself is slow work, for you can't make them understand" (46). Obtaining a supply of acceptable food was problematic for Fitzgerald because beef was issued only once a week and had to be transported to Alaska on the regular steamer, which was often delayed. Consequently, for several days each week, the Americans had to buy food in the native market. There, things were "cheap enough," but Fitzgerald had no liking for the game food at the market. She seemed to resent having to rely on the natives for food and was uneasy about her inability to control her food supply.

In some of her letters, Fitzgerald describes events in the Tlingit village, providing a brief account of what she terms a "pow-wow" conducted between two clans to settle an interclan dispute (67). Here, the Tlingit sought recompense in the form of goods or lives for serious injuries suffered by one clan at the hands of another. Fitzgerald describes how the Sitka natives, while out hunting seals, had shot and killed a "squaw" of a neighboring tribe, mistaking her for a seal in the water. Fitzgerald reports (67) that "blankets or blood" were demanded for the killing, and that the victim's tribe had arrived in "war canoes" and demanded one thousand blankets for the dead woman. Fitzgerald assumes the offenders' tribe would not "comply with a manifestly unreasonable demand" (67) and that war might result. However, her reading of Tlingit cultural practice must have been flawed, because in her next letter she informs her mother that the affair was settled peacefully by the exchange of blankets.

Passing through the Russian part of town one day on a walk, Fitzgerald encounters a group of fifty or one hundred natives:

> Such wretches! They are the most horrible looking things you can imagine. They crouch down in a corner somewhere or on some steps, six, eight or a dozen in a bunch, each rolled in a dirty blanket or squirrel robe. Their faces are painted every way imaginable. . . . The women all have rings in their noses and their lower lip pierced with a silver pin . . . they all go barefooted over the ice and snow and the children that are too young to hold blankets around them are almost entirely naked. (83)

In another expedition, in January 1875, she visits a store and goes behind the counter to look at furs and "Indian curiosities" (84). Noting that the store was full of natives who had brought things to trade, she wishes her mother could

he would return to the wild if he "should live a year to two with any savage tribe" (11).

On his trip to Alaska, Howard visits Fort Wrangell and its small garrison, where the commander reports to him that white men are making home-brewed liquor which they sell to both Euro-Americans and natives. Howard meets with natives from a village adjacent to the garrison who complain that the army had forcibly taken away their favorite chief, Fernandeste. In his terror at being abducted, Fernandeste had taken his own life. The dead chief's clan had been goaded and insulted by other natives for not seeking revenge or compensation for Fernandeste's death and had attempted to kill a white man as an act of retaliation. Still seeking compensation for the death, the natives had communicated their demands to the general and received a letter from him promising a settlement. Now that the general has come, they ask him for recompense of one hundred blankets and the dead body of the chief (which the general has thoughtfully brought with him). Howard writes that he "graciously yielded to the natives' fervent entreaty" (1972, 305). Overcome by the beneficence of the general, according to Howard, the natives' moods change completely and they perform a dance depicting the events and the financial settlement. Howard recounts that the natives then beg him for a teacher such as they hear exists elsewhere in the territory (306). In concluding his account, the general, an amateur ethnographer of the period, provides the reader with a description of native houses, and explains his interest in their totem poles.

The general moves on to Sitka, where his previously complacent narrative of cultural superiority begins to reveal a note of unease. It seems that crime control measures are required in the capital. After hearing from the local citizenry, the general instructs the capital's military commander to "introduce a little home-rule and a few police regulations" (306). Later, he meets the Sitka Tlingit chief Anahootz, who, according to Howard, tells him, "My people are just beginning to arrive at what I have long desired—amity with the whites and with each other under the protection of a good commander" (308). In his response, Howard extols education as the most efficacious means of learning white ways, at which this chief also asks for a good teacher, for whom he promises to build a schoolhouse. Howard, apparently overcome by passion for education, addresses all the natives on the topics of education and industry, and claims that his polemic is received with "a universal response, hearty and happy" (308).[6]

The Sitka Tlingit, says Howard (308), showed evidence of "extreme poverty" and "vicious indulgence," though we are left to wonder what this might be. The general apparently believes that providing a teacher, education, and industry will cure their ills. Howard shows some anxiety about native "indulgence," perhaps fearing that contact with the natives might contaminate him with the same degeneracy. Traveling on to visit the Chilkat, the general tells the tribe of the benefits to be gained by securing a teacher, and, after visiting the Kake, Howard turns toward home, summarizing his trip as a visit to many tribes whom he found much the same: "usually well fed and kindly disposed, but prone to believe the abundant superstition of natives and still depraved, most of them, by the grosser vices of savage life" (316). In universalizing native cultures and experiences, the general manages alterity by homogenizing it. He conducts his civilizing mission among people he regards as primitive and childlike, concluding that natives must be educated in the white man's ways if they are to avoid poverty and a depraved life. He presents them as grateful subjects, perfectly under his control.

ORDERING AND DISPLACING CULTURES

In the early period of colonization, policies predominated that sought to assimilate natives through education or to criminalize or contest cultural practices that did not meet Euro-American norms and expectations. At the same time, natives were encouraged to become economically dependent on the imported culture and to neglect their own customs and traditions in favor of Euro-Americans ways (Krause 1956, 46–47). Instead of fostering traditional practices, such as those that promoted dispute resolution, the Americans championed a strategy that emphasized materialism and dependency within the introduced economy. Unlike the Russians, who had lived among the native populations, the Euro-Americans did not invest time or energy in familiarizing themselves with native cultures. U.S. colonizers rejected the idea of peaceful coexistence, fearing the disorder manifested in the figure of "the savage" with his "untamed nature or barely contained human passion" (Fitzpatrick 1992, 81). Instead, they devised and implemented an ordering process that constantly asserted and affirmed their cultural superiority. Laws, policies, social practices, and discourse separately and in combination regulated the lives and customs of the Alaskan Natives in the interests of the colonizers. The colonizers adopted a range of measures that included labeling traditional practices deviant and punishing those who observed them, rendering local ways of social control redundant, outlawing native languages, and undermining the traditional subsistence lifestyle by promoting reliance on imported foodstuffs and material goods.

The Tlingit acknowledged Euro-American power but did not welcome it. At the time of takeover, many sought to resist the colonization of their lands. In 1898, in Juneau, having had time to reflect on the nature of their colonizers, they were given an opportunity to voice their grievances to the governor. Tlingit Chief Kadashan is reported as saying that "[W]hite people are smart; our people are not as smart as white people. They have a very fine name; they call themselves white people. Just like the sun shining on this earth.

They are powerful . . . It is not right for such powerful people as you are to take away from poor people like we are, our creeks and hunting grounds" (in Daley and James 1998, 366).

In the ordering process, the powerful colonizers criminalized customs and traditional practices with the aim of civilizing or advancing "peoples defined as inferior" (Engel Merry 1998, 18). It did not matter that the Tlingit and other cultures possessed highly developed and complex norms and rules governing conduct, because, as Peter Fitzpatrick has observed, "the most complex of resident legal cultures were taken over with an unquestioning confidence by colonial administrators" (1992, 110). In Alaska, acts that were labeled deviant included speaking and writing indigenous languages in mission schools. S. Hall Young, the first Presbyterian minister recruited for Alaska, expressed a typical attitude toward native language: "The Tlingits never had a written language. While the figures on their totem poles and on their blankets and baskets expressed certain crude ideas, they could not convey messages or thoughts to one another. Their language . . . like the Chinook was ridiculously inadequate to express any thought" (quoted in Cox 1991, 23).

Forcing the children to learn English enabled the colonizers to instill in them Euro-American values and aspirations, and encouraged them to abandon their traditional culture so that "they would most rapidly get away from their heathen customs and advance in civilization. Those who know no English are great sticklers for old customs" (Mitchell 1997, 95). The decree on language use was strictly enforced. For example, when a Quaker missionary in Douglas heard a pupil speaking Tlingit, he would soak a sponge with hot peppers and bitter-tasting resin and rinse the pupil's mouth out to remove the foul language (95). Such methods appear to have worked, since, in 1887, the *Alaskan* newspaper reported that the natives were accepting the decree "with good grace and they were now anxious, both old and young, to adopt the new language and follow in the footsteps of civilization" (95).

The Christian missions regarded education as "the primary means of enticing young Native Americans to reject tradition and seek conversion" (Hoxie, Mancall, and Merrell 2001, 158). If natives failed to attend school, where they were expected to acquire these new values, their parents were sanctioned with criminal penalties. In 1881, for example, Captain Glass, naval commander at Sitka, ordered all native children between the ages of five and nineteen to attend school. To enforce this decree, each village house was allocated a number and all inhabitants in each house counted. Children were required to wear a tin marker inscribed with their house number around the neck (Krause 1956 [1875], 228). A child found on the street during school hours would be detained by the native police, who would inspect the tag and note it. The following day, the head of that child's household would be summoned by the teacher to explain his or her absence from school, and, if the explanation failed to satisfy, a fine of a blanket or a day in jail was imposed (Krause 1956 [1875], 228; Mitchell 1997, 75).

Moreover, there were clearly gendered concerns in the colonizers' bid to educate the indigenous population. As the primary socializers of small children, women were thought crucial to the colonial enterprise. Thus, Presbyterian Isaac Baird wrote, "the girls will need the training more than the boys as they will wield a greater influence in the future. If we get the girls we get the race" (159).

In promoting a policy of assimilation through education, the army administration marched in line with the strategy formulated by General George Washington, who proposed that Indian policy comprise three elements that included transforming the natives' thinking and behavior to match that of whites (Mitchell 1997, 18).[7] Thus, federal policy on natives in Alaska as administered by the U.S. Bureau of Education enticed the natives to consume a range of imported foods and other goods and to adopt a material culture quite different from their own. The local subsistence economy waned, and natives had to compete for low-paying jobs at Euro-American centers of population, and so most worked as poorly skilled laborers. This, and not education, was their principal assimilation experience (99).

Dr. Sheldon Jackson, the first general agent of education for the territory, emphasized "moral education," which encompassed the adoption of Western courting and marriage customs, and acceptance of the white work ethic and the economics of American society (Cox 1991, 24). As elsewhere in America and abroad, missionary teachers believed that the best means of educating native children was to remove them from their parents (93–94). Rather than destroying families, such practices were, in the colonizers' view, beneficial to the native population. Jackson thus defined the purpose of his industrial training and boarding school at Sitka: "as the people make progress, catch the spirit of civilization and come under the influences which emanate from the schools, they gradually begin to give up their old methods of living, and adopt the American" (cited in Cox 1991, 26). Specifically, industrial training would ensure that native men would earn a sufficient income to buy the consumer goods that would make them American, and that the women would be trained to become productive housewives.

Despite the missionary and official pressure for culture change, the cultures of Alaska persisted, because they adapted and sometimes resisted social change as they had always done. Andrei Znamenski (1998), discussing Russian Orthodox missionary activity in the period 1896–1907, points out that current research has shown that Alaskan Natives actively borrowed and experimented with elements of the various religions for their own benefit and, through this syncretic approach, incorporated foreign religion into their cultural worldviews. Thus religion was shaped to meet indigenous needs. Similarly, after 1867 the natives indigenized Orthodoxy and, because Tlingit words and concepts had to be used to convey the nature of the imported religion, "Christianity reached the natives through a screen of traditional beliefs" (Kan 1985, 208). Moreover, the missionaries themselves approached the task of conversion somewhat half-heartedly because very few of them, even those who had spent a long time in the southeast of the territory, could speak Tlingit. Scholars now see indigenous societies as having experimented with Western religions and reinterpreted them to converge with their own cultures. They were creative in adopting some parts of the religious tenets and discarding others, and followed a "complex process of intercultural exchange" (Znamenski 1999, 7).

The early missionaries were disturbed by a number of native customs and traditions that appeared to challenge Euro-American values of gender and class. For example, a couple could divorce with ease if they considered themselves incompatible. Customary practice also accepted sexual relations between unmarried adolescents (Cox 1991). Other traditions with both economic and social significance, such as the potlatch, were mysterious and incomprehensible, and American officials actively challenged them (Remsberg 1975). Military commanders too were troubled by what they perceived as resistance to the ordering process, such as intraclan fighting among the Tlingit, and tried to stop these contests by issuing warnings of severe punishment (Remsberg 1975).[8] Customary notions such as a belief in blood vengeance, retaliation, and compensation gravely worried the Americans (Remsberg 1975, 292). The natives thought in terms of collective guilt, and wanted compensation or "an eye for an eye." For instance, the natives insisted on compensation for attacks upon them by American traders. The army, however, considered such demands bribery at best and extravagant blackmail at worst, and were always reluctant to give in.[9] In general, officials refused to pay them compensation and insisted that disputes be settled in "the American way" (Remsberg 1975, 295).

Native crimes like petty thefts and armed robbery reinforced an American perception that basic lawlessness lay deep in the Indian character. However, most criminal prosecutions involving natives were for violations of liquor laws or for offenses committed while intoxicated; alcohol was the cause of most of what the army perceived as crime and disorder in the territory during the first eighteen years after acquisition (Hunt 1987).[10] In criminal trials, accused natives relied on explanations consistent with native custom, but the American courts insisted that the civilizing process made such explanations illegitimate. In one of the first murder trials in the territory, the accused, Kie, had killed his wife and was convicted of manslaughter and sentenced to ten years in prison (Hunt 1987). He appealed to the circuit court in San Francisco, arguing that killing his wife in the particular circumstances of his case was justified by tradition and custom. Although the circuit court refused to consider the issue of custom as a defense, it did note the effect of recent white incursions into Alaska. The court advised Congress to institute a legal regime that, in the case of "minor offenses peculiar to their social life and condition," would allow custom to regulate proceedings (Hunt 1987, 35). Nonetheless, the court's overall finding on the defense was that the aim of the 1884 Organic Law granting civil government to the territory was to "impart to this people the elements of our civilization" so that they might "not be allowed to practice with impunity such acts of barbarity" as did the Kie (35).

The Americans were particularly concerned about a form of bondage within Tlingit culture that they equated with Euro-American slavery (Hunt 1987). An early civil case featured Sah Quah, who had been captured and sold into slavery when a boy. After many years, Quah petitioned the court for release. His owner pleaded that he and his tribe were uncivilized natives and that their own laws and customs governed their communities; buying, selling, and holding slaves was one such custom, and the civil authority lacked jurisdiction over them. The judge ruled against these arguments and held that the practice of slavery was intolerable in a civilized Christian community. This appeal to Christian morality as the basis for condemning slavery was, of course, somewhat compromised by the missionary practice of capturing native children and removing them from their homes and communities for education and assimilation. In one instance, U.S. Attorney Haskett made this parallel with cross-cultural slavery explicit when he decided that missionary Sheldon Jackson's practice of removing native children to his home in Sitka as boarders for five years amounted to indentured servitude (Hunt 1987, 18). Having located some native parents of children who said they did not understand the custody papers they had signed, Haskett filed petitions to free the children. A judge found for Haskett.[11]

Interactions between Alaskan Natives and the missionaries and government officers often reinforced the American perception that Alaskan Natives were lawless people practicing customs inimical to Euro-American ways. In the early period in Sitka, most exchanges between natives and Americans involved army officers and troops. For the military, the civilizing mission was often treated as an opportunity to promote alcohol abuse among the natives, sexually exploit native women, and practice the immorality and depravity that the surgeon's wife and the general placed exclusively within the native community. One commentator describes the army as being "as dissolute a lot of rascals as ever wore the army uniform," who did "more to provoke disorder than to prevent it" (Hulley 1970, 209). Similarly, in 1855, a traveler through Alaska wrote that, although the Tlingit were pleasant to him and his guide, they showed only "unconcealed hostility" toward American soldiers (Teichmann 1963, 214). Soldiers encouraged the local production of a homebrew known as hooch. At Wrangell, the deputy customs collector alleged that troops made a business of manufacturing liquor, which they sold to the natives (Nielson 1988, 20). Dr. E. J. Bailey, the medical director of the Department of Alaska, thought that a "greater mistake could not have been committed than placing troops in their (the Indians') midst" (quoted in Nielson 1988, 20).

The rape of native women by soldiers was a special cause of concern (Remsberg 1975, 283). Army officers tried to keep their men out of the villages, and troops were not allowed outside the stockade after dark without prior approval. Court martial records, however, show the ineffectiveness of these orders, and it proved impossible to keep the troops away from the Tlingit women. Thus, while the administration and the army officially attacked native customs they deemed depraved and uncivilized, they permitted native women to be preyed upon, abused, and vilified.

Conclusion: Tracing the Impact of Colonialism Today

Over the past two decades, an increasing number of researchers have theorized the economic, social, and political consequences of the colonization of American Indians and Alaskan Natives.[12] This chapter contributes to that body of literature by examining several ways the native cultures of Alaskan were ordered, disrupted, and displaced to further the American colonial project. As it has shown, records of the past and autobiographical accounts of the period reveal that laws, policies, and practices of colonial administrators and the military together and individually defined cultural practices as deviant and Alaskan Native cultures as beyond "civilization." These records and accounts thus provide practical examples of the manner in which colonizers, "in drawing racial, sexual and class boundaries . . . and actually formulating these as integral to the maintenance of colonial rule, defined authority and legitimacy through the difference rather than commonality of rulers and 'natives' " (Mohanty et al. 1991, 16).

Of course, a theoretically-informed appreciation of the colonial project in Alaska must also acknowledge that all cultures change, and that some of these developments were occurring even before the Euro-Americans arrived. Culture does not remain permanently "traditional." It is a mutable and active process. Studies of social change "always associate change with European contacts or some colonial presence" and most accounts of social change involving the colonization of peoples are written as if there is no continuity between the *before* of colonial encounters and the *after* (Thomas 1989, 11). In my view, theorists of colonialism and North American indigenous cultures ought to bring into their accounts the concrete forms of adaptation and change generated by these cultures during the colonial project, to add greater insight to the theoretical understanding. Theoretical accounts can also be enriched by focusing on the colonizers themselves, and here I agree with Rabinow (1986, 259), who calls for studies of colonialism to focus more on "the cultural complexity of colonial life as it varied from place to place at different historical periods" (258). The autobiographical accounts of the surgeon's wife and the general thus supplement records of the colonial project with tangible evidence of intricate cultural phenomena and exchanges revealing how "we can only understand the social life of other cultures through the prison of our own linguistic and conceptual apparatus" (Beirne 1983, 385). More than that, however, such accounts provide a firm foundation for examining indigenous experiences today.

For example, similar practices of cultural differentiation that were first established during the initial ordering process can be found in the contemporary prison environment. In the Alaskan prison system, those few Euro-Americans who are confronted with Alaskan Native cultures engage in analogous processes of ordering the native, of fear of the Other, and of cultural boundary-marking; in turn, their actions continue to be met with a cultural adaptation akin to that which sustained Alaskan Natives during the early part of the colonial project in Alaska. In prison, Alaskan cultures are subjected to an ordering process by prison staff who interpret behavior and belief according to Euro-American values and expectations. Relations between guards and Alaskan Native women are mediated through the lens of difference; all Alaskan cultures are regarded as homogeneous, and many prison staff regard the women as childlike and in need of protection. Thus the guards affirm past colonial practices, attitudes, and values toward Alaskan Native cultures. In the prison context (and elsewhere), culture is regarded as unchanged and unchanging, and cultural meanings channeled into the values and thinking of the dominant culture.

Just as the surgeon's wife read Tlingit culture by confining it within a pre-existing Euro-American discourse that made it intelligible to her, so do prison staff arrive at conclusions about Alaskan Native attitudes to treatment and to the prison regime in response to a Euro-American discourse about cognitive treatment programs and reform of the self (Banks 2002). For example, when native women follow their cultural learning practices of watching and learning through observation, rather than actively participating in treatment programs, the staff interpret their conduct as nonparticipation and therefore as resistant to treatment.

The staff, like the general, experience a sense of unease and anxiety associated with the colonial project and with the ordering of the Other. Thus, when women attempt to demonstrate respect by maintaining their distance, staff construe such conduct as unfriendliness: "(t)hey won't look you in the eye, don't show emotions, won't cry, some will laugh but look away. They keep to themselves. You don't even know they are there unless you go to them." They resent the women's quietness and unwillingness to display emotional patterns found in Euro-American culture, preferring the women to confide in them and take responsibility for their deviance in explicit forms.

The ordering process in the early colonial period required natives to become competent in the English language to mark their cultural assimilation. Today, fluency in the Euro-American language of "treatment" renders a native woman reformed and ready for release from the Alaskan prison. Alaskan Native women must undertake a series of treatment programs that stress individuality, accountability, and confrontation, values that are respected and even cherished in Euro-American cultures. Above all, the women must demonstrate knowledge of the techniques of participation, and of the language and responses to counseling, in cognitive programs designed for Euro-American women.

Just as the early colonizers refused to recognize all cultures as legitimate and valued, so the prison authorities of today continue to read Alaskan cultures through a lens of perceived cultural superiority and supremacy. Prison norms and rules deny cultural difference. Any discrete cultural programming for Alaskan Natives is regarded by most staff as conferring "special treatment." Confronted with these practices and beliefs, incarcerated Alaskan Native women and men follow a complex process of intercultural exchange by tenaciously asserting their cultures while remaining acutely aware that they must adapt to the ordering process that began with the American takeover of their lands.

NOTES

1. The acquisition of territories by the United States was authorized and regulated by the Northwest Ordinance of 1787, which provided that new territories were to be given the status of districts and have their officials appointed by the president until the white male population reached five thousand (Nielson 1988, 15–16).

2. Writing in 1875, explorer Dr. Aurel Krause pointed out that, although Tlingit certainly did smell strongly compared to whites, Tlingit had been accustomed to taking sweat baths even before contact with whites and "the need for bodily cleanliness was not completely foreign" to them (1956 [1875], 113).

3. According to Krause, when engaging with other Tlingit or non-Tlingit, the Tlingit was quiet and evenhanded. Haste or curiosity was regarded as improper conduct and words came slowly, and it was only through tragic emotion that speech became expressive (Krause 1956 [1875]). In fact, Chinook was not a true language but a kind of trade Creole or pidgin of the Northwest Coast, limited in its scope. Olson (1967, preface, v) writes that "the Tlingit language is an extremely difficult one and trader and missionary alike depended on the Chinook jargon. While this served admirably for purposes of trading, attempts to explain Christianity by means of it must have been merely ridiculous."

4. The ability of the Tlingit at Sitka to withstand extremes of climate, and their physical strength, were considerable (Krause 1956 [1875], 103). Krause cites the examples of Tlingit carrying packs of one hundred pounds through mountain passes, and spending the night in the open with little clothing or covering in temperatures of minus twenty-to-thirty degrees Celsius.

5. Krause (1956 [1875], 115) observed that the Tlingit had a highly developed sense of ownership but theft was not considered a disgraceful act. If the thief returned the

stolen property he would not be punished further and did not lose the respect of his peers. The thief who was caught, however, was shamed by his lack of skill. In theory, stealing did not exist within clans as all resources were held in common (Oberg 1934, 214). However, if a man took individual assets like tools, he had to return them.

6. Anahootz reminded Howard that he had been doing his best to live peacefully with the whites even though nine of his people had been killed or wounded by whites, and complained that the storekeepers in the town treated them "like dogs," because they were paid for their labor with "a little hard tack or flour and if they complain are kicked from the stores" (Mitchell 1997, 53).

7. The first element was protection of the natives from exploitation and land seizure, reflected in laws that prohibited trade with the natives except by licensed persons and voided all land sales except those effected under government authority. The second was an effort to persuade the natives to cede more land to the government on a voluntary basis (Mitchell 1997, 18).

8. Few murders took place in Tlingit society until alcohol arrived. Murder among the Tlingit was punished by death when committed outside the clan. If the victim was of low rank and poor reputation, the injured clan could be compensated for the death by a payment in goods. If the victim was of high rank, then the death of a man of equal standing was required. The man selected to die did so willingly, as to die for the honor of one's clan was thought an act of great bravery (Oberg 1934, 211).

9. In one such incident in 1872, two traders escaped death after sixty armed natives, intent on avenging a tribesman allegedly injured by whites, shot at their schooner and threatened to seize their ship, kill the crew, and plunder the cargo if the Americans did not pay very high prices for their furs (293). The traders managed to escape.

10. In the Pribiloff Islands, the Americans would not tolerate drunken Aleuts and at first lectured them about the evils of drinking. Later, they undertook investigations by searching houses and assigning work as punishment for possessing home brew. They also imposed fines and placed intoxicated persons in irons, as well as threatening them with exile (Jones 1980, 26). The Aleuts refused to conform. Nancy Lurie has described Indian drinking as "the world's longest on-going protest demonstration" (Lurie in Jones 1980, 26).

11. In response to this adverse decision Jackson actively lobbied against the judge and prosecutor in Washington, and the outcome was a presidential removal from office of the judge and the prosecutor (Hunt 1987, 18).

12. See, for example: LaPraire 1987; Saggers and Gray 1998; Mitchell 1997; Ross 1998; Razack 1998; Furniss 1999; and Rabinow 1986.

WORKS CITED

Banks, Cyndi. 2002. Doing time in Alaska: Women, culture, and crime. In *It's a crime: Women and justice*, 3rd edition, ed. Roslyn Muraskin. Upper Saddle River, NJ: Prentice Hall.

Beirne, Piers. 1983. Cultural relativism and comparative criminology. *Contemporary Crisis* 7: 371–391.

Cox, James. 1991. *The impact of Christian missions on indigenous cultures: The "real people" and the unreal gospel.* Lewiston, NY: Edwin Mellen Press.

Daley, Patrick, and Beverly James. 1998. Missionary voices as the discursive terrain for native resistance. *Journal of Communication Inquiry* 22: 365–384.

Engel Merry, Sally. 1998. The criminalization of everyday life. In *Everyday practices and trouble cases*, ed. Austin Sarat, Marianne Constable, David Engel, Valerie Hans, and Susan Lawrence, 14–39. Evanston, IL: Northwestern University Press.

Fitzpatrick, Peter. 1992. *The myth of modern law*. London: Routledge.

Furniss, Elizabeth. 1999. *The burden of history: Colonialism and the frontier myth in a rural Canadian community*. Vancouver, BC: UBC Press.

Howard, Oliver. 1972 [1907]. *My life and experiences among our hostile Indians: A record of personal observations, adventures, and campaigns among the Indians of the great West, with some account of their life, habits, traits, religion, ceremonies, dress, savage instincts, and customs in peace and war*. New York: Da Capo Press.

Hoxie, Frederick, Peter Mancall, and James Merrell, eds. 2001. *American nations: Encounters in Indian country, 1850 to the present*. New York: Routledge.

Hulley, Clarence Charles. 1970. *Alaska: Past and present*. Portland, OR: Binfords and Mort.

Hunt, William. 1987. *Distant justice: Policing the Alaskan frontier*. Norman, OK: University of Oklahoma Press.

Jones, Dorothy Knee. 1980. *A century of servitude: Pribilof Aleuts under U.S. rule*. Washington, DC: University Press of America.

Kan, Sergei. 1985. Russian Orthodox brotherhoods among the Tlingit: Missionary goals and native response. *Ethnohistory* 32: 196–223.

Krause, Aurel. 1956. *The Tlingit Indians: Results of a trip to the Northwest coast of America and the Bering Straits*. Seattle, WA: University of Washington Press.

LaPrairie, Carol. 1987. Native women and crime: A theoretical model. *Canadian Journal of Native Studies* 7: 121–137.

Laufe, Abe, ed. 1962. *An army doctor's wife on the frontier*. Pittsburgh, PA: University of Pittsburgh Press.

Lautaret, Ronald. 1989. *Alaskan historical documents since 1867*. Jefferson, NC: McFarland and Company.

Mitchell, Donald. 1997. *Sold American: The story of Alaska Natives and their land, 1867–1959: The army to statehood*. Hanover, MA: University Press of New England.

Mohanty, Chandra Talpade, Ann Russo, and Lourdes Torres. 1991. *Third World women and the politics of feminism*. Bloomington: Indiana University Press.

Nielson, Jonathan. 1988. *Armed forces on a northern frontier: The military in Alaska's history, 1867–1987*. New York: Greenwood Press.

Oberg, Kalervo. 1934. Deviance and normality: Crime and punishment in Tlingit society. *American Anthropologist* 36: 145–156.

Olson, R.L. 1967. *Social structure and social life of the Tlingit in Alaska*. Berkeley and Los Angeles: University of California Press.

Rabinow, Paul. 1986. Representations are social facts: Modernity and post-modernity in anthropology. In *Writing culture: The poetics and politics of ethnography*, ed. James Clifford and George Marcus. Berkeley and Los Angeles: University of California Press.

Razack, Sherene. 1998. *Looking white people in the eye: Gender, race, and culture in courtrooms and classrooms*. Toronto, ON: University of Toronto Press.

Remsberg, Stanley. 1975. United States Administration of Alaska: The Army Phase, 1867–1877. A study in federal governance of an overseas possession, Vol. 1. PhD diss., University of Wisconsin`Madison.

Ross, Luana. 1998. *Inventing the savage: The social construction of Native American criminality*. Austin: University of Texas Press.

Saggers, Sherry, and Dennis Gray. 1998. *Dealing with alcohol: Indigenous usage in Australia, New Zealand, and Canada*. Cambridge: Cambridge University Press.

Teichmann, Emil. 1963. *A journey to Alaska in the year 1868*. New York: Argosy-Antiquarian.

Thomas, Nicholas. 1989. *Out of time: History and evolution in anthropological discourse*. Cambridge: Cambridge University Press.

Turner, Bryan. 1994. *Orientalism, postmoderism, and globalism*. New York: Routledge.

Znamenski, Andrei. 1998. Native culture through Orthodox eyes: Russian missionary Ioann Bortnovsky on the Dena'ina and Ahtna, 1896–1907. *Alaska History* 13: 1–26.

———. 1999. *Shamanism and Christianity: Native encounters with Russian Orthodox missions in Siberia and Alaska, 1820–1917*. Westport, CT: Greenwood Press.

CHAPTER 3

Colonialism and Its Impact on Mexicans' Experiences of Punishment in the United States

Martin G. Urbina and Leslie Smith

AS THE DOMINANT ECONOMIC AND MILITARY FORCE in the region, the United States has for many years reaped the benefits of official and unofficial practices of colonialism. Claiming sovereignty over territory and people beyond its own boundaries in order to facilitate economic and political domination over their resources, labor, and markets, it has also legitimized and promoted a belief system where nativist views, customs, and cultures have been treated as superior to all others. Externally, the United States' might has been shored up through a combination of immigration policies, economic treaties, and military action. Internally, almost all institutions and interactions reflect the majority interest, as racial and ethnic differences established in the colonial era have successfully made race, ethnicity, and color a basis for group position in the contemporary United States.

As many scholars have observed, prisons and the system of punishment have been particularly adversely affected by these views. The impact on the African American population is well rehearsed (see Young and Spencer, Messerschmidt, and Flavin, this volume). What is less frequently discussed, however, is their effect on the 12.5 percent of the population that is Latino(a).[1] In part because we tend to theorize without nuance, and because ethnicity has received insufficient attention in academic literature, the story of Latinos and Latinas in the American legal system remains incomplete. Yet clearly something is going on. From 1985 to 2001, for example, the percentage of Latinos(as) in state or federal prisons increased from 10.9 to 15.6 percent (Bonczar 2003). In 2001, one in ten Latinos between the ages of thirty-five and forty-four had at some point been incarcerated (Bonczar 2003). By 2003, nearly one in three persons held in federal prisons was Latino(a). If current incarceration rates continue, about one in six Latinos, and two in one hundred Latinas, born in 2001 are expected to go to prison at some point in their lifetimes (Bonczar 2003).

Despite being bracketed together as "Latino" or "Hispanic," many different groups comprise the Latino(a) population, and each receives distinct treatment within the U.S. legal system.[2] At least part of the variation in the punishment of Cubans, Mexicans, Puerto Ricans, and South and Central Americans may be explained historically. For example, both Puerto Rico and Mexico were deeply affected by the process and influence of colonialism, but, unlike Mexico, the island of Puerto Rico was not conquered in war by the United States. Rather, it was ceded to the United States in a "political transaction" through which it received formal recognition as a colony without the "benefits" of total invasion. In comparison, the experience of Cubans in the United States has been defined by notions of socialism and democracy and by the frequently antagonistic relationship between the U.S. government and that of Fidel Castro (see Ruddell and Urbina 2004).[3] In this chapter, we focus on the treatment and experiences of Mexicans and Mexican Americans, who are the largest Latino(a) group in the United States. Mexicans constitute 9 percent (25,300,000) of the total U.S. population and approximately 63 percent of the Latino(a) population (U.S. Census Bureau 2005). The chapter reveals how the treatment of Mexicans and other Latinos(as) is dictated in part by complex webs and histories of colonialism. It also illustrates why the concepts of social control and punishment need to be broadly conceived to take into account persistent measures, like racial profiling and border control, that are often used as punitive mechanisms against a population.

THE LEGACY OF COLONIALISM

Long before the United States sought to control Mexican territory, European nations pursued a vigorous regime of colonial expansion. What began as an internal process—exemplified by the Spanish *reconquista*—gradually extended its reach across oceans, with the "voyages of discovery." The apex of power was reached in the early twentieth century, when 84 percent of the earth's surface was controlled by European nations (Shohat and Stam 1994).

Colonizing practices, in which large swaths of foreign territory were appropriated and indigenous peoples and cultures were destroyed, needed some justification. In this regard, racism quickly became colonialism's ally as well as its product. The "conviction of our superiority, not merely our mechanical, economic, and military superiority, but our moral superiority," enabled colonialists to portray, to themselves and to their compatriots back home, indigenous people as lacking order, intelligence, sexual modesty, material civilization, and even history (Jules Harmand, as quoted in Shohat and Stam 1994, 18). Thus, the Anglo-American war against the Native American population was justified by Indians' "savagery," while Mexicans were labeled "bandidos" and "greasers" when Americans sought to take over their territory. Prejudices once reserved for African Americans and Native Americans were transferred to the mestizo Mexicans, as many whites decried "mixed blood" and blamed the decline and "degeneracy" of Mexicans on miscegenation.

Colonial racism had several other ramifications, including a desire to rank not only people, but artifacts and cultural practices. Colonized people were blamed for their condition, while colonialists, refusing to empathize with people struggling for survival, were skeptical of their claims of oppression and systematically devalued their lives (Shohat and Stam 1994; see Banks, this volume). As the rest of this chapter will demonstrate, these byproducts of colonial rule continue to shape and define the treatment of Mexicans and Mexican Americans in the U.S. criminal justice system.

MEXICO AND COLONIALISM

Mexico endured successive foreign conquests—first by Spain, in 1519, and then by the United States, in 1848. Although the U.S. war against Mexico was justified by the idea of "Manifest Destiny," which posited that the whole North American continent should belong to Anglos because Anglos were a superior race (Trujillo 1974), the reasons for the conflict were predominantly economic. The United States declared war on Mexico in 1846 to acquire the resource-rich territories of Texas and California, along with the connecting desert terrain. A long course of mutual distrust was about to begin.

The Treaty of Guadalupe Hidalgo ended the brutalities that came with war, while ushering in a new form of domination, suppression, and subordination. When the Mexican-American War ended in 1848, there were close to seventy-five thousand Mexicans living in the conquered territory, from California to Texas (Weber 1998). Those who opted to remain in the United States were given the choice of U.S. or Mexican citizenship; if no choice was made within a year, they would automatically become U.S. citizens. However, these guarantees were not fulfilled. Instead, many Mexicans lost rights to their land and were exploited as a cheap labor force for the expanding U.S. economy. When some tried to resist, police and the military were called in to preserve "law and order," and, if that did not suffice, local Anglo populations formed vigilante committees.

The suppression of Mexicans occurred also at the level of culture as they became targets of countless negative characterizations. A *New York Times* headline of 1882, for example, described "[Mexicans'] hatred of Americans, their dense ignorance, and total unfitness for citizenship" (Gomez 2000, 1143). They were viewed as "criminal" because of their "Indian blood," "low intelligence," and "feeblemindedness." Mexicans, it was asserted, were impulsive, passive, cruel, superstitious, lazy, and cunning. They were ruthless bandits, preying on American citizens. This particular idea, as well as the slogan

"Remember the Alamo," persist today (Urbina 2003b; Muñoz, Lopez, and Stewart 1998).

CONTROL AND PUNISHMENT
IN THE UNITED STATES

Prejudiced assumptions about the nature of Mexicans continue to mar relations between Anglos and Mexican Americans, and have significant implications for how the latter are treated in the criminal justice system (Trujillo 1974; see also Hagan and Palloni 1999; Díaz–Cotto 1996; Steffensmeier and Demuth 2001; Aguirre 2004). The perceived or actual immigrant status of many Mexicans and other Latinos(as) also means that they are subject to the forces of border control, while the growing population of Latinos is threatening to some Anglo-Americans who fear competition for jobs and the decreasing primacy of Anglo-American culture (Steffensmeier and Demuth 2001). The complex intersections of race, ethnicity, language, and immigration status create a heady mix in which forces of social control and state coercion operate with extreme punitiveness. Likewise, the participation of the military, the police, immigration officials, and certain sections of the Anglo community in the social control of Mexicans, an overlapping involvement that dates to the nineteenth century, continues today.

For many years, for example, Mexican Americans have served as a convenient scapegoat for crime rates in many cities. Criminalizing Mexicans has been of particular benefit for those employers who use the threat of raids and deportation as a tool of intimidation and control (see Calavita, this volume). During economic downturns, many Mexicans, including U.S. citizens, have been deported from the country, especially from California and Texas, where the Mexican population is concentrated (Gutierrez 1997). At other times, Mexican workers are shipped back to Mexico after the season's field work is done. In 1996 in Jackson Hole, Wyoming, local police and Border Patrol agents raided numerous restaurants and took into custody 153 Latino workers, nearly one-third of whom were legal residents or U.S. citizens (Parenti 1999). Such actions unnerve undocumented immigrants and legal residents alike, serving to keep workers unorganized. Indeed, in the dangerous and dirty labor markets of food processing and agriculture, employers often prefer poor and criminalized workers who, because of their legal status, are unable to demand greater salaries or improved labor conditions (Parenti 1999, 154).

Likewise, there tends to be heavier police deployment and militarization of policing practices in Mexican American neighborhoods (see Sanchez, this volume). A recent study of 114 U.S. cities, for example, found that "the constellation of social conditions that . . . Hispanics confront amplifies the police's perceptions of minority threat and increases the use of coercive controls such as excessive force" (Smith and Holmes 2003, 1055). As a result, Mexicans and

Mexican Americans experience higher arrest rates and punitive racism and discrimination. They are often subject to illegal practices and biased discretion and frequently are unable to make bail or hire lawyers (see Acuna 1998; Urbina and Kreitzer 2004).

Language barriers are also particularly difficult. After the 1848 conquest, Mexican Americans struggled with Anglos for the survival of their culture and language. Imposing the English language became a tool for subordinating the newly conquered population; those who did not readily comply were punished and viewed as threats to the state's security and authority (Perea 2004). Today, language remains a concern of Mexicans, and Latinos(as) in general throughout the United States (Urbina 2004a; Perea 2004, 1425). As Juanita Díaz-Cotto (1996) observes, "It is not uncommon for law enforcement officials to regard the speaking of a foreign language as defiance" (56). It is not surprising then, that Latinos(as) have been punished for speaking Spanish in some prison facilities (DeJesus-Torres 2000). Due process challenges to limited or non-English-speaking Latino(a) defendants start before the trial actually begins. Language barriers may influence whether a defendant is forced to provide a voluntary confession to the police, consent to a police search, waive the right to trial by jury, or fully understand the elements and consequences of the charge, the Constitutional rights waived, and the significance of a plea in plea bargaining negotiations. In some situations, communication is a problem behind prison walls and may result in difficulties between inmates and correctional officers. Until mechanisms are set in place to control for these issues, Mexicans will not receive the full benefits of due process, negotiation, and basic human rights.

The treatment of Mexicans in the U.S. legal system is better documented than it is for Cubans and Puerto Ricans, yet information is still minimal. Most studies of punishment have excluded Latinos and Latinas, or scholars have classified Latinos(as) into either "white" or "black" categories in punishment research. This practice has, in effect, silenced attempts by Latinos(as) to show that they are victimized both by crime and by criminal justice agencies (Aguirre and Baker 2000).

Information about incarceration likewise rarely distinguishes among the various Latino(a) ethnic groups. Evidence strongly suggests, however, that Latino(a) men and women face harsher punishment than do whites (see Díaz-Cotto, this volume). Nationally, in state prisons and local jails, Hispanics are incarcerated at nearly twice the rate of whites; in some states, the rate is six or seven times higher (Beck, Karberg, and Harrison 2002). Muñoz et al. (1998) examined several rural Nebraskan counties and found that Latinos(as) had significantly higher proportions of individuals charged with misdemeanor offenses, and that they received both a higher mean number of charges and higher mean fines and days' probation. A study of criminal cases between 1981 and 1990 in California showed that 20 percent of white defendants charged with crimes providing for the option of diversion received that decision, while only 11 percent of similarly situated Latinos were placed in such programs (Weich and Angulo 2000). Federal statistics also indicate that, although non-Latinos are likely to be released prior to trial in 66 percent of cases, Latinos are released only 26 percent of the time (Weich and Angulo 2000). This has important implications for trial outcomes, as pretrial detention is known to increase vulnerability to conviction and imprisonment (Hagan and Palloni 1999).

Most seriously, differential treatment is widespread in the matter of capital punishment (Urbina 2003a, 2003c). In the case of *Saldano v. Texas*, prosecutors relied on the expert testimony of a psychiatrist who "testified about statistical factors which have been identified as increasing the probability of future dangerousness. He noted that African Americans and Hispanics are overrepresented in prisons compared to their representation outside of prison [and] testified that because the appellant is Hispanic, this was a factor weighing in the favor of future dangerousness" (Weich and Angulo 2000, 196).

The U.S. Supreme Court eventually vacated the judgment against Saldano after Texas conceded error. Of the nineteen identifiable Latinos executed between 1975 and 1995, sixteen were of Mexican origin (Urbina 2004b), and as of 2004, fifty-one Mexican nationals were on death row in the United States (International Court of Justice 2004). In part, this overrepresentation could be explained by data showing that, between 1890 and 1986, the number of appeals to a higher court was much lower (vis-à-vis other ethnic and racial groups) for Mexicans (Aguirre and Baker 1989). Further, not only were the majority of Mexicans executed between 1975 and 1995 inadequately represented throughout the legal process (including the appeals process), but they were executed in violation of international treaties (Urbina 2004b).

The treatment of Mexican youths by the juvenile justice system also suggests bias. A California study revealed that, with the exception of status offenses, both Mexican boys and girls received the most severe dispositions in all offense categories (Pope and Feyerherm 1981). More recently, a 1998 New Mexico study found strong positive ethnic effects at various processing points—e.g., poor Mexican boys and girls have an especially high likelihood of referral to the formal juvenile justice system (Bond-Maupin and Maupin 1998). Lastly, a 2005 study reports harsher sanctions not only against Mexican youths in some cases, but also against Puerto Ricans, Colombians, and Ecuadorians (Urbina 2005).

RACIAL PROFILING AND
THE U.S. BORDER PATROL

Many Mexicans and Mexican Americans come into contact with the criminal justice system due to racial profiling. Just as African Americans are the target of pretextual traffic stops and searches in the infamous "driving while black" scenarios, Latinas(os) also suffer under the biased scrutiny of police officers across the country. Most often, Latinas(os) are stopped by police on the suspicion that they are drug smugglers, undocumented immigrants, or both. The racial profiling of Mexican-origin persons as foreigners in the United States unfairly burdens all people of Latin American ancestry or appearance, because they are more likely than other persons to be stopped and interrogated about their immigration status, even though the vast majority of Latinos(as) are U.S. citizens or lawful immigrants (Johnson 2000).

The practice of racial profiling is not simply left to the discretion of individual police officers. Sometimes, this practice is mandated or given legitimacy by the highest levels of authority. Carl Williams, the former superintendent of the New Jersey State Police, defended racial profiling by claiming that "mostly minorities" traffic in marijuana and cocaine (Weich and Angulo 2000). Although the U.S. Supreme Court ruled in *United States v. Brigoni-Ponce* that a person's "appearing" Mexican is not sufficient to justify stopping a Mexican American, the Court's written opinion stated that "*the likelihood is high that a person who appears to be of Mexican origin is an alien*" [authors' emphasis] (Aguirre 2004). Elsewhere, the *Sacramento Valley Mirror* published the contents of a 2000 memo obtained from the U.S. Forest Service. The document directed U.S. Forest Service officers to detain Latinas(os) driving through Mendocino National Forest as possible drug smugglers (Aguirre 2004). Indeed, few who appear to be Latino(a) are immune from racial profiling, as evidenced by accounts from a federal judge, the mayor of Pomona, California, and a lawyer, each of whom was stopped by the Border Patrol on suspicion of being an "illegal alien" (Aguirre 2004).

Each year, numerous Mexicans die while trying to cross into the United States along the 2000-mile border. In addition to facing the possibilities of heat stroke, drowning, or dehydration associated with border crossing, Mexicans must risk encounters with U.S. Border Patrol agents and other law enforcement entities. The brutality of such groups in the 1990s, which was extensively documented by both Amnesty International and Human Rights Watch, included unjustified shootings, rape, and beatings (see Amnesty International 1998; Human Rights Watch 1992, 1993, and 1995). In San Ysidro, California, for example, a 23-year-old Mexican man was shot by a Border Patrol agent, who claimed that the man had thrown a rock at him. However, a jury in U.S. District Court found the wounded Mexican not guilty of the charge. In another incident, Border Patrol agents shot a boy whom, once again, they claimed was throwing rocks at them. As with many of the shootings by the border police, the bullet entered the boy's body from the back.

Violence toward Mexicans can be found everywhere along the border. In the late 1980s, a Border Crime Prevention Unit organized jointly by the

San Diego police and the Border Patrol shot thirty-one individuals (nineteen died), all Mexican citizens, in five years (Shorris 1992). One surviving witness described how INS agents sat him in a chair, handcuffed him from behind, and pushed his face toward some dog feces on the floor, saying, "That's what you are" (Shorris 1992, 273; see also Gutierrez 1997; Rodriguez 1993). Numerous cases of sexual assault of Latinas, perpetrated by INS officials and Border Patrol agents, have also occurred on the U.S.–Mexico border. Many women describe being raped as the price they had to pay to cross the border without being apprehended or deported, or to avoid having their documents confiscated (Falcon 2001, 34).

Regardless of individual perspective, it appears that "serious violations of the rights of Mexican nationals were found to be the norm rather than the exception" (Garcia y Griego 1997, 69). Thus, Border Patrol agents and their tactics have become a major threat for many Mexicans, some of whom are U.S. citizens. Since the terrorist attacks of September 11, 2001, the situation appears to be worsening as more and more barriers are being implemented under the rationale of "national security" (see Welch, this volume; Bosworth, this volume). New border vigilante groups like the "Minuteman Civil Defense Corps" and the "Friends of the Border Patrol" have been established; some of these have been implicated in violent attacks of their own. On October 2004 in Douglas, Arizona, for example, a border vigilante detained members of two families, threatening them with a loaded rifle and verbally abusing them; the victims were U.S. citizens, one of whom was a veteran of the U.S. Navy (Border Action Network 2004).

Militarized immigration enforcement is no longer relegated to border areas, as law enforcement and INS authorities cooperate in patrols and raids.[4] In 1997, 120 miles north of the U.S.–Mexico border, in Chandler, Arizona, police and Border Patrol agents began an immigration "round-up," stopping Latino(a) drivers and pedestrians at random, conducting warrantless searches, harassing and sometimes beating victims. The Arizona attorney general condemned the raid, noting that the only criterion at work was skin color; eighteen Latinos(as) filed lawsuits thereafter (Parenti 1999). Because of increased cooperation between local police and INS agents, "Latinos who run stop signs can be checked for immigration papers and undocumented jaywalkers now live under the threat of deportation" (Parenti 1999, 145). In addition to being unjustly targeted for immigration checks and unlawful searches, Mexicans and Mexican Americans are often the victims of police brutality. Latinos(as) complain of police officers using their firearms unnecessarily, and of using excessive physical force, resulting in severe injuries and death in some cases. Authorities also subject Latinos(as) to verbal abuse, using ethnic slurs (e.g., "spic" or "wetback"), and employing violent epithets against women like "bitch," "whore," and "slut" (Díaz-Cotto 2000, and this volume). Latinas have also been raped and sexually harassed by police officers, who sometimes tell women that they will drop charges in exchange for sexual favors (Díaz-Cotto 1996).[5]

CONCLUSION

Once the United States set out to acquire the rich and fertile territories of the present-day Southwest, war with Mexico was inevitable, and seen as a worthy sacrifice in the fulfillment of Manifest Destiny. The presence of tens of thousands of Mexican citizens on those lands presented no more of an obstacle than had the Native Americans to the first European settlers. The Mexicans, like the Native Americans before them, were vilified by the invading Anglo-Americans, with the implication that such people did not deserve the land in the first place. Promises of citizenship and property were easily given, and just as easily taken away without cause. When these Mexican residents refused to be subjugated, ideological and physical repression were used to forcibly subdue the population. From the viewpoint of the conquerors, there was no alternative to assimilation and Anglo-American dominance, other than elimination or deportation.

Today, discrimination against Mexicans (and Latinos[as] in general) persists. Anglos often cite concerns about Mexicans "taking away" jobs. Latinos(as) are stopped on the street or in their cars because they look like "illegal aliens" or are suspected of being delinquents and criminals. Some fear the possibility of Mexicans attaining elected and/or appointed positions. More recently, observers have claimed that the so-called Mexican "sleeping political giant" is threatening to "wake" (de la Garza and DeSipio 2004). In the last few years, not only has the number of voting Mexicans increased significantly, but, according to the U.S. Census Bureau (2004), naturalized Mexican Americans are more likely to vote than are U.S.-born citizens.[6] Consequently, politicians have begun to woo the Mexican vote.[7]

Although some progress has been made, Mexicans continue to have limited economic and political resources in the United States. Mexican Americans earn far less than Anglo-Americans, even after three generations, because they are less educated than almost all other racial and ethnic groups (Grogger and Trejo 2002). They are also, as this article has shown, overrepresented throughout the criminal justice system.

In sum, the process and influence of colonialism as well as the legacy of hate after the Mexican-American War have manifested themselves in subtle and, at times, overt forms of domination, manipulation, and control. Measures to control the rising number of Mexicans and Mexican Americans in the United States have less to do with actual threats to jobs or real connections to crime than politicians sometimes argue. Rather, they reflect the ruling Anglo majority's fear of losing power and numeric advantage. Today, the racist practices initiated under colonialism persevere in the quest for further conquest and domination.

NOTES

1. Since "Latino(a)" carries less political baggage than the term "Hispanic," we will use the former to refer to people of Spanish heritage who are not Anglo or African American. People of Spanish heritage can be of any "color"; therefore we use the term "Anglo-American" or "Anglo" when referring to nonminorities, and "African American" when referring to the black population that is not of Spanish heritage or Anglo.

2. Of fifty-three ethnic studies conducted in the last sixty years, thirty-four treated Latinos(as) as a monolithic group, fifteen concentrated only on the Mexican experience, four examined Puerto Ricans, and only one study considered the treatment of Colombians, Dominicans, and Cubans (Urbina forthcoming).

3. Initially, skin color was a defining factor in the treatment of these populations. While still significant, skin color has, however, become secondary to the influence of class and legal status, especially for Puerto Ricans and Cubans. For other Latinos and Latinas, especially those who have arrived recently, experiences with the U.S. legal system are heavily influenced by immigration issues (see Bosworth, this volume). Similarly, within each ethnic group, certain segments of the community have been targeted for extreme punishment. The harsh treatment meted out to Puerto Rican Nationalists, the Cuban Marielitos, and those Mexicans who have been executed has typically been rationalized as the elimination of a threat to social order, though in reality it has more to do with the historical effects of colonialism, and with current efforts to preserve the status quo.

4. Corruption along the border is thought to be widespread. According to a May 2005 *Los Angeles Times* story, sixteen U.S. law enforcement officers and soldiers were caught in an FBI sting, smuggling cocaine from Mexico in a case involving "widespread bribery and extortion conspiracy" (Varabedian 2005); most have pled guilty. The defendants had been employed by a number of agencies, including the U.S. Army, the Arizona Army National Guard, the U.S. Bureau of Prisons, the Arizona Department of Corrections, a local Arizona police department, and the Immigration and Naturalization Service (INS). The Justice Department reported that the defendants "used their color of authority to prevent police stops, searches, and seizures of narcotics as they drove the cocaine shipments on highways that passed through checkpoints." The defendants pleaded guilty to transporting 1,232 pounds of cocaine and accepting $222,000 in cash for their activities.

5. Mexican women have been treated as second- and third-class citizens since their incorporation into the United States in 1848 (Acuna 1988; Segura and Pasquera 1998; see Díaz-Cotto, this volume). Some scholars argue that Chicanas suffer "triple oppression" because they are part of a historically marginalized and subordinated ethnic group (Segura and Pasquera 1998; see also Madriz 1997). Much of the attention paid to Latina women in general revolves around their sexuality, usually dichotomizing them into "Madonnas" or "whores." Academic research has largely neglected the subject of their treatment in the criminal justice system, choosing to focus instead on domestic violence among Mexican and Mexican American families and drug use among Chicanas.

6. According to the INS, 207,750 Mexicans applied for citizenship in 2000, representing around a quarter of the total (839,944) applications (Immigration and Naturalization Service 2000, table 49). Likewise, between 1996 and 2000 the number of Latino(a) voters increased by approximately 20 percent.

7. The George W. Bush administration nominated and appointed a number of ultra-conservative Latinos and Latinas to office, including Latinos(as) who have little or no understanding of the Latino(a) community (see Acuna 1988, 1998; de la Garza and DeSipio 2004).

WORKS CITED

Acuna, Rodolfo. 1988. *Occupied America*. 2nd edition. New York: Harper Collins.

———. 1998. *Sometimes there is no other side: Chicanos and the myth of equality*. Notre Dame, IN: University of Notre Dame Press.

Aguirre, Adalberto. 2004. Profiling Mexican American identity: Issues and concerns. *American Behavioral Scientist* 47: 928–42.

Aguirre, Adalberto, and David Baker. 1989. The executions of Mexican American prisoners in the Southwest. *Social Justice* 16: 150–161.

———. 2000. Latinos and the United States criminal justice system: Introduction. *The Justice Professional* 13: 3–6.

Amnesty International. 1998. *United States of America: Human rights concerns in the border region with Mexico*. Amnesty International (AI Index: AMR 51/03/98).

Beck, Allen, Jennifer Karberg, and Paige Harrison. 2002. *Prison and jail inmates at midyear 2001*. Washington, DC: Bureau of Justice Statistics.

Bonczar, Thomas. 2003. *Prevalence of imprisonment in the U.S. population, 1974–2001*. Washington, DC: Bureau of Justice Statistics.

Bond-Maupin, Lisa, and James Maupin. 1998. Juvenile justice decision-making in a rural Hispanic community. *Journal of Criminal Justice* 26: 373–384.

Border Action Network. 2004. *Border vigilantes armed with assault weapons terrorize local Douglas families and children*. Available at: http://www.borderaction.org.

DeJesus-Torres, Migdalia. 2000. Microaggression in the criminal justice system at discretionary stages and its impact on Latino(a)/Hispanics. *Justice Professional* 13: 69–89.

de la Garza, Rodolfo, and Louis DeSipio, eds. 2004. *Muted voices: Latinos and the 2000 elections*. Lanham, MD: Rowman & Littlefield.

Díaz-Cotto, Juanita. 1996. *Gender, ethnicity, and the state: Latina and Latino prison politics*. Albany, NY: State University of New York Press.

Falcon, Sylvanna. 2001. Rape as a weapon of war: Advancing human rights for women at the U.S.–Mexico border. *Social Justice* 28: 31–50.

Garcia y Griego, Manuel. 1997. The importation of Mexican contract laborers to the United States, 1942–1964. In *Between two worlds: Mexican immigrants in the United States*, ed. David Gutierrez. Wilmington, DE: Jaguar Books.

Gomez, Laura E. 2000. Race, colonialism, and criminal law: Mexicans and the American criminal justice system in territorial New Mexico. *Law and Society Review* 34: 1129–1202.

Grogger, Jeffrey, and Stephen Trejo. 2002. Falling behind or moving up? The intergenerational progress of Mexican Americans. Available at: http://www.ppic.org/publications/PPIC160/ppic160.abstract.html.

Gutierrez, David, ed. 1997. *Between two worlds: Mexican immigrants in the United States*. Wilmington, DE: Jaguar Books.

Hagan, John, and Alberto Palloni. 1999. Sociological criminology and the mythology of Hispanic immigration and crime. *Social Problems* 46: 617–632.

Human Rights Watch. 1992. *Brutality unchecked: Human rights abuses along the U.S. border with Mexico*. New York: Human Rights Watch.

———. 1993. *Frontier injustice: Human rights abuses along the U.S. Border with Mexico persist amid climate of impunity*. New York: Human Rights Watch.

————. 1995. *Crossing the line: Human rights abuses along the U.S. Border with Mexico persist amid climate of impunity.* New York: Human Rights Watch.

Immigration and Naturalization Service. 2000. *2000 statistical yearbook of the Immigration and Naturalization Service.* Washington, DC: U.S. Department of Justice.

International Court of Justice. 2004. Press release 2004/16: Avena and other Mexican nationals (*Mexico v. United States of America*). Available at: http://www.icj-cij.org.

Johnson, Kevin. 2000. The case against race profiling in immigration enforcement. *Washington University Law Quarterly* 78: 675–736.

Kingsolver, Ann E. 2001. *NAFTA stories: Fears and hopes in Mexico and the United States.* Boulder, CO: Lynne Rienner.

Madriz, Esther. 1997. *Nothing bad happens to good girls.* Berkeley and Los Angeles, CA: University of California Press.

Muñoz, Ed, David Lopez, and Eric Stewart. 1998. Misdemeanor sentencing decisions: The cumulative disadvantage effect of "gringo justice." *Hispanic Journal of Behavioral Sciences* 20: 298–319.

Parenti, Christian. 1999. *Lockdown America: Police and prisons in the age of crisis.* London: Verso.

Perea, Juan F. 2004. Buscando America: Why integration and equal protection fail to protect Latinos. *Harvard Law Review* 117: 1420–1469.

Pope, Carl, and William Feyerherm. 1981. Race and juvenile court dispositions: An examination of initial screening decisions. *Criminal Justice and Behavior* 8: 287–301.

Rodriguez, Luis J. 1993. *Always running: La vida loca: Gang days in L.A.* New York: Simon and Schuster.

Ruddell, Rick, and Martin Urbina. 2004. Minority threat and punishment: A cross-national analysis. *Justice Quarterly* 21: 903–931.

Segura, Denise A., and Beatriz M. Pasquera. 1998. Chicana feminists: Their political context and contemporary expression. In *The Latino studies reader: Culture, economy, and society*, ed. Antonia Darder and Rodolfo Torres. Malden, MA: Blackwell Publishers.

Shohat, Ella, and Robert Stam. 1994. *Unthinking Eurocentrism.* London: Routledge.

Shorris, Earl. 1992. *Latinos: A biography of the people.* New York: W. W. Norton.

Smith, Brad, and Malcolm Holmes. 2003. Community accountability, minority threat, and police brutality: An examination of civil rights criminal complaints. *Criminology* 41: 1035–1064.

Steffensmeier, Darrell, and Stephen Demuth. 2001. Ethnicity and judges' sentencing decisions: Hispanic-black-white comparisons. *Criminology* 39: 145–178.

Trujillo, Larry D. 1974. La evolucion del "bandido" al "pachuco": A Critical examination and evaluation of criminological literature on Chicanos. In *Latinos in the United States*, ed. Antoinette Sedillo Lopez. New York: Garland.

United States Census. 2004. Record numbers registered and voted in 2002 election, Census Bureau reports. Available at: http://www.census.gov/Press-Release/www/releases/archives/voting/002278.html.

————. 2005. *Facts for features.* Available at: http://www.census.gov/Press-Release/www/releases/archives/facts_for_features_ special_editions/001739.html.

Urbina, Martin. 2003a. *Capital punishment and Latino offenders: Racial and ethnic differences in death sentences.* New York: LFB Scholarly Publishing.

————. 2003b. History of U.S. race and ethnic relations. In *Capital punishment and Latino offenders: Racial and ethnic differences in death sentences.* New York: LFB Scholarly Publishing.

————. 2003c. Race and ethnic differences in punishment and death sentence outcomes: Empirical analysis of data on California, Florida, and Texas, 1975–1995. *Journal of Ethnicity in Criminal Justice* 1: 5–35.

————. 2004a. Language barriers in the Wisconsin court system: The Latino(a) experience. *Journal of ethnicity in criminal justice* 2: 91–118.

————. 2004b. A qualitative analysis of Latinos executed in the United States between 1975 and 1995: Who were they? *Social justice* 31: 242–267.

————. 2005. Transferring juveniles to adult court in Wisconsin: Practitioners voice their views. *Criminal Justice Studies: A Critical Journal of Crime, Law and Society* 18: 1–26.

————. (forthcoming). Latinos(as) in the criminal and juvenile justice systems. *Critical Criminology*.

Urbina, Martin, and Sara Kreitzer. 2004. The practical utility and ramifications of RICO: Thirty-two years after its implementation. *Criminal Justice Policy Review* 15: 294–323.

Varabedian, Ralph. 2005. U.S. soldiers, law officers snared in border drug sting. *L.A. Times*, May 13.

Weber, David. 1998. Many truths constitute the past: The legacy of the U.S.–Mexican War. Available at: http://www.pbs.org/kera/usmexicanwar/mainframe.html.

Weich, Ronald, and Carlos Angulo. 2000. Racial disparities in the American criminal justice system. Citizens' commission on civil rights. Available at: http://www.cccr.org.

PART TWO

Slavery

CHAPTER 4

Multiple Jeopardy

The Impact of Race, Gender, and Slavery on the Punishment of Women in Antebellum America

Vernetta D. Young and Zoe Spencer

THROUGHOUT HISTORY, punishment has been used as a form of social control. In the United States, penalties have been shaped by colonization, patriarchy, and slavery, each of which has also stratified the nation into groups based on race and ethnicity, gender, and class. A review of the perspectives and practices of punishment predominating in the pre–Civil War era shows how strategies were designed not only to discourage crime, but also to induce conformity. White women were encouraged to adhere to gender norms and the "cult of true womanhood," while free and enslaved black women were continually reminded of their vulnerable position. The multiple jeopardies faced by black women, in which as women they were expected to follow gender norms, yet as blacks were not protected by chivalric paternalism, reveal clearly how punishment is shaped by an intersection of race, gender, and class.

COLONIAL AMERICA

Settlers from England founded the first American colony in Jamestown, Virginia, in 1607, with just 105 women and men. An additional 101 colonists settled in Massachusetts in 1620; by 1636, New York, Maryland, and Rhode Island had added to these numbers. Most of the first colonists were men. Those few women who arrived with them typically had been forced to leave their homelands. They either were fleeing poor living and working conditions or were petty criminals—prostitutes and thieves—who had been officially pardoned and deported to help populate the new colonies (Blumenthal 1973). These women, who made up about one-quarter of all convicts sent to America, came as indentured servants. Their presence was thought necessary to persuade male laborers and settlers to remain in the colonies (Moller 1945; Galenson 1978).

This same indentured servant system brought the first Africans to the colonies as early as 1619. Africans in America continued as indentured servants until 1640, when Maryland became the first colony to institutionalize slavery. Thereafter, the practice of slavery expanded until 1790, by which time slaves accounted for about 92 percent of the total black population. From the early 1800s to around 1850, the slave population decreased due to manumission, escape to the North, and the loose enforcement of the Fugitive Slave Laws of 1793 that permitted the Underground Railroad to flourish. By 1860, the original population trend had reversed and the free black population outnumbered the slave population (Berlin 1974; Brugger 1988).

The colonists sought to control those who violated the law as they had in England. To that end, they relied upon a range of strategies including the death penalty, nonlethal corporal techniques, and noncorporal punishments that sought primarily to humiliate and mark out those who had transgressed society's norms. The status of the offender—e.g., whether the person was a free white, a white indentured servant, a free African, an African indentured servant, an African slave, a man or a woman—determined the specific nature of the punishment he or she received. Under slavery, plantation owners and their overseers handled the punishment of slave offenders, and tended to favor, above all, the whip (Keve 1986). Free blacks were dealt with in the criminal justice system, although informal, racist vigilante justice was also common, in which groups of white men "punished" black men for perceived transgressions of the racial and gender order (see Messerschmidt, this volume).

In states such as Maryland, which had a significant population of both slaves and free blacks, the criminal justice system and the system of plantation or slave owner "justice" operated simultaneously. Local sheriffs handled cases involving violations of the general criminal code by both the free black population and the white population. They also dealt with violations that were specific to the free black population. In 1831, for example, the Maryland legislature made it illegal for a free black to keep or carry a firelock without a license or to attend religious meetings not conducted by whites (Laws of Maryland 1831, Chapter 323). Similarly, in 1857 this group was prohibited from using any rowboats on the Potomac without a license or written permission (Laws of Maryland 1857, Chapter 356).

Race was not the only factor shaping strategies of punishment at this time. Rather, the antebellum period was marked by a struggle to determine how best to deal with women who violated the law. Most methods and instruments of punishment had been created for men. Establishing which women were to be punished, how they were to be chastised, and for what offenses proved challenging.

Many white women of the antebellum period, particularly those of middle- or upper-class status, were protected by the "cult of true womanhood" that emphasized traditional gender roles of piousness, purity, submissiveness, and domesticity (Welter 1966). Provided she adhered to these notions, a white woman was entitled to basic religious and moral rights and privileges. She was also usually shielded from the punitive gaze of society. Such advantages, however, came at a repressive price. Following the Christian notion that God is the head of the church and man is the head of the woman, white women were considered property, first of their fathers and then of their husbands. They could neither vote nor hold public office. They were also not allowed to own property in their own names, bring a suit in court, or have rights over their children. Moreover, the "cult of true womanhood" was shaped by class values, meaning that poor and working class white women could never live up to its ideals, even though many aspired to do so (Hewitt 2002).

If a white woman acted in a manner contrary to the traditional gender role notions and expectations, she risked social censure and harsh punishment. Depending on the nature of her transgression, it could be dealt with in the domestic setting or in the courts. A husband, for example, was free to beat his wife to ensure obedience or conjugal privileges (Hine and Thompson 1999). Those white women who committed criminal offenses were automatically labeled and defined as morally suspect, though the kind of punishment they received depended on the nature of their crime. Women who committed adultery or other offenses that broke with the gender order, such as infanticide, were usually punished more harshly than white men for comparable offenses, whereas those who perpetrated other less obviously gendered crimes, such as fraud or theft, were frequently dealt with more leniently (Feinman 1983).

Such repression of white women pales when compared to the everyday treatment of most black women. Under the institution of slavery, these women were not considered human beings. They had very limited control over their productive, reproductive, and sexual being, and no right to mother their own children (see Flavin, this volume). Instead, they were no more than property to be bought and sold in the market, and subject to the control and domination of their owner. As property, black women were subject to methods and practices of "breaking," control, and punishment that were frequently harsher and more sadistic than the punitive measures used for convicted criminals. Everyday penalties they faced included intimidation, separation from family, starvation and other forms of deprivation, whipping and scarring, rape, mutilation, amputation, and death. Some plantation owners developed unique forms of punishment to deal with their female slaves, going so far as to dig a hole into which a pregnant woman's swollen stomach would fit so that her fetus would not be harmed during a beating (Hine and Thompson 1999, 84).

By the 1820s, slavery had been abolished in the Northern states and shortly thereafter members of the abolitionist movement began agitating for an end to slavery throughout the country. The women's rights movement was launched almost simultaneously. These challenges to the institutions of slavery and patriarchy may have influenced the manner in which women, black and white, were controlled. Although it is difficult to speculate about the impact of these ideas on the punishment of women during the antebellum periodm since much of the detail about the treatment of women concentrates only on the post–Civil War period (Rafter 1985; Butler 1997), specific cases from the historical record suggest that the intersections of race and gender resulted in certain women being treated more harshly than others. The next sections will explore the racial and gendered nature of sanctions meted out to offenders at this time.

CAPITAL PUNISHMENT

Punishment by death was a central component of the first colonial criminal justice system. Although considerable debate surrounds the details of early executions, the Espy file, a data file of executions performed under civil authority in the United States, is considered by many to be the most comprehensive source (Espy and Smykla 1987). According to the Espy file, women accounted for close to one-quarter of all executions at the turn of the eighteenth century. By the turn of the nineteenth century, however, the proportion of women executed decreased to less than 10 percent (1987). From 1632 to 1861, there were 3,805 total executions in the colonies; of these, 271, or 7 percent, of those put to death were women. Black women comprised a majority of women executed (close to 60 percent), followed by white women (who accounted for about one-third of all female executions). The remaining executions were of Native American and Hispanic women, with a small percentage of cases in which race was not reported.

Although both men and women, black and white, were subject to capital punishment, they were usually executed for different types of crimes. Thus, while men were commonly put to death for murder, robbery, piracy, and a range of theft offenses, women were most likely to receive the death penalty for murder (poisoning) and witchcraft (Keve 1986). Women also were executed for conspiracy to murder, accessory to murder, arson, housebreaking, robbery, slave revolts, adultery, concealing birth, and other, unspecified felonies. More significant to the gender disparity, women could be—and in two cases were—burned at the stake for adultery or murdering a spouse, while men typically were not punished for such actions (Kurshan 1996).

There were also some telling racial differences in the types of offenses that resulted in execution. For example, the Espy file indicates that the only person put to death for adultery was a white woman. This case perhaps reflects the institutionalized nature of white men's extramarital sex with slave women, serving as it did as a means of domination, and also as a strategy for creating more property and labor. In the five cases of concealed births mentioned in the files, four of the offenders were identified as white, and the offender's race was not reported in the fifth case. Giving birth out of wedlock was, in other words, considered much more of a social problem for white women than for anyone else.

The seriousness of the punishments assigned to adultery and concealing a birth suggest efforts to maintain patriarchal control over white women's marital, sexual, and reproductive behaviors, and hence preserve the purity of the family. For black women, the focus of control was different. Their punishments were aimed at maintaining the institution of slavery by reducing the possibility of resistance, rebellion, and insurrection, and by ensuring that the life and property of the slave owner/white property owner was protected above all else. Thus, all of the cases of arson, as well as twelve cases of poisoning, involved black female offenders. These two groups of offenses involved black women destroying the life and property of whites, since the victims of poisoning were white and, in the arson cases, the target was usually the home or property of the white master. These cases also could have been seen as indications of moves toward insurrection and as particularly threatening to the status quo.

According to the Espy file, twenty-six women—all white—were executed for witchcraft. Reports indicate that these women were generally older, over forty, and likely to be single as the result of either divorce or widowhood (Karlsen 1987; Kurshan 1996). Most of the women who were punished for this offense "had expressed dissatisfaction with their lot, if only indirectly. Some were not sufficiently submissive in that they filed petitions and court suits, and sometimes sought divorces. Others were midwives and had influence over the well-being of others, often to the chagrin of their male competitors, medical doctors. Still others exhibited a female pride and assertiveness, refusing to defer to their male neighbors" (Kurshan 1996, 1). The treatment of these women, in other words, suggests a harsh societal response to white female independence.

Other archival material indicates that black women accused of witchcraft were generally treated more leniently than whites. In an article on witchcraft in colonial New England, for example, Timothy McMillan (1994) describes how two black women, Mary Black and Candy, were accused and convicted of witchcraft but were both sentenced to imprisonment and later freed by the governor. McMillan attributes the more moderate treatment of blacks accused of witchcraft to a number of factors, including their value as property, the preconceptions by whites of blacks as morally inferior, and whites' fear of the believed magical powers of blacks.

Although a number of methods of capital punishment were in use in England at this time, hanging remained predominant in the colonies throughout the nineteenth century. Burning, for example, accounted for less than 4 percent of all executions, and most of those subjected to this method were slaves (Espy and Smykla 1987). Once again such treatment reveals a gender bias, as all but two of the thirteen executions by burning were enslaved black women. In general, enslaved women were punished at least as severely as enslaved men, and in some instances, it appears their punishments were even more excessive. As Angela Davis observes, "when men were hanged, the women were burned alive" (Davis 1971, 12).

Until the mid-nineteenth century, executions were conducted in public, both as a warning to others and as an additional punishment for the offender. The humiliation of such publicity was not lost on its subjects. Thus, in 1860, as one woman was led out of the jail, she pleaded with her escort for cover from the viewers' eyes even though there was a fence around the gallows: "Don't let a crowd see me. I am willing to meet my God, but I don't want to have a crowd see me die" (Bessler 1997, 64). When women were put to death, such "spectacles of suffering" were often sexualized, as women were forced to parade in thin gowns for the edification and, no doubt, titillation of their audience (Spierenburg 1984; Newman 1983). The added degradation of being forced to "expose" oneself in an environment in which "true womanhood" was portrayed as the gender ideal effectively unsexed the female offender, rendering her as less than a woman.

Other Corporal and Non-Corporal Punishments

In addition to the death penalty, settlers had a dizzying array of corporal and noncorporal sanctions from which to choose. Such choice usually was driven, once again, by the race, gender, and class of the offender. Although the whipping post was the most common corporal punishment employed against all populations, the use of other corporal techniques, including the pillory, branding and maiming, the cleft-stick on forked tongue, branks and gags, bilboes, and the bridle varied by gender, race, and economic standing. Noncorporal punishments, designed to humiliate individuals rather than cause them any lasting physical pain, typically were not used against slaves. These penalties, many of which were used against white women and free black women, included the ducking stool, stocks, sitting in the gallows, gagging, fines, banishment, and being forced to wear a placard that declaimed the person's infamy.

Until the early twentieth century, whippings could be administered for a range of offenses. Most whippings occurred in full public view, but in Rhode Island women were whipped in the jail yard and only women were allowed to watch (Earle [1896] 1968). The number of lashes depended upon the status of the offender and the type of offense. In the colonies, crimes of immorality received up to forty lashes, whereas crimes of insubordinate behavior, mutiny, or falsely accusing the mistress of acts of unchastity, were punished by one hundred lashes on the bare back (Preyer 1982). Servants and slaves tended to receive the greatest number of lashes overall, while sometimes those of higher social standing avoided such humiliation altogether. For example, prison historian Paul Keve documents a criminal case of fornication in Accomack County, Virginia, in which the man was fined and required to do penance in church, whereas the woman, who apparently was a servant and thus could not afford to pay a fine, received thirty lashes and was shipped out (Keve 1996). State penal codes also revealed a greater willingness to subject black women, slave or free, than white women to corporal punishment. Thus, whereas the 1827 revised penal code of Illinois prohibited the whipping or pillorying of white women, the same legislation permitted these techniques when disciplining black women (Dodge 1999, 6).

As noted earlier, in most instances owners disciplined slaves on the plantation. When trials were public, the punishment of slaves was usually corporal (Keve 1986). These public punishments of slaves were usually the result of an alleged affront, physical or verbal, toward someone outside the plantation, or a violation that would lead to the likely transfer of the slave to another plantation.

The pillory was another method of discipline favored by the colonists. Used primarily for economic crimes such as counterfeiting, fraud, and forgery, this sanction involved locking the offender in full public view in a wooden device that contained openings for the head and hands (Newman 1978). Although more frequently administered to male offenders, it was used for some women, often in conjunction with other penalties. Consider this example from the early records of Maryland: "when Elizabeth Greene, the wife of William Greene forced a servant boy in her employ to forge a receipt, or discharge a debt . . . when the jury found Elizabeth guilty of forgery, the court ordered 'set on the pillory and loose one of her ears.' After this punishment had been inflicted, Elizabeth was to be imprisoned for twelve months and to pay double costs and damages 'to the party grieved,' if the latter should make this demand" (Semmes 1938, 31–32).

Other strategies existed to control nuisance or public order crimes. The bridle, an iron cage fitted over the head with a sharp front plate, was used against men and women for swearing, drunkenness, and sarcasm (Newman 1978), whereas the branks, a similar contraption, often of great weight, with a spiked or flat tongue of iron placed in the mouth over the tongue, was usually reserved only for female offenders (Buford and Shulman 1992). According to the *Records of the Massachusetts Bay Colony:* "6 September, Boston 1636. Robert Shorthouse for swearinge by the bloud of God was sentenced to have his tongue put into a cleft stick, and soe stand for halfe an houre & Elizabeth wife of Thomas Applegate was censured to stand with her tongue in a cleft stick for half an houre for swearinge, railinge and revilinge" (Earle [1896] 1968, n.p.).

Finally, the ducking stool was widely utilized in Virginia, the Carolinas, and Pennsylvania (Newman 1978). Until the late 1800s, this technique, in which the offender was tied to a chair at the end of a plank and ducked into water, was used to publicly punish "scolds" or individuals—most of whom were white women—who "often slander and scandalize their neighbors, for which their poor husbands are often brought into chargeable vexatious suits and cast in great damages" (Earle [1896] 1968).

Noncorporal punishments typically were not used against enslaved black men and women because to do so would have been both futile and counter-productive. Punishments aimed at public humiliation would serve little purpose because slaves had already been subject to the perpetuation of stereotypes about their inferiority that served to legitimize their enslavement. And because, as slaves, they were the property of a white man, banishment would not only be economically unfeasible, but would have imposed on the property owner's rights. Lastly, since slaves were, by definition, unpaid, they would lack the ability to pay any fines.

The colonists also distinguished between free and enslaved blacks in administering penalties. For example, although both slave and free black women were apt to be whipped for criminal violations, only black slave women were likely to be punished by branding, especially with the hot poker (Saunders 1978). Banishment, a sanction never used for slaves, was something administered to free blacks, particularly those convicted of perjury and adultery (McManus 1993). These offenders were removed to the western territories or to "Barbados or some far away place" (Newman 1978).

Toward the end of the eighteenth century, support for corporal punishment and those noncorporal techniques aimed at public humiliation gradually waned, and reformers began to look for more humane ways of dealing with the increasing criminal population. In response to changing sensibilities and new economic needs, states began to build and open prisons, penitentiaries, and reformatories. These new institutions, many of which remain with us today, continued to be shaped by intersections of race, gender, and class. Thus, though a large proportion of women sentenced to Newgate Prison in New York from 1797 to 1891 were black (44 percent), female convicts in the South during the same period were overwhelmingly white, since slave owners punished their slaves privately (Rafter 1985, 141). Indeed, it was not until the abolition of slavery that the black prison population grew in the South.

INCARCERATION

Although both men and women's facilities were filthy and overcrowded, female inmates were subject to additional abuses. First, in part because of their small numbers, and in part due to racist assumptions of black women's innate depravity, those few women who were incarcerated endured great hardship and neglect. Social, economic, and political disadvantages experienced by women in the larger society were reflected in their treatment in prisons. As historian Nicole Rafter (1985, 155) observes, the "in-prison treatment of black and white women demonstrates that partiality was extended mainly to whites . . . And partiality toward whites contributed to development of a bifurcated system, one track custodial and predominantly black, the other reformatory and reserved mainly for whites. As always, however, racism harmed the favored as well as the castigated group."

Thus, despite the influence of Elizabeth Fry's critical report on women in prison in England that was published in 1827, the majority of U.S. women prisoners languished in poor, sometimes dangerous conditions well into the nineteenth century. They tended to be housed together, usually in sections of men's establishments, regardless of their age or type of offense, without adequate supervision or security precautions. Many were forced to have sex with male prisoners and staff. In 1826, as a result of this kind of treatment, Rachel Welch became pregnant while in solitary confinement in Auburn Penitentiary, New York. The case of Welch, flogged after childbirth by a prison official, is frequently cited as an illustration of the additional suffering of women housed in men's prisons (Feinman 1983; Kurshan 1996).

An early women's reformatory opened in Massachusetts in 1877. Designed particularly for women "convicted of being vagrants, common drunkards, lewd and wanton and lascivious behavior, common nightwalkers, and other idle and disorderly females" (Lekkerkerker 1931, 92–94), it provided the model for subsequent institutions established throughout the Northern states. In the South, however, black women freed from domestic slavery rapidly found themselves targeted by the Black Codes and vagrancy laws in a new form of state slavery. As sociologist William DuBois observed in 1901, the convict-lease system allowed states to maintain control over and criminalize freed blacks. Working in concert, often with former plantation owners, the state passed the labor of convicted black women and men over to entrepreneurs, and put the convicts to work rebuilding the South. Women and men built roads, picked cotton, and mined, all for no pay and in the most abject of conditions (Work 1913, Lichtenstein 1996; Myers 1998).

In time, the South developed its own penitentiaries, often on the site of former plantations. Mississippi's Parchman Penitentiary, which opened in 1901, provides the most notorious example of this kind of institution, one that became synonymous with brutality and institutionalized racism (Oshinsky 1997). Women confined here, almost all of whom were black, reproduced their earlier roles under slavery, forced into sexual unions with staff, and working in the cotton fields during harvest time.

In Maryland during the antebellum period, 90 percent of all white female prisoners were incarcerated for two offenses: 54 percent for property crimes (larceny, arson, horse stealing, and burglary), and 42 percent for the miscellaneous "else" category (Young 2001). Almost all of those incarcerated for the latter category were incarcerated for "vagrancy," a term Nicole Rafter (1985) suggests was a euphemism for sexual promiscuity. This view is supported by Friedman (1993), who reported that women were arrested for fornication, adultery, lewd cohabitation, common night-walking, all offenses against chastity, and petty crimes.

Black women in Maryland at this time were more likely to be incarcerated for lesser offenses such as larceny than for any other crime. Over three-quarters were incarcerated for property crimes, followed by much smaller proportions for other crimes: 10 percent for unspecified felonies, 8 percent for miscellaneous, and 4 percent for violent crime (Young 2001). Unlike their white counterparts, black women who committed offenses against morality were generally ignored.

CONCLUSION

Slavery and the cult of true womanhood established disparate punitive structures from the early colonial period. Sex and race, as well as status and class, determined both the types of behavior labeled criminal and the mode of punishment individuals received. Blacks, male and female, free and slave, were punished most harshly, while white women were sometimes protected by adhering or appealing to gender norms. The constructed notions of race, gender, and class created a multiple jeopardy that remains with us today. The "war on drugs," for example, that has defined criminal justice policy in the late twentieth and early twenty-first centuries, pivots on harsher penalties for crack cocaine, which blacks are more likely than whites to use. As a direct result of targeting this kind of drug use over others, the incarcerated female population has increased significantly, with a particularly dramatic growth in the numbers of black and Hispanic women incarcerated (see Díaz-Cotto, this volume).

As an historical study like this illustrates, punishment can only be understood when placed in its social context. Responses to crime and crime itself are always driven by a broader web of ideas shaped by race, gender, and class. Only if we can document and analyze how these factors intersect can we hope to address the negative impact of the multiple jeopardy many woman face in their experiences of the justice system.

WORKS CITED

Berlin, Ira. 1974. *Slaves without masters: The free Negro in the antebellum South*. New York: Pantheon Books.

Bessler, John. 1997. *Death in the dark: Midnight executions in America*. Boston, MA: North-eastern University Press.

Blumenthal, Walter. 1973. Brides from Bridewell: Female felons sent to colonial America. Rutland: Charles E. Truttle.

Brugger, Robert. 1988. *Maryland: A middle temperament.* Baltimore, MD: The Johns Hopkins University Press.

Burford, E. J., and Sandra Shulman. 1992. *Of bridles and burnings: The punishment of women.* New York: Saint Martin's Press.

Butler, Anne. 1997. *Gendered justice in the American West: Women prisoners in men's penitentiaries.* Urbana: University of Illinois Press.

Colvin, Mark. 1997. *Penitentiaries, reformatories, and chain gangs: Social theory and the history of punishment in nineteenth-century America.* New York: St. Martin's Press.

Corzine, Jay, James Creech, and Lin Corzine. 1983. Black concentration and lynchings in the South: Testing Blalock's power-threat hypothesis. *Social Forces* 61: 774–796.

Davis, Angela. 1971. Reflections on the black woman's role in the community of slaves. *The Black Scholar* 3: 2–15.

Dodge, Mara. 1999. One female prisoner is of more trouble than twenty males: Women convicts in Illinois prisons, 1835–1896. *Journal of Social History* 32: 907–930.

DuBois, W. E. B. 1901. The spawn of slavery. *Missionary Review of the World* 14: 737–745.

Earle, Alice. [1896] 1968. *Curious punishments of bygone days.* Montclair, NJ: Patterson Smith. http://www.getchwood.com/punishments/curious/index.html. Retrieved on November 18, 2005.

Espy, M. W., and John Smykla. 1987. *Executions in the United States, 1608–1991: The Espy file* (machine-readable data file). Ann Arbor, Michigan: Inter-University Consortium for Political and Social Research.

Feinman, Clarice. 1983. An historical overview of the treatment of incarcerated women: Myths and realities of rehabilitation. *Prison Journal* 63: 12–26.

Friedman, Lawrence. 1993. *Crime and punishment in American history.* New York: Basic Books.

Galenson, David. 1978. British servants and the colonial indentured system in the eighteenth century. *Journal of Southern History* 44: 41–66.

Gibson, Campbell, and Kay Jung. 2002. *Historical census statistics on population totals by race, 1790 to 1990, and by Hispanic origin, 1970 to 1990, for the United States, regions, divisions, and states.* Washington, DC: U.S. Census Bureau.

Harm, Nancy. 1992. Social policy on women prisoners: An historical analysis. *Affilia Journal of Women and Social Work* 7: 90–108.

Hewitt, Nancy. 2002. Taking the true woman hostage. *Journal of Women's History* 14: 156–162.

Hine, Darlene Clark, and Kathleen Thompson. 1999. *A shining thread of hope: The history of black women in America.* New York: Broadway Books.

Karlsen, Carol. 1987. *The devil in the shape of a woman.* New York: W. W. Norton.

Keve, Paul. 1986. *The history of corrections in Virginia.* Charlottesville: University Press of Virginia.

Kurshan, Nancy. 1996. Behind the walls: The history and current reality of women's imprisonment. In *Criminal injustice: Confronting the prison crisis,* ed. Elihu Rosenblatt. Boston, MA: South End Press.

Lekkerkerker, Eugenia. 1931. *Reformatories for women.* The Hague–Batava: J. B. Woeters Groningen.

Lichtenstein, Alex. 1996. *Twice the work of free labor: The political economy of convict labor in the New South.* New York: Verso.

Maryland. 1831. *Laws of Maryland.* Ch. 323.

————. 1857. *Laws of Maryland*. Ch. 356.

McManus, Edgar. 1993. *Law and liberty in early New England: Criminal justice and due process, 1620–1692*. Amherst: University of Massachusetts Press.

McMillan, Timothy. 1994. Black magic: Witchcraft, race, and resistance in colonial New England. *Journal of Black Studies* 25: 99–117.

Moller, Herbert. 1945. Sex composition and correlated culture patterns of colonial America. *William and Mary Quarterly* 2: 113–153.

Myers, Martha A. 1990. Black threat and incarceration in postbellum Georgia. *Social Forces* 69: 373–394.

————. 1998. *Race, labor, and punishment in the New South*. Columbus: Ohio State University Press.

Oshinsky, David M. 1997. *Worse than slavery: Parchman Farm and the ordeal of Jim Crow justice*. New York: The Free Press.

Newman, Graeme. 1978. *The punishment response*. Philadelphia, PA: J. B. Lippincott.

————. 1983. *Just and painful: A case for the corporal punishment of criminals*. New York: Macmillan.

Preyer, Kathryn. 1982. Penal measures in the American colonies: An overview. *American Journal of Legal History* 26: 326–353.

Rafter, Nicole. 1985. *Partial justice: Women in state prisons, 1800–1935*. Boston, MA: Northeastern University Press.

Records of Massachusetts Bay Colony. http://www.getchwood.com/punishments/curious/chapter-8.html. Retrieved November 18, 2005.

Saunders, Robert. 1978. Crime and punishment in early national America: Richmond, Virginia, 1784–1820. *Virginia Magazine of History and Biography* 86: 33–44.

Semmes, Raphael. 1938. *Crime and punishment in early Maryland*. Baltimore, MD: Johns Hopkins University Press.

Spierenburg, Petrus Cornelis. 1984. *The spectacle of suffering: Executions and the evolution of repression: From a preindustrial metropolis to the European experience*. Cambridge: Cambridge University Press, 1984.

Welter, Barbara. 1966. The cult of true womanhood, 1820–1860. *American Quarterly* 2: 151–174.

Work, Monroe. 1913. Negro criminality in the South. *Annals of the American Academy of Political and Social Sciences* 49: 74–80.

Young, Vernetta D. 2001. All the women in the Maryland state penitentiary: 1812–1869. *Prison Journal* 81: 113–132.

CHAPTER 5

"We Must Protect Our Southern Women"

ON WHITENESS, MASCULINITIES, AND LYNCHING

James W. Messerschmidt

The Negro meets no resistance when on a downward course. It is only when he rises in wealth, intelligence and manly character that he brings upon himself the heavy hand of persecution.

—Frederick Douglass, "Lynch Law in the South" (1892)

THIS CHAPTER EXAMINES LYNCHING as a form of extrajudicial punishment during Reconstruction (1865–1877) and its immediate aftermath. As I shall argue, lynching was a response to the perceived erosion of white male domination that had flourished under slavery, and an attempt to recreate what white supremacist men imagined to be the loss of their unchallenged supremacy. Disguised in chivalric intimations, as retribution for the alleged rape of a white woman by an African American man, lynching enforced racial dominance as well as gender hierarchies between men and women and gender hierarchies among men.

SLAVERY

Slavery produced a white supremacist discourse and practice that declared the physical, intellectual, and moral superiority of whites over blacks (see Young and Spencer, this volume). It legally bound all blacks to the patriarchal "white father" and cut slaves off from all birthrights they might have enjoyed as members of a community. Male and female slaves were without social status or political and economic power; they could not own property, earn a living for themselves, or participate in public and political life. Slavery conveyed to all blacks that the fullness of humanity would never be available to them, and overtly sought to reduce them to dependent, passive, childlike characters.

The master-slave relation constructed a masculine power hierarchy in which the "white master" was *the* representative of hegemonic masculinity. At the same time, cultural ideology and discourse claimed that the most "advanced" races had evolved the most pronounced gender differences. A white "civilized" planter woman (the mistress) thus represented the highest level of womanhood—delicate, spiritual, exempt from heavy labor, ensconced in and dedicated to home. In contrast, a white "civilized" planter man (the master) was the most manly creature ever evolved—firm of character and self-controlled, who provided for his family and steadfastly protected "his" woman and children from the rigors of the workaday world.

Participation in politics was also an essential practice for defining white men (hegemonic masculinity) in relation to black men (subordinate masculinity) and to all women. The notions of "womanhood" and "blackness," in other words, served as negative referents that united all white men. Political parties were fraternal organizations that bonded white men through their whiteness, thus, at times, overcoming class differences. Paula Baker (1984, 628) explains, "Parties and electoral politics united all white men, regardless of class or other differences, and provided entertainment, a definition of manhood, and the basis for a male ritual. Universal white manhood suffrage implied that because all [white] men shared the chance to participate in electoral politics, they possessed political equality. The right to vote was something important that [white] men held in common."

According to scientific and popular discourse, the "savage races" had not evolved the proper gender differences that whites possessed, and this was precisely what made them savage (Russett 1989). Indeed, slavery denoted black males and females as more alike than different—"genderless as far as the slaveholders were concerned" (Davis 1983, 5). In the middle of the nineteenth century, seven of eight slaves (men and women alike) were field workers, both profitable labor units for the master. Perhaps as a result, black slaves did not construct the gender differences of the white planter class. The race and gender divisions of labor and power in slavery caused black women not to view themselves as the "weaker sex" or the "housewife," nor to construct black men as the "family head" and the "family provider" (Davis 1983, 8). By failing to conform to dominant gender ideals, black male slaves were defined as less than men and black female slaves less than women (Bederman 1995).

This construction of racial boundaries through gender also had a sexual component. White southerners differentiated themselves from "savages" by attributing to the latter a sexual nature that was more sensual, aggressive, and beastlike than that of whites. Influenced by the Elizabethan image of "the lusty Moor," white southerners embraced the notion that blacks were "lewd, lascivious, and wanton people" (D'Emilio and Freedman 1988, 35). Both their gender similarity and animal-like sexuality, white supremacist discourse declared, "proved" blacks were a subordinate species; therefore, it was natural that races must not mix and that whites must dominate blacks. Both scientific and popular thought supported the view that whites were civilized and rational, while blacks were savage, irrational, and sensual (Jordan 1968; Takaki 1982). Indeed, it was this notion of racial corporeality that defined inequality between whites and blacks and constructed what Frankenberg (1993) labels an "essentialist racist discourse." Such a discourse constructed blacks as "fundamentally Other than white people: different, inferior, less civilized, less human, more animal, than whites" (61). The articulation and deployment of essentialist racism as the dominant discourse for thinking about race marks the moment when race was constructed as *difference*: alleged white biological superiority justifies economic, political, and social inequalities in slavery.

Not surprisingly, social and legal regulations affecting interracial sexuality, such as prohibiting marriage between black men and white women, served to produce and cement racial identities. Slavery "heightened planter insistence on protecting white women and their family line, from the specter of interracial union" (D'Emilio and Freedman 1988, 94). The commitment in slave society was protection of white female virtue and containment of white female sexuality within white, marital, reproductive relations. In contrast to this draconian social control of white women, southern white men of the planter class faced few restrictions on their heterosexual desire. "Most southern moralists condoned white men's gratification of lust, as long as they did so discre[et]ly with poor white or black women. Polite society condemned the public discussion of illicit sex, but men's private writings reveal a good deal of comfort with the expression of pure sexual desire, unrelated to love or intimacy" (95).

The rape of black female slaves by white masters rivaled the enforced separation of families as the most provocative event in black family life (Jones 1986). Slaves endured each day the pervasive fear that such assaults were possible, especially given the easy circumstances under which they could be committed. For example, one Louisiana master would enter the slave cabin and tell the husband "to go outside and wait 'til he do what he want to do." The black husband "had to do it and he couldn't do nothing 'bout it" (37–38). As Angela Davis (1983, 23–24) points out, rape of black women was a weapon of domination and repression "whose covert goal was to extinguish slave women's will to resist, and in the process, demoralize their men." Indeed, sexual abuse of slave women in the presence of slave husbands/fathers made the point that slave men were not "real men" (Genovese 1974, 482).[1] Thus, greater regulation of white women's sexuality was matched by greater sexual privilege for white men, and "provided white men with both a sexual outlet and a means of maintaining racial domination" (D'Emilio and Freedman 1988, 94).[2]

Moreover, although denigration of interracial sexuality evoked the notion of virility—the sexually active black male as a threat to white women (Fox-Genovese 1988)—this clearly was overshadowed by the social control of white female sexuality noted earlier. As Elizabeth Fox-Genovese (291) points out, "The presumed threat of black male sexuality never provoked the wild hysteria and violence in the Old South that it did in the New." Thus, although approximately three hundred lynchings were recorded between 1840 and 1860, less than 10 percent involved blacks (the majority were of white abolitionists). Black lynching was carried out primarily in the wake of an insurrection scare, not because of sexual liaisons with white women and, therefore, was insignificant numerically prior to Reconstruction (Dray 2002; Genovese 1974).

Indeed, during slavery black men could be acquitted or pardoned for raping white women (Hodes 1991).[3] Although occasionally some accused of raping white women suffered lynching, the vast majority were tried in the court system (Schwarz 1988; Spindel 1989). Records suggest that antebellum courts proceeded with relative restraint in such cases, occasionally acknowledging that some black-white sexual relationships were consensual (Dray 2002). Similarly, not all rape trials resulted in conviction, and appellate courts in every Southern state "threw out convictions for rape and attempted rape on every possible ground, including the purely technical. They overturned convictions because the indictments had not been drawn up properly, because the lower courts had based their convictions on possibly coerced confessions, or because the reputation of the white victim had not been admitted as evidence" (Genovese 1974, 34).

The latter ground, the reputation of the *white* victim, is telling. The sexual conduct of slave men seemed to matter less to white southerners than did the sexual conduct of white women. White women who were not pure and chaste when unmarried, and those who did not observe decorum when married, were severely admonished (Fox-Genovese 1988).[4] Indeed, the sexual reputation of the white woman was so important to the white community that, even if the evidence was clear that a black-on-white rape did in fact occur, if the victim was of "bad character," the black rapist quite possibly would go free. James Hugo Johnston (1970, 258), in his study of miscegenation in the South from 1776–1860, was "astonished" at the number of rape cases in which "white citizens of the communities in which these events transpired testify for the Negro and against the white woman and declare that the case is not a matter of rape, for the woman encouraged and consented to the act of the Negro."

The case of Carter, a "Negro man slave," in antebellum Virginia, and Catherine Brinal, the white female victim, is an excellent example (Johnston 1970, 259–260). Carter was found guilty of the rape of Brinal and sentenced to death. Yet the judge determined that Carter was the "proper object of mercy" because community members testified that Ms. Brinal "was a woman of the worst fame, that her character was that of the most abandoned inasmuch as she (being a white woman) has three mulatto children, which by her own confession were begotten by different Negro men; that from report she had permitted the said Carter to have peaceable sexual intercourse with her, before the time of his forcing her" (259–260). In this case, the social control of the white woman's sexuality outweighed the concerns over the behavior of the slave (Hodes 1991). Leniency accorded to black male slaves in such cases appears to reflect their value as property (Dray 2002, 39–40).

White slave masters and black male slaves constructed unique types of racial masculinity (hegemonic vs. subordinate) during slavery by occupying distinct locations within the particular race and gender divisions of labor and power. Both male groups experienced the everyday world from their proprietary positions in slave society and, consequently, there existed patterned ways in which race and masculinity were constructed and represented. The meaning of "white masculinity," in other words, hinged on the existence of a subordinated "black masculinity." [5]

RECONSTRUCTION

The passage of the Thirteenth Amendment (1865) outlawed slavery; with emancipation, former slaves became "African Americans." Through the process of Reconstruction, the Union attempted to restore relations with the Confederate states. Arguably the most crucial issue of Reconstruction was the political status of former black slaves as African Americans. Former slaves immediately began asserting independence from whites by forming churches, becoming politically active, strengthening family ties, and attempting to educate their children (Zinn 1980). In fact, emancipation was defined in terms of the ability of former slave men and women to fully participate in U.S. life. This meant not only acquiring citizenship rights as African Americans, but also living out the gender ideals dominant in U.S. society. In particular, for African American men, there was a euphoric desire to seize the rights and privileges of citizenship and, thereby, hegemonic masculinity.

Under slavery, black men were unable to be economic providers or to participate in social and political affairs. Their family authority ultimately was inferior to that of the white master. With emancipation, their authority within the African American family grew, and beliefs that men and women should inhabit separate spheres consolidated. By 1870, the majority of African Americans lived in two-parent patriarchal family households, in which African Americans embraced the new "cult of domesticity," women worked primarily in household labor, and men became public representative of the family.[6] African American former slave men now considered it a badge of honor for their wives to work at home, and thereby gained considerable power within the

household (Foner 1988). To former slave men, the ability to support and protect a family was synonymous with manhood. Embracing this ideology, the
Freedman's Bureau appointed the husband as "head of household," assigning
to him sole power to enter into contractual labor agreements for the entire
family.[7] Moreover, the Freedman's Bureau Act of 1865 assigned the right for
allotment of land primarily to males (women could claim land only if unmarried) (87).[8] In short, the phenomenon of "separate spheres" as discourse for
hegemonic masculinity and emphasized femininity provided the definitional
space needed for gender practices by African Americans no longer denied the
right to maintain family bonds (Wiegman 1993).

The Reconstruction program contemplated that the freedom of African
American men included their "natural" social superiority over African American
women, and served to perpetuate gender divisions common in nineteenth-
century U.S. society (Wiegman 1993). Thus, only African American men
served as delegates to statewide organized constitutional conventions (held in
1867 and 1868), where they demanded equality with whites—from access to
public education to the right to bear arms, serve on juries, establish newspapers, assemble peacefully, and enter all avenues of agriculture, commerce, and
trade. And African American men were quite successful. Not only did they
help write Southern state constitutions, but by 1868 African American men
could serve on juries, vote, hold political office, and rise to political leadership
(in the Republican party); African American women, like their white counterparts, could not (Foner 1988).

By 1869, former slave voting accounted for two African American members of the U.S. senate and twenty congressmen: eight from South Carolina,
four from North Carolina, three from Alabama, and one each from the other
former Confederate states (Zinn 1980). Moreover, the Fourteenth Amendment (ratified in 1868) declared that "all persons born or naturalized in the
United States" were citizens, and that "no state shall make or enforce any law
that shall abridge the privileges or immunities of citizens of the United Sates;
nor shall any State deprive any person of life, liberty, or property, without due
process of law; nor deny to any person within its jurisdiction the equal protection of the laws." Also, in the late 1860s and early 1870s, Congress enacted
several laws making it a crime to deprive African Americans of their rights,
and requiring federal officials to enforce those rights. These laws gave African
Americans the right to contract and buy property (Zinn 1980).

The move, then, from slavery to citizenry resulted in African Americans
attempting to take control of conditions under which they labored, to free
themselves from economic and political subordination to white authority,
and to carve out the greatest possible measure of economic autonomy. Many
African American men refused to continue working under the direction of
an overseer, and hundreds refused to sign labor contracts with their former

The case of Henry Lowther presents yet another example of white supremacist male concern with political, economic, and sexual independence of African American men. Lowther was a forty-year-old ex-slave in Georgia who in 1870 was both a member of the Republican Party and economically independent. Lowther was arrested for conspiracy to commit murder and, at 2 A.M. one morning, approximately 180 Klansmen came to the jail and carried off Lowther to a swamp. Lowther explained to the Joint Select Committee (*Condition of affairs* 1871, pt. 6: 357) what happened next: "Every man cocked his gun and looked right at me. I thought they were going to shoot me, and leave me right there. The moon was shining bright, and I could see them. I was satisfied they were going to kill me, and I did not care much then. Then they asked me whether I preferred to be altered or to be killed. I said I preferred to be altered."

After castrating him, the Klansmen left Lowther in the swamp to bleed to death. He made it home, however, and survived to recount the violence to the committee. Asked by the committee why the Klan came to jail for him, Lowther (pt. 6: 359, 362) gave three reasons: "They said that no such man as me should live there . . . I worked for my money and carried on a shop. They have been working at me ever since I have been free. I had too much money. They said I had taken too great a stand against them in the Republican Party. They said I was going to see a white lady." Finally, in a similar case, ex-slave Bill Brigan was taken from his home in 1870 by the Klan on suspicion of involvement with white women in Georgia; Brigan was "tied down on a log and they took a buggy-trace to him, and whipped one of his seeds [testicles] entirely out and the other nearly out" (pt. 6: 359).

How can we begin to make sense of such white mob violence directed primarily toward African American men exhibiting political, economic, and sexual independence? During Reconstruction, African American male participation in the political/economic arena as competitors threatened white masculine status. The "invasion" of African American men into these critical hegemonic masculine spheres posed a very real threat to white men's monopoly over politics and jobs; one way to discourage such competition and reestablish racial and masculine meanings and practices was to use violence to remind African American men of their subordinate Otherness. In other words, white men secured both a specific type of "whiteness" and a specific type of "maleness" by emphasizing the subordinate status of African American male competitors. White supremacist masculinity was defined through the collective practice of lynching. Mob violence helped white supremacist men define who they were by directing hostility toward African American men as a symbol of what they were not. In the particular social context of Reconstruction, African American male accountability to race and sex categories would become salient. Politically and economically independent African American men confounded the possibility of differentiating men according to race and, therefore, undermined the legitimacy of white male supremacy. Whippings, lynchings, and castrations conveyed to African American men that white men were ready to punish the slightest deviation from tolerated lines marking their "subordinate masculinity." When African American men dared step over these lines, they were made examples of what was acceptable and of what was expected from the entire race (Harris 1984).

Although not all white males engaged in such violence, the unique social setting of Reconstruction increased the likelihood of this particular type of violence, since white supremacist masculinity was so effectively being challenged.[11] Mob violence communicated widely held indignation against African American men for invading a white male bastion, and for threatening the economic and social status of white men.

Under slavery, political participation and economic independence was an ideal arena for differentiating racial masculinities; engaging in these activities demonstrated clearly that players were "white" and "real men." By implication, in the Reconstruction South, African American males engaging in the same activities diluted this masculine and race distinction: If African American men were permitted to do what "real men" (white men) did, the value of this practice to accomplishing white masculinity was effectively compromised. And because part of "doing difference" (West and Fenstermaker 1995) meant creating racial differences and therefore racial boundaries among men, by maintaining and emphasizing the subordinate status of African American men through violence, white men were attempting to restore those distinctions and thus to preserve the peculiarity of white supremacist masculinity. Mob violence served to solidify, strengthen, and validate white supremacist masculinity and simultaneously to exclude, disparage, and subordinate African American masculinity. Indeed, it reinforced the commonality of white males as against the pernicious Other.

Finally, the case studies reveal a heightened and intense white male concern with every interaction between white women and African American men, especially if it indicated even the slightest possibility of interracial sexuality. In other words, under the conditions of Reconstruction, attention to relationships between white women and African American men was intensified. The African American male had joined with the white female as the major targets of sexual regulation. It is to this regulation that we now turn.

RACE, SEXUALITY, AND THE CHIVALRIC PHALLACY

Most chroniclers of lynching say little about those lynchings that occurred during Reconstruction, preferring to examine primarily lynchings from the late 1880s. Those who have studied the Reconstruction period, however, find that "the practice was widespread" (Rable 1984, 98). Richard Maxwell Brown (1975, 214, 323) writes that, from 1868 through 1871, the Klan engaged in large-scale lynching of African American men. He records over 400 Klan lynchings of African Americans in the South over this time: 291 in 1868, 31 in 1869, 34 in 1870, and 53 in 1871. Similarly, George C. Wright (1990, 41–42) reports in his study of Kentucky that more than one-third of the lynchings that occurred in that state (117 of 353) happened between 1865 and 1874, "with 2 years alone, 1868 (with 21) and 1870 (with 36), accounting for the extremely high number of 57." And more recent estimates suggest that as many as 20,000 African Americans may have been lynched by the Klan during Reconstruction (Dray 2002).

Moreover, in the 1880s and 1890s, the number of lynchings gradually increased (though never reaching the 1868 level). During those years, the heyday occurred in the early 1890s, when, in 1892, the largest number (106) of African American lynchings occurred (Tolnay and Beck 1995, 271).

The vast majority of victims during this period (1880–1900) were charged with alleged sexual offenses against white women (Brundage 1993; Tolnay and Beck 1995). As Brundage (1993, 58) reports in his study of lynching from 1880–1930, "white Southerners maintained that rape was the key to lynching" whether or not a rape actually occurred. Rape became such an elastic concept within the white community during Reconstruction and its immediate aftermath that it stretched far beyond the legal definition to include "acts as apparently innocent as a nudge" (61). For example, "On November 8, 1889, a mob lynched Orion Anderson in Loudoun County, Virginia, for an alleged attempted "assault" of a 15-year-old white girl. In fact, the black youth, a friend of the girl, had merely donned a sack on his head and frightened her while she walked to school" (61).

Perhaps more telling, the following event illustrates the intense white supremacist male interest in sexuality between white women and African American men. When a sixteen-year-old white girl became pregnant by her African American male lover, the girl's father had the African American male "promptly arrested for rape even though the girl adamantly refused to accuse him. While he was being transported to the county jail, a mob seized him and hanged him. The tragic affair ended when the young girl committed suicide by taking an overdose of sleeping pills" (Brundage 1993, 62).

In addition, lynchings for any such interaction suggesting interracial sexuality increasingly included sexual mutilation (Dowd Hall 1979, 1983). As Brown (1975, 151) shows, "the lynching of Southern blacks routinely came to be accompanied by the emasculation of males." Indeed, the typical lynching became a white community celebration, with men, women, and children cheering on the mutilation and hanging, burning, or both, at the stake. As Raper (1969, 12) shows, white women spectators figured prominently in the ordeal, inciting "the men to do their 'manly duty' " and "inspiring the mobs to greater brutalities."

The lynching process extended for several hours, during which the African American male suffered excruciating pain from torture, mutilation, and castration committed throughout the ordeal by certain white supremacist males. The finale featured spectator scavenging for "souvenirs" of African American body parts (Brown 1975, 217–218).

The 1889 lynching of Sam Holt in Newman, Georgia, provides an effective example (Ginzburg 1988, 11–14). Holt was charged and detained for the alleged rape of a white woman. Soon a mob of whites gathered outside the jail, and the sheriff of the town "turned the Negro over to the waiting crowd" (13). Although the alleged rape victim "was not permitted to identify the Negro" because "it was thought the shock would be too great for her," a procession quickly formed and the doomed man marched at the head of the shouting crowd (approximately two thousand white people) down several streets (11–13). Eventually a tree was chosen, and Holt was tied from a branch facing the crowd. Immediately his clothes were torn from him and a heavy chain was wound around his body. The local press reported what happened next (12): "Before the torch was applied to the pyre, the Negro was deprived of his ears, fingers, and genital parts of his body. He pleaded pitifully for his life while the mutilation was going on, but stood the ordeal of the fire with surprising fortitude. Before the body was cool, it was cut into pieces, the bones were crushed into small bits, and even the tree on which the wretch met his fate was torn up and disposed of as 'souvenirs.' The Negro's heart was cut into several pieces, as was also his liver."

None of the white male lynchers attempted to disguise their appearance, and there was no effort to prevent anyone from seeing who lighted the fire or mutilated and castrated the body. On the contrary, there was a festival atmosphere. Finally, on the trunk of a nearby tree was pinned a placard that read "We Must Protect Our Southern Women."

Under conditions of "emancipation," African American male sexuality, viewed as dangerous and animal-like, grew to become an even greater threat assiduously waiting to be unleashed. By opposing this embodiment of evil, white supremacist men affirmed their version of morality and virtue, and at the same time their status as white men. Lynching reconstructed African American men as "natural," "animalistic" rapists; by resolutely and "bravely" avenging the alleged rape of pure white womanhood, Southern white men framed themselves as chivalric patriarchs, avengers, and righteous protectors (Dowd Hall 1983).

As demonstrated, hegemonic white male masculinity was measured by a man's ability to control, provide for, and protect his home—especially the white woman at the center of it. Under conditions of Reconstruction and its immediate aftermath, interracial sexuality represented the loss of all this. Thus, when a white man acted to save "his woman" from the bestial African American male, he constructed himself as savior, father, and keeper of racial purity (Harris 1984). White women were regarded as being at risk, and had to be protected in the name of the race. By this commitment, white men taught "their women" that there was nothing to fear by capturing the source of that fear, torturing it, and killing it (20). In this way, white supremacist men regained patriarchal hegemonic masculine status by determining what was wrong with society, ferreting it out, and reestablishing the norm as it had existed before the interruption (20).

Lynching for rape upheld white privilege and underpinned the objectified figure of white women defined as "ours" and protected by "us" from "them" (Fraiman 1994, 73). These beliefs formed what Fraiman (73) calls the white male chivalric phallacy: preservation of white masculine supremacy was refigured as protection of white females for white males. Over and over, Klan members and other white supremacists told the Joint Select Committee (*Condition of affairs* 1871, pt. 2) that "females shall ever be special objects of our regard and protection." Using the white woman's emblem as the keeper of racial purity, these white men cast themselves as protectors of civilization, thereby reaffirming not only their role as social and familial "heads," but also their paternal property rights (Wiegman 1993). In this view, interracial sexuality destroyed what it meant to be a man because white masculinity was inextricably tied to race: To be a man was to be a white man who had sole access to, and the duty to protect, white women. The lynching and castrating of African American men, founded on the protection of white women, was central to securing white male power and identity and, thereby, reconstructing a hierarchical masculine difference between white and African American men.

Moreover, in the context of the nineteenth-century feminist movement, the necessity for disrupting potential bonds between white women and African American men was critical (Wiegman 1993). The women's movement challenged hegemonic white masculinity by agitating for female access to activities traditionally reserved for men, in particular white men, from economic to political equality. For example, during Reconstruction, Susan B. Anthony and Elizabeth Cady Stanton founded not only the National Woman Suffrage Association but also *The Revolution*, which became one of the best-known independent women's newspapers of its time. The motto of the weekly was: "men, their rights and nothing more; women, their rights and nothing less." In addition to discussions of suffrage, *The Revolution* critically examined topics ranging from marriage to sexuality.[12]

It was also during the 1870s and 1880s that the "New Woman" appeared in U.S. society (Smith-Rosenberg 1985, 26). The New Woman was single, highly educated, and economically autonomous; she eschewed marriage, fought for professional visibility, and often espoused innovative and radical economic and social reforms (245). As Smith-Rosenberg (1985, 245) shows, the New Woman "challenged existing gender relations and the distribution of power" and, therefore, "challenged men in ways her mother never did." Indeed, according to Michael Kimmel (1987, 270), one white male response to this visible and outspoken feminist movement, as well as to the New Woman, was "to push women out of the public domain and return them to the home as passive, idealized figurines."

This focus by Kimmel (1987), however, overlooks the practice of lynching and castrating African American men. Violence against alleged black rapists earned white men positions of superiority over white women as well as over African American men; thus lynching equated the preservation of race with passive femininity. The lynching scenario constructed white women as frail, vulnerable, and wholly dependent for protection on chivalric white men. In this way, lynching and the mythology of the "black rapist" reproduced race and gender hierarchies during a time when these very hierarchies were threatened by both the New Woman and the newly independent African American male. Protection of white women reinforced femaleness and thus the notion of "separate spheres," while simultaneously constructing racial boundaries between white and African American men (Harris 1984). Lynching, then, was a white male resource for "doing difference" (West and Fenstermaker 1995) between men and women and among men. Accordingly, lynching the "black rapist" not only constructed African American men as subordinate to white men, but simultaneously perpetrated the notion of separate spheres and inequality between white men and white women.

Yet, this still leaves unanswered the reason for castrating African American males in public spectacles. Arguably, the increased reliance on public castration made clear the profound white supremacist male distress over masculine equality and similarity with African American men. As Robin Wiegman (1993, 450) eloquently puts it: "Within the context of white supremacy, we must understand this threat of masculine sameness as so terrifying that only the reassertion of a gender difference can provide the necessary disavowal. It is this that lynching and castration offer in their ritualized deployment, functioning as both a refusal and a negation of the possibility of extending the privileges of patriarchy to the black man."

Both race and masculine differences were reproduced through the practice of lynching and castration by ultimately emasculating the African American male body. African American masculine equality and similarity was discredited symbolically through publicly displayed castrated bodies. Possible sameness with white men was compromised violently in favor of continued primacy of white masculine supremacy (Wiegman 1993); the practice of lynching and castration provided a resource for the physical enactment of white masculine hegemony. And as Wiegman (449, 465) concludes, castration consigned African American men "to the fragmented and decidedly feminized realm of the body," while simultaneously the white male retains "hegemony over the entire field of masculine entitlements."[13]

CONCLUSION

Reconstruction created the social context for constructing an alarmist ideology about African American male sexuality, with the resulting pronounced public mob violence employed by white supremacist men.[14] White supremacist men bonded into lynching mobs that provided arenas for an individual to prove himself a white man among white men. During the economic turbulence of Reconstruction and its immediate aftermath, gender and race became extraordinarily salient and thus white supremacist men developed strong ties with their neighbors, with their acquaintances, and with those whom they perceived to be like themselves. In particular, participation in mob violence demonstrated that one was a "real white man." Within the social context of the white male mob, this hegemonic white supremacist masculinity—as a particular type of "whiteness"—was sustained by means of collective practices that subordinated African American men and, therefore, a specific African American masculinity. Indeed, the individual style of the white male mob member was somewhat meaningless outside the group; it was the lynching mob that provided meaning and currency for this type of white masculinity. White supremacist men, then, were doing a specific type of whiteness and masculinity simultaneously as they were doing lynching—the three merged into one entity.

The collective struggle for supremacy over African American men was a means with which to gain recognition and reward for one's white masculinity, and mob violence was a situational resource for surmounting a perceived threat by reasserting the social dominance of white men. Lynching the "bestial black rapist" reconstructed racial masculinities in hierarchical terms of essential, biological inequality. In short, these white supremacist men gained status, reputation, and self-respect through participation in mob lynchings, which symbolically, especially through the ritual of castration, disclaimed an African American male's right to citizenry, freedom, and self-determination.

NOTES

1. Nevertheless, slave men often attempted to protect slave women from such violence. As Jacqueline Jones (1986, 37) shows, the literature is "replete with accounts of slave husbands who intervened at the risk of their own lives to save wives and children from violence at the hands of whites."
2. Anne Firor Scott (1970, 54–55) argues that many white women found this sexual double standard difficult to accept, and engaged in premarital and extramarital affairs.

3. In this slave society, rape meant the rape of white women—for it was not a crime to rape black women. Consequently, when a black man raped a black woman, only his master could punish him, not the court system (Genovese 1974; see Flavin, this volume).

4. Throughout the North and South during this period, the largest proportion of women arrested were charged with such "moral misbehavior" as adultery, fornication, and bastardy (Spindel 1989, 82–86).

5. Both slave men and free blacks recognized this purported subordinate masculinity. A central theme of the abolitionists' attack on slavery was that it robbed black men of their manhood. And male slaves who agitated for freedom demanded their "manhood rights," equating freedom and equality with manhood (Horton 1993, 83–85). Moreover, black men who enlisted in the Union Army and fought in the Civil War conceptualized the practice as marking a watershed in the construction of "true" black masculinity. As Cullen (1992, 77) found in his examination, exhibiting "real manhood surfaces again and again as an aspiration, a concern, or a fact of life" for these black soldiers.

6. Because African Americans were involved increasingly in sharecropping, however, it became necessary for African American women to contribute to family income. Thus, a "separate spheres" ideology was at best a temporary phenomenon (Foner 1988, 86).

7. In March 1865, Congress created the Bureau of Refugees, Freedmen, and Abandoned Lands, which became known as the Freedman's Bureau, to protect the interests of African Americans in the South, and to help them obtain jobs and establish African American hospitals and churches.

8. Many African American women resisted this forced patriarchal component of African American family life (Foner 1988, 88).

9. Examples are the Black Codes or local ordinances in the South that restricted African American movement, prohibited planters from luring African Americans away from existing jobs with promises of better pay and working conditions, and allowed for the arrest of African Americans not lawfully employed, who would then be hired out to the highest bidder and kept in virtual bondage until the fine was paid off (Dray 2002, 34–35).

10. In 1871, Congress appointed a joint committee to investigate violence against African Americans in the former Confederate states. Witnesses testified that throughout the late 1860s white male terrorism was directed primarily against politically active and economically independent African American men who refused to defer to white supremacist men, who engaged in any conduct that indicated a sexual liaison with white women, or both. This government document is one of the few primary sources on white mob violence during Reconstruction.

11. Indeed, many close relationships between whites and African Americans developed during Reconstruction, and even during the antebellum period non-slaveholding whites and blacks interacted on a social level, a religious level, and an economic level. For an interesting discussion of interracial alliances forged among those involved in crime in the antebellum South, see Lockley (1997).

12. For an informative account of the racism inherent in this "first wave" of the feminist movement, see Davis (1983, 46–86).

13. In addition to this antifeminist response, Kimmel (1987, 269–277) outlines two additional responses by men: a "masculinist" response that urged a greater participation by men in the rearing of boys, and a "profeminist" response that embraced feminist principles as a solution to this "crisis" of masculinity.

14. The legacy of this racist violence has been extensive "legal lynchings" by the state. For example, between 1930 and 1967, 455 men were executed for rape in the

United States; 405 were African American men, and all victims of the convicted rapists were white women (Wolfgang and Riedel 1975). Moreover, a number of these cases have proven to be miscarriages of justice, in which innocent men were executed (Bedau and Radelet 1987).

Works Cited

Ayers, Edward. 1984. *Vengence and justice: Crime and punishment in the nineteenth-century American South.* New York: Oxford University Press.

Bedau, Hugo, and Michael Radelet. 1987. Miscarriages of justice in potentially capital cases. *Stanford Law Review* 40: 21–179.

Baker, Paula. 1984. The domestication of politics: Women and American political society, 1780–1920. *American Historical Review* 89: 620–647.

Bederman, Gail. 1995. *Manliness and civilization: A cultural history of gender and race in the United States, 1880–1917.* Chicago, IL: University of Chicago Press.

Brown, Richard Maxwell. 1975. *Strain of violence: Historical studies of American violence and vigilantism.* New York: Oxford University Press.

Brundage, William Fitzhugh. 1993. *Lynching in the New South: Georgia and Virginia, 1880–1930.* Chicago, IL: University of Chicago Press.

The condition of affairs in the late insurrectionary states: Report and testimony to the Joint Select Committee. 42nd Cong., 2nd Sess. 13, 1871.

Cullen, Jim. 1992. "I's a man now": Gender and African American men. In *Divided houses: Gender and the Civil War,* edited by Catherine Clinton and Nina Silber, 76–91. New York: Oxford University Press.

Davis, Angela. 1983. *Women, race, and class.* New York: Vintage.

D'Emilio, John, and Estelle B. Freedman. 1988. *Intimate matters: A history of sexuality in America.* New York: Harper and Row.

Douglass, Frederick. 1892. Lynch law in the South. *North American Review* 155: 17–24.

Dowd Hall, Jacquelyn. 1979. *Revolt against chivalry: Jessie Daniel Ames and the women's campaign against lynching.* New York: Columbia University Press.

———. 1983. "The mind that burns in each body": Women, rape, and racial violence. In *Powers of desire: The politics of sexuality,* ed. Ann Snitow, Christine Stansill, and Sharon Thompson, 328–349. New York: Monthly Review Press.

Dray, Phillip. 2002. *At the hands of persons unknown: The lynching of black America.* New York: Random House.

Foner, Eric. 1988. *Reconstruction: America's unfinished revolution, 1863–1877.* New York: Harper and Row.

Fox-Genovese, Elizabeth. 1988. *Within the plantation household: Black and white women of the Old South.* Chapel Hill: University of North Carolina Press.

Fraiman, Susan. 1994. Geometrics of race and gender: Eve Sedgwick, Spike Lee, and Charlayne Hunter-Gault. *Feminist Studies* 20: 67–84.

Frankenberg, Ruth. 1993. *White women, race matters: The social construction of whiteness.* Minneapolis: University of Minnesota Press.

Genovese, Eugene. 1974. *Roll, Jordan, roll: The world the slaves made.* New York: Random House.

Ginzburg, Ralph. 1988. *100 years of lynching.* Baltimore, MD: Black Classic.

Harris, Trudier. 1984. *Exorcising blackness.* Bloomington: Indiana University Press.

Hodes, Martha. 1991. *Sex across the color line: White women and black men in the nineteenth-century American South.* PhD diss., Princeton University.

Horton, James. 1993. *Free people of color: Inside the African American community.* Washington, DC: Smithsonian Institution Press.

Johnston, James Hugh. 1970. *Race relations and miscegenation in the South, 1776–1860.* Amherst: University of Massachusetts Press.

Jones, Jacqueline. 1986. *Labor of love, labor of sorrow: Black women, work, and the family from slavery to the present.* New York: Vintage.

Jordan, Winthrop. 1968. *White over black: American attitudes toward the Negro, 1550–1812.* Chapel Hill: University of North Carolina Press.

Kimmel, Michael. 1987. Men's responses to feminism at the turn of the century. *Gender and Society* 1: 261–283.

Lockley, Tim. 1997. Partners in crime: African Americans and non-slaveholding whites in antebellum Georgia. In *White trash: Race and class in America*, ed. Matt Wray and Annalee Newitz, 57–72. New York: Routledge.

Rable, G. C. 1984. *But there was no peace: The role of violence in the politics of Reconstruction.* Athens: University of Georgia Press.

Raper, Arthur. 1969. *The tragedy of lynching.* New York: Negro University Press.

Russett, Cynthia Eagle. 1989. *Sexual science: The Victorian construction of womanhood.* Cambridge, MA: Harvard University Press.

Schwarz, Phillip. 1988. *Twice condemned: Slaves and the criminal laws of Virginia, 1705–1865.* Baton Rouge: Louisiana State University Press.

Scott, Anne Firor. 1970. *The southern lady: From pedestal to politics, 1830–1930.* Chicago, IL: University of Chicago Press.

Smith-Rosenberg, Carroll. 1985. *Disorderly conduct: Visions of gender in Victorian America.* New York: Oxford University Press.

Spindel, Donna. 1989. *Crime and society in North Carolina, 1663–1776.* Baton Rouge: Louisiana State University Press.

Takaki, Ronald. 1982. *Iron cages: Race and culture in nineteenth-century America.* New York: Alfred A. Knopf.

Thorpe, Earl. 1967. *Eros and freedom in Southern life and thought.* Durham, NC: Seeman.

Tolnay, Stewart, and E. M. Beck 1995. *A festival of violence: An analysis of southern lynchings, 1882–1930.* Chicago: University of Illinois Press.

Trelease, Allen. 1971. *White terror: The Ku Klux Klan conspiracy and Southern Reconstruction.* New York: Harper and Row.

West, Candace, and Sarah Fenstermaker. 1995. Doing difference. *Gender and Society* 9: 8–37.

Wiegman, Robin. 1993. The anatomy of lynching. *Journal of the History of Sexuality* 3: 445–467.

Wolfgang, Marvin, and Marc Riedel. 1975. Rape, race, and the death penalty in Georgia. *American Journal of Orthopsychiatry* 45: 658–668.

Wright, George. 1990. *Racial violence in Kentucky, 1865–1940: Lynchings, mob rule, and "legal lynchings."* Baton Rouge: Louisiana State University Press.

Zinn, Howard. 1980. *A people's history of the United States.* New York: Harper and Row.

CHAPTER 6

Slavery's Legacy in Contemporary Attempts to Regulate Black Women's Reproduction

Jeanne Flavin

THE CONTEMPORARY STRUGGLE over black women's reproductive rights bears a disturbing resemblance to that which took place under slavery, marked as it is by racist stereotyping, paternalism, and insidious forms of control.[1] Slavery and punishment have served similar functions, permitting the state to exert control over black people's lives while at the same time communicating messages about which social arrangements and what conduct are acceptable. Although a low-income black woman's reproductive capacity does not break any laws, the policies governing her reproduction are often punitive in nature.

Today, low-income black mothers in the United States are blamed for a huge range of social problems, including "violent crime; the illegal drug epidemic; the decline of families, communities, and schools; the growth of rampant immorality; and even poverty itself" (Neubeck and Cazenave 2001, 3). Women's own poverty is frequently attributed to their "lack of responsibility" or "poor choices" rather than to dropping wages and institutionalized discrimination. This misplaced blame has led to tightening controls over black women's reproductive lives, as manifested by practices such as family caps, the prosecution of pregnant women who use drugs, court orders banning women addicted to drugs from procreating, and the separation of mothers from their children.

In mainstream discourse, reproductive rights are frequently reduced to access to abortion. For black women, however, these rights have more often been about the right to conceive, to be pregnant, and to raise children without unwarranted government interference than about the right to terminate a pregnancy. The narrow focus on abortion occurs to the particular detriment of black and Hispanic women, whose reproduction is most likely to be regulated by formal institutions such as the welfare system and the criminal justice system. As this chapter aims to show, the situation today is not a new one. Arguments that we need to restrict and even criminalize some women's behaviors to ensure the healthy reproduction of this nation have been around for over two hundred years.

REPRODUCTIVE CONTROL UNDER SLAVERY

During slavery, owners profited not only from the labor of enslaved women but also from these women's ability to give birth to more slaves. A blunt statement by slaveholder and former president Thomas Jefferson illustrates this: "I consider a woman who brings a child every two years as more profitable than the best man on the farm" (quoted in Roberts 1997, 25), as does the recollection of former slave Willis Cofer that "A good young breedin' 'oman brung two thousand dollars easy, 'cause all de marsters wanted to see plenty of strong healthy chillun comin' on, all de time . . . A nigger what warn't no more'n jes' a good field hand brung 'bout two hundred dollars" (quoted in Mellon 1988, 287–288). Especially after the 1808 ban on importing slaves, the replenishment of the enslaved labor force through childbearing led to black women's reproductive capacity "being subject to social regulation rather than to their own will" (Roberts 1997, 22–23). This social regulation of enslaved women took numerous forms and involved many specific mechanisms of control. Attention to some of these forms and mechanisms sheds light on the similar functions served by contemporary practices.

Owners enforced their expectations that slave women would produce children, using strategies of varying degrees of coercion. Some offered incentives to pregnant slaves such as extra rations or a lighter workload. Others spared pregnant women especially harsh disciplinary measures. In rare cases, masters might grant women who had already given birth to a requisite number of children permanent freedom from field work. "When the family increases to ten children living," a Georgia planter explained, "I require no other labor from the mother than to attend to her children" (quoted in Schwartz 2000, 20). Elsewhere, a former slave recalls "Long Peggy," who was freed after she bore twenty-five children (Smith 1988, 148).

In addition to exerting control over fecundity, owners determined whether a pregnancy was to be acknowledged and, if so, how. An owner could not afford completely to ignore a slave woman's physical health, because to do so would jeopardize her reproductive capacity and thus seriously threaten his future earnings. At the same time, however, owners wanted to maximize the physical labor they extracted from enslaved women. They also believed that slaves' inherent character defects made them more prone to deception. To avoid being duped by a slave woman "playing the lady," some owners insisted on examining a "patient" thoroughly (or summoning a physician to do so) before excusing her from work. Others simply ignored slave women's reports of fatigue or nausea. Some permitted women to do lighter labor such as mending clothes. Still many other accounts indicate slave women were expected to perform strenuous field work until they went into labor. Schwartz (2000), for example, describes former slave James Williams's published account of incidents in which pregnant women were whipped for failing to complete their duties, and subsequently miscarried or died. Schwartz suggests that the public criticism of slavery that sprang from Williams's account may have dissuaded some owners from using especially harsh disciplinary measures.

Owners also tried to control the medical care a woman received during and after the delivery. Some slaveholders were willing to undergo the expense of a physician in the case of an extremely complicated delivery, but resisted paying physicians' fees to attend to more routine problems. Some owners even studied medicine in an effort to monitor slaves' pregnancies with less expense.

The so-called "Father of Modern Gynecology," Dr. J. Marion Sims, conducted surgical experiments in his Alabama backyard hospital for slaves. Area slave owners sent slaves to Sims so he could attempt to return them to their original value; in return, Sims was able to experiment on the women, inventing instruments and medical procedures (Kapsalis 2002). Sims was particularly concerned with vesico-vaginal fistulas which often result from prolonged childbirth. Although women of all races develop fistulas, Sims and other physicians of the time tended to blame enslaved women's condition on their reluctance to call on white male physicians during labor, in favor of seeking help from midwives or black "root doctors," or from other trusted members of slave communities. Physicians and slave owners conveniently overlooked the fact that midwives often welcomed a physician in the case of difficult deliveries but planters and slave owners ultimately determined whether or not a physician was summoned.

By his own admission, Sims's interest in fistulas stemmed from economic rather than humanitarian concerns regarding the condition of slave women, namely, fears that a fistula "unfits her for the duties required of a servant" (Sims, quoted in Kapsalis 2002, 267).[2] This is true of most of the concessions granted to enslaved pregnant women: instead of stemming from owners' concern and care for enslaved women's humanity, they reflected the owners' recognition of a correlation between a heavy workload and an increased risk of miscarriage or the delivery of a sickly or stillborn infant.

Once a child was born, "owners kept up their meddling," historian Marie Jenkins Schwartz recounts in *Born in Bondage* (2000, 42). Again, it was slave owners, not mothers, who decided the answers to questions such as: When would a new mother return to work? How would children be fed, clothed, and sheltered, and by whom? Where would new parents and their infant live?

What tasks would women perform while they were excused from difficult farm chores? Who would nurse the babies or nurture older children, and under what conditions? What education would children receive? Who would supervise them? How much time would they spend with their parents? What relationships would they have with other children? What skills would they learn? Would children be separated temporarily or permanently from their families, and under what circumstances?

Plantation owners used threats of sale even in mundane circumstances. A Virginia ex-slave, Cornelius Garner, describes how the master used the threat of family dissolution to maintain peace and quiet on Sundays on the plantation. The master selected the family with the most children and warned that he would sell all of the children unless they were kept quiet. "Dat threat," Garner observed, "was worsen prospects of a lickin' " (quoted in Gutman 1976, 148).

Although owners' control over slave women was far-reaching and oppressive, it was not complete. Owners had the final say in most matters, but men and women slaves often pushed their owners to provide them with certain levels of protection and care. Slaves applied pressure through a variety of means, ranging from, for instance, raising a chorus of requests for accommodations, to such tactics as breaking tools, committing arson, refusing to work, or running away, until owners promised to spare pregnant women harsh treatment (Schwartz 2000, 24). Many owners succumbed at least in part to such actions not out of benevolence but "out of [owners'] necessity to discipline and morally justify a system of exploitation" (Genovese 1976, 4).

Enslaved women also found ways to resist the control over their fertility and reproduction. One woman explained that she used to have a baby every year but "when I had six, I put a stop to it, and had only one every other year" (quoted in Gutman 1976, 85). Enslaved women engaged in a wide range of practices designed to prevent or terminate a pregnancy, including violent exercise, root concoctions, camphor, turpentine, vaginal douches made with cockleburr roots and bluestone, and magical methods (e.g., keeping a copper coin under the tongue during sex) (Gutman 1976). Owners complained that whole families failed to have any children, or that few children had been born for an extended period of time. Some enslaved women falsely claimed pregnancy or did not report their miscarriages, in hopes of temporarily obtaining lighter tasks or extra rations (Kapsalis 2002, 268).

Resistance also came in the form of physical confrontation. Slave women fought against physical and emotional abuse by their owners, even though their actions were often met with violence. Rose Williams describes how she resisted the master forcing her to take a slave "husband" for the purpose of bearing children. When her "husband" approached her bed, she hit him over the head with a poker. Although she had two children by him, Rose Williams left the man and never married, declaring that the Lord would have to "forgive dis cullud woman, but have to 'scuse me and look for some others for to 'plenish the earth" (Williams 1988, 132).

Owners recognized that the cooperation of adult slaves in the workplace and the training of younger slaves required that at least some of the wishes of slaves be taken into consideration. Yet the predicament slave parents faced was undeniable: "When they encouraged owners to ensure their children's health and safety, they relinquished what they viewed as their parental prerogatives" (Schwartz 2000, 208).

CONTEMPORARY CHALLENGES TO BLACK WOMEN'S REPRODUCTIVE RIGHTS

Although contemporary society by and large condemns slavery, we are much less willing to recognize that similarly oppressive patterns continue to be exercised today. As during slavery, contemporary efforts to regulate black women's reproductive capacities encompass all aspects of reproduction from conception through child-raising. Although scholars of punishment have paid substantial attention to how incarcerated women's lives are controlled and regulated (see Britton 2003; McCorkel 2003; Roth 2004a) less attention has been given to the ways in which other institutions regulate women's lives, e.g., the welfare system and the child protective system. The control exercised by these systems is exercised with the full support of large sectors of the voting public, politicians, the media, policymakers, social service agencies, and the courts. Operating interdependently, these structures construct low-income black women as "irresponsible" individuals who should be prevented from conceiving, and, in some cases, from raising a child.

Complicating matters, contemporary discussions tend to steer clear of any direct mention of race, and instead insist that the problem of poverty and single-parent families is "color-blind" or "race-blind." But declaring something to be the case does not make it so. One cannot discuss poverty without describing a reality that is not only disproportionately experienced by black women, but also is conceptualized in racialized (and racist) ways. Consequently, any discussion of poor women's reproduction is essentially—though not exclusively—a discussion of poor black women. In turn, these discussions, declarations of race-blindness notwithstanding, are colored by historic patterns of control over poor black women getting pregnant, having children, and raising them. Although the policies described below affect many women who are not black, the roots of these policies are entrenched in concerns about black women's reproductive capacity.

While, during slavery, black women's fecundity was encouraged, contemporary efforts seek to limit it. Once slavery was abolished and black women's capacity to bear children lost its economic value to dominant-class whites, black women's childbearing was devalued and discouraged by European Americans

(Neubeck and Cazenave 2001, 152). Public and private incentives designed to pressure women to use long-term contraceptives, and welfare reform measures such as "family caps" provide evidence that economic interests and deeply seated biases continue to reign, over humanity and recognition of black women's bodily and personal integrity.

The eugenics movements of the twentieth century advocated the systematic and involuntary sterilization of "undesirables" for official reasons ranging from mental impairment to promiscuity to poverty. Between the early 1900s and the 1970s, at least 60,000 Americans (and perhaps as many as 100,000 to 150,000) in more than thirty states were sterilized against their will (Sinderbrand 2003; May 1995; see also Calavita, this volume). These efforts often targeted black women and other women of color. During the first half of the twentieth century, compulsory sterilization was aimed at "feeble-minded" and "genetically inferior" women. Many eugenic theorists equated racial inferiority with sexual degeneracy. At the time, many women were incarcerated in prisons or other institutions for engaging in nonmarital sexual behavior. As Elaine Tyler May notes, "Nonmarital sexual activity was a code for class and a marker for hereditary inferiority. There is no evidence that middle-class or affluent women were ever labeled feebleminded or sterilized against their will" (May 1995, 203). After World War II, institutional sterilizations declined, but the practice continued outside of institutions. Sterilizations were disproportionately performed on Native American, black, and Hispanic women, and justified by claims that this would save taxpayers' money by lowering welfare costs.

Evidence of the consequences of nativist fears is also found in more recent history. In 1990, Norplant received FDA approval. Within two years, over a dozen state legislatures proposed measures such as implanting women on welfare and those convicted of drug or child abuse with Norplant (Roberts 1997). All states and the District of Columbia made Norplant available through Medicaid. Many clinic staff emphasized the benefits of Norplant, while downplaying side effects such as depression, weight gain, and prolonged and heavy bleeding. Disadvantaged women's requests to have Norplant removed were met with opposition from clinic staff. Medicaid policy in some states authorized doctors' removal of Norplant only in cases of medical necessity. Norplant was eventually removed from the market in 2002.

In the wake of successful court challenges and wider public awareness of the medical complications associated with Norplant, overt federal and state efforts to sterilize poor women have become less popular. At least one private effort, however, continues to gain strength. Since 1997, Project Prevention has reinforced the racialized economic divide in our responses to women's reproduction by paying over one thousand drug-using women (and a few dozen men) two hundred dollars each for getting sterilized or using long-term birth control, such as Depo-Provera, Norplant, or IUDs. Project Prevention is funded largely by wealthy conservatives such as talk-show host Dr. Laura Schlessinger (Yeoman 2001). The program was originally named Children Requiring a Caring Kommunity or C.R.A.C.K., reflecting the founder's focus on crack cocaine rather than on substances like alcohol and tobacco that also pose a threat to fetal health but are more commonly used by white and middle-class women. Although C.R.A.C.K. was pitched as a sincere effort to improve the quality of women's and children's lives, evidence suggests otherwise. The program used to give clients more money if they were permanently sterilized than if they undertook a form of temporary sterilization such as Norplant. Further, the outreach strategies of Project Prevention/C.R.A.C.K. reveal the race-based roots of the program. Outreach efforts target communities of color, while ignoring drug and alcohol use in white communities. In Oakland, California, for example, billboards were placed in African American neighborhoods (Allina 2002). In 1998, founder Barbara Harris was quoted as saying: "We don't allow dogs to breed. We spay them. We neuter them. We try to keep them from having unwanted puppies, and yet these women are literally having litters of children" (Vega 2003). Project Prevention's website (www.projectprevention.org) reports that the organization relies heavily on referrals from probation offices, jails, drug treatment programs, methadone clinics and law enforcement agencies; staff receive fifty dollars for referring people to Project Prevention. This arrangement is troubling for a variety of reasons, not the least of which is that it supplies a financial incentive for state agents to encourage women to forgo their reproductive rights.

Although the popularity of privately-funded efforts such as Project Prevention has not been accompanied by similar government efforts in recent years, abuses of power by the state still occur. In July 2003, a Michigan judge ordered a woman to submit to a medically "verifiable" method of birth control (such as Norplant, Depo-Provera, or an IUD) in an abuse and neglect proceeding regarding her two children (*Family Independence Center v. Renee Gamez* 2003).[3] The Family Court alleged that Renee Gamez had physically neglected her children due to drug use. The judge argued that, because Gamez's drug use made it likely that she would bear a child with special needs, the state had a compelling interest in ordering her to be placed on birth control as part of the parent/agency reunification agreement.

In a friend of the court brief, the Michigan branch of the American Civil Liberties Union (ACLU) outlined some of the problems inherent in court-mandated contraceptive use. First, the Constitution protects a woman's right to make reproductive decisions free from unwarranted government intrusion. Just as the court cannot force a woman to have an abortion against her will, it cannot make her submit to a contraceptive method. Second, other, less intrusive, and more directly relevant means exist to protect children and rehabilitate troubled parents, such as counseling and supervised parenting times. Third, arguing—as the judge did in *Gamez*—that a prohibition on having an additional child is justified if any risk exists that the child might have "special needs," raises the question of whether the state may limit the procreation of parents who have a family history of genetic disorders, or of mothers who are on prescription medicine (e.g., for seizures) that may have adverse effects on a fetus.

Other actions assume different, and arguably more insidious, forms. In *Welfare Racism*, for example, sociologists Kenneth J. Neubeck and Noel A. Cazenave (2001) suggest that the authors of the Personal Responsibility and Work Opportunity Reconciliation Act of 1996 (PRWORA) aimed not only to force indolent black mothers receiving welfare to take jobs (or gain "work opportunities"), but also to discourage poor people of color from reproducing.[4]

Around half of all states have enacted "family caps" or "child exclusion" policies. Normally, states set the amount of public assistance payments based on factors such as the number of family members and the sources and amount of income. In states that have family cap laws, however, a woman who has another child while she is already receiving public assistance does not receive an increased payment. Forcing some women to raise an additional child without extra income, the argument goes, will deter other women on welfare from having more children. Basically, family caps aim to promote birth control through the prospect of increased impoverishment (Neubeck and Cazenave 2001, 159). No evidence exists to indicate that women have children in order to make money (Children's Defense Fund 2004). It is not surprising, then, that the General Accounting Office (GAO) reported that "[W]e cannot conclude that family cap policies reduce the incidence of out-of-wedlock births" (GAO 2001, 3). In fact, the same GAO report cited anecdotal evidence that family cap laws may unintentionally harm children above and beyond requiring they live in more impoverished families. All states with family cap policies have procedures to enroll eligible children in Medicaid and food stamps programs even when their families' benefits have been capped. Some women are not aware of this. They may be less likely to report the birth of children subject to the family cap to a caseworker; thus making it less likely that these children will be enrolled in or receive public benefits to which they are entitled.

At the same time that federal and state governments have endeavored to discourage low-income women from getting pregnant and having children, they have limited poor women's ability to terminate an unwanted or unplanned pregnancy. Medicaid offers comprehensive reproductive health care, including family planning, prenatal care, and services related to childbirth. Yet, since 1976, the Hyde Amendment has prevented low-income women (who are disproportionately women of color) from receiving an abortion federally funded through Medicaid (except in a few cases such as rape or incest).[5] All but seventeen states also restrict public funding for abortion.

By selectively withholding benefits to a woman who needs to end her pregnancy but not to one who elects to carry her pregnancy to term, politicians are able to impose their own choices on poor women (ACLU 2003). Consequently, many women who seek abortions are not able to obtain them. The situation is particularly bleak for women being charged or held in jails and prisons across the country. In many jail systems, women must first secure a court order in order to secure an abortion, a process which can take weeks or potentially months and may require the payment of lawyer's fees. Further, even with a court order, many counties will not transport pregnant inmates to abortion facilities or cover the cost of the abortion.

Rachel Roth (2004a) surveyed forty-four states and the District of Columbia and conducted a LexisNexis search of relevant state statutes, administrative regulations, and attorney general opinions to find out the status of abortion policies in prisons and jails. State policies vary widely, even within the same federal circuit. New Jersey, for example, has clearly articulated and readily available policies. New Jersey not only provides abortions for prisoners who are up to eighteen weeks of pregnancy, but also makes all arrangements. By contrast, in Delaware, not only must women pay for abortions, but they are charged $100 for transportation and security, which is provided by "moonlighting" correctional officers on Saturdays. At least one-third of all states have no official written policy governing incarcerated women's access to abortion. Another study found that over one in four pregnant women who used cocaine (and around one in sixteen other women) who gave birth in Washington, DC, hospitals considered abortion when they discovered they were pregnant, but could not afford it (Flavin 2002).

Once a low-income black woman becomes pregnant, states have sought to control her behavior during pregnancy, as illustrated by the response to pregnant women who use illegal drugs. Since the 1980s, over two hundred women in more than thirty states have been arrested and charged for their alleged drug use or other actions during pregnancy (Center for Reproductive Law and Policy 2000). In some of these cases, charges were dropped before trial, but, in many others, women have been pressured into pleading guilty or accepting plea bargains, some of which have resulted in incarceration. Upon appeal, most courts have found that prosecutions of women for their conduct during pregnancy are without legal basis or unconstitutional. In at least one case, however, the state supreme court involved upheld a woman's criminal child neglect conviction and eight-year prison sentence for drug use during pregnancy, even though the woman, Cornelia Whitner, had asked the criminal court to place her in drug treatment and ultimately gave birth to a healthy child (*Whitner v. South Carolina* 1998).[6]

Proponents of prosecution, court intervention, increased medical surveillance, and other measures designed to recognize "fetal rights" claim that such
measures are necessary to protect the fetus from harm. Even a cursory examination of this claim, however, reveals the flawed assumptions upon which it is
based. For example, although maternal cocaine use does add risk of poor fetal
outcomes to pregnancy, cocaine exposure does not automatically result in
poor fetal health. In contrast to the devastating impact predicted by sensationalist media accounts, meta-analyses (i.e., studies of many other studies) examining the effects of prenatal cocaine exposure have found *small or no effects* on
physical growth, cognition, language skills, motor skills, behavior, attention,
affect, and neurophysiology (Frank et al. 2001; Lester, LaGasse, and Seifer
1998). Children exposed to cocaine in utero "are not hopelessly damaged and
destined to become a burden to society" (Lester, LaGasse, and Seifer 1998,
634). In fact, research suggests that poverty, environment, and their correlates,
such as poor nutrition and tobacco use, influence children's development as
much or more than prenatal exposure to drugs (Frank et al. 2001). Unfortunately, such medical information is lost on people like the South Carolina state
court judge who, after reviewing the prosecution of a woman who had used
cocaine while pregnant, observed "Now this little baby's born with crack.
When he is seven years old . . . they can't run. They just run around in class like
a little rat. Not just black ones. White ones too" (quoted in Paltrow 2001, 247).

On a strictly pragmatic level, it is not clear how arresting a woman *after*
she gives birth can be expected to have a retroactive impact on the previous
nine months of her pregnancy. Similarly, "protecting the fetus" by incarcerating pregnant women wrongly assumes that jails and prisons offer high-quality
prenatal care programs, nutritional diets, and violence- and drug-free environ-
ments. As for any possible deterrent effect caused by fear of prosecution and
imprisonment, the nature of addiction (and the corresponding lack of effective drug treatment on demand) makes it more likely that a woman will be
deterred from seeking prenatal care and drug treatment, for fear of being punished, than be deterred from using drugs.

In light of the flawed logic and limitations of punitive policies, many states
have moved away from prosecution and punishment. Instead, they encourage
reporting maternal drug use to child protective services. The federal government's Administration for Children and Families (ACF) recognizes that drug
use does not automatically render someone an unfit parent, and that parental
substance abuse in and of itself should not be equated with child maltreatment. Consequently, ACF stipulates that parental substance abuse should not
be reported to child protective services as a form of child maltreatment unless
there is reason to believe that the parent's alcohol or other drug abuse is so
severe that the child has been or is likely to be harmed due to such substance
abuse, *or* unless other specific state legislation exists (NCCANI 2003). Therein

lies part of the problem. Such legislation *does* exist in many states, although the conditions that trigger mandatory reporting laws vary widely. Some states require only a positive toxicology screen at birth or physical signs of addiction or dependence, while other states require an assessment of the newborn's imminent risk of harm or need for protection.

Although in some respects an improvement over use of the criminal justice system to enforce expectations of how pregnant women should act, use of the child welfare system (and the welfare system's use of family caps) changes the site of reproductive control, but not the impact. Poverty and institutional racism continue to collude and seriously undermine low-income black women's ability to raise their own children. In particular, the increased use of foster care and the involuntary termination of parental rights undermine black women's attempts to raise their children, often with long-lasting and detrimental effects.

In 2003, around 906,000 children were found to be victims of child maltreatment, mostly neglect. Only one in four child victims of maltreatment are black, yet black children comprise nearly 35 percent of the 523,000 children in foster care (DHHS 2005a, 2005b).[7] In *Shattered Bonds: The Color of Child Welfare* (2002), Northwestern University law professor Dorothy Roberts asks why black children are disproportionately likely to be removed from their parents and placed under state supervision. Why is the child welfare system focused, not on assisting parents to take care of their children, but on punishing parents for their failures by threatening to take their children away? Why does our system focus on "protecting" children by blaming their parents, rather than truly promoting children's welfare? Roberts concludes that America has tolerated the destructiveness of separating parents from their children *because* of the color of America's child welfare system. "This protective function falls heaviest on African American parents," Robert asserts, "because they are most likely to suffer from poverty and institutional discrimination and to be blamed for the effects on their children" (Roberts 2002, 74).

Studies suggest that many women are poor, not because they have children, are lazy and make bad choices, but rather because dropping wages have made it increasingly difficult for female-headed households to escape poverty. Contrary to popular belief, the average family on welfare is no larger than the average nonrecipient's family and people do not get rich on welfare. Over 70 percent of the families receiving TANF in 2001 had only one or two children.[8] The maximum TANF benefit for a family of three in a typical state was only $362/month, with a possible food stamp benefit of an additional $288/month. This provides a combined annual income of $7,800, far below the federal poverty guideline of around $14,000 for a family of three. Nor do welfare programs drain government budgets; they constitute only about 1 percent and 2 percent of federal and state budgets, respectively (Armas 2003;

Children's Defense Fund 2004; APA 2003). Misconceptions about poor women persist in large part because they contribute to an ideology that "has helped to create and to maintain invidious distinctions between welfare recipients and other workers, thereby supporting seriously constrained policy . . . The fact that [the stereotype associated with 'typical welfare recipient'] is both so strong and so far from the reality of the lives of most welfare recipients is a key to understanding the increasingly punitive nature of welfare policy since the early 1980s" (Rose 2000, 144).

Welfare reform's work requirements and family cap laws make it extremely difficult for the poorest welfare recipients to take care of their children. Children are removed because of inadequacy of income more than for any other factor (Lindsey 1994). Poverty makes it more likely that a child will be exposed to poor nutrition, health problems, unsafe housing, and other threats to her physical well-being. Inadequate housing or lack of housing also causes children to remain in foster care longer.

In addition to ideology, political trends contribute to the long-term or permanent separation of children from their parents (Roberts 2002). Specifically, state and federal child welfare systems' original focus on family preservation has shifted to a focus on "freeing" children in foster care for adoption, by accelerating the termination of parental rights. The mass incarceration of black adults also has contributed to the long-term or permanent separation of children from their parents.

In the past quarter-century, the government has responded to the deficiencies of an overburdened child welfare system, and the harm it can cause to children and their families, in two distinct ways. In 1980, the Adoption Assistance and Child Welfare Act (AACWA) focused on keeping children safely in their families and safely reuniting children in foster care with their biological families. In 1997, AACWA was amended by the Adoption and Safe Families Act (ASFA). Instead of trying to reduce the number of children languishing in foster care by safely keeping families together, ASFA promoted adoption and the speedier termination of parental rights.[9] ASFA orders state governments to begin termination proceedings if efforts to reunite the family do not work within fifteen months. In other words, ASFA encourages judges to enforce statutory deadlines related mainly to the length of time a children has spent out of parents' custody, not to child abuse. This is all the more troubling when one considers that victims of severe abuse are only a tiny minority of children in foster care; most children in foster care are removed from their homes because of poverty-related neglect (GAO 1999). Moreover, most children want to remain with their biological parents, regardless of the circumstances; involuntary separation can cause deep psychological harm (see Roberts 2002).

Although federal law still requires states to make reasonable efforts to reunify children with their families, it also urges states to make concurrent efforts to prepare them for adoption. It is one thing to remove barriers to the adoption of children who are already available to be adopted, and quite another to treat the legal relationship between children in foster care and their parents as a barrier to adoption (Roberts 2002, 113). Researchers at Chapin Hall Center for Children at the University of Chicago predict that the number of children adopted from foster care in Illinois, Michigan, Missouri, New Jersey, and New York will exceed the foster care caseloads in those states some time between 2004 and 2006 (Anonymous 2002). At present, far more children in foster care are eligible for adoption than are successfully placed. According to the Urban Institute, in 1999, only around one in three of the half million foster care children available for adoption were successfully placed. Younger, white, or Hispanic females were more likely to be adopted than other children. Agencies' efforts to recruit black families may not be fruitful since black parents already adopt foster children at a rate double their proportion in the population (Green 2003).

The erosion of the black family through the extensive use of foster care is exacerbated by the disproportionately high rates of incarceration of black women and men. In 1999, 1.4 million children had a father in a state or federal prison, another 126,000 children had a mother in prison. Most mothers are incarcerated for nonviolent drug or property offenses. Two-thirds of women lived with their children prior to being incarcerated; one-third of all mothers lived alone with their children prior to arrest (Mumola 2000). While most children of incarcerated fathers live with their mothers, most children of incarcerated women live not with their father but with a grandparent or other relative, often a grandmother (Snell and Morton 1994; Mumola 2000).

Under TANF, a grandmother (or other relative) can only receive assistance for sixty months in her lifetime. If she has exhausted this limit while raising her own children, she can no longer receive TANF to care for, say, her incarcerated daughter's child. One possible solution is formally to place the children of incarcerated parents in foster care with the grandmother. After all, states are already directed to place children with relatives whenever possible, and the average foster care payment is typically greater than the average monthly payment under TANF. To receive foster care assistance, however, the children must be in state custody. Thus a grandmother needing financial assistance and supportive services to care for her grandchild may have to allege the child's mother neglected, abused, or abandoned the child, which may later contribute to the termination of the incarcerated mother's parental rights.

The courts may consider incarceration to be an aspect of abandonment and thus a justification to terminate parental rights. ASFA permits exceptions to the fifteen-month termination rule if a child is living with a relative or if other "compelling reasons" exist. But even if children do reside in a relative's home, caseworkers are unlikely to invoke these exceptions unless the child has a close and sustained relationship with the incarcerated parent, *and* the case-worker is aware of it. Further, around 10 percent of incarcerated mothers' children are in foster homes and do not qualify for such an exemption (Mumola 2000; Crary 2003). Once the mother of a child in foster care has been incarcerated at least fifteen months, state governments are mandated to start termination proceedings (NCCANI 2002).

Many obstacles exist that interfere with incarcerated women's ability to maintain contact with their children and the caseworkers, including limited access to telephones, restriction to making collect calls, lack of message-taking services for inmates, mothers' relocation to another facility, children's move to another foster home, imprisonment in geographically remote areas (making it difficult to transport children for visits), lack of adequate space and staff to permit child-parent visits, corrections' failure to produce parents for Family Court hearings even when the termination of parental rights is at stake. Women's lack of legal assistance to help guide them through the complex process also limits their ability to be effective advocates for themselves. Martha L. Raimon of the Women's Prison Association observes that, without adequate information about the incarcerated women's circumstances and their relationships with their children, "foster care agencies make vital decisions about the children's future simply based on the number of months spent in foster care and without a meaningful inquiry into what is best for the children. Stated differently, permanency is sacrificed in the name of expediency" (Raimon 2000, 425). Although incarcerated mothers can seek exemptions from termination, child-protection agencies in many states do not routinely encourage such efforts. "Instead of looking closely at the circumstances, agencies push the button for termination," Raimon notes. "It's faster, it's cleaner, it doesn't take as much work. I'm afraid we're sucking large numbers of children and parents down a black hole who otherwise could have maintained their family ties" (quoted in Crary 2003).

The criminal justice system, welfare system, and child welfare systems have become inextricably intertwined. Incarceration and poverty do not have a "ripple effect" on black families, so much as a tsunami effect. Congressional testimony and sensationalist media coverage of a few (admittedly horrific) cases contribute to the perception that low-income black women—not just those who are incarcerated—are unfit mothers. At the same time, foster and adoptive parents, who often have better incomes and less chaotic lives, are idealized. ASFA and the policies described earlier depend upon and perpetuate a belief in a false dichotomy that pits parents' rights against children's rights. No evidence exists to suggest that ASFA and other measures provide any overall social benefit for children. Moreover, seeing the situation as a dichotomy precludes serious consideration of how material and social assistance to mothers stands to benefit children as well (Stein 2000, 590).

What drives child welfare and other reproductive policies appears not to be a genuine and deep-seated concern about the physical and emotional well-being of children so much as the expression of a thinly veiled attempt to dictate what constitutes a "good mother," particularly when the mother in question is poor and black. Although prenatal exposure to alcohol is a leading cause of mental retardation, only four states currently require that fetal alcohol syndrome be reported (NCCANI 2003). Some states specifically mention prenatal drug exposure in their statutes defining child abuse and neglect but limit the definition of "drug exposure" to illegal substances. Around thirty-four states make exemptions for parents who choose not to seek medical care for their children because of their religious beliefs, but only around one-third of states' definitions of neglect grant exemptions for poverty. That is, in a minority of states, if a family living in poverty was not providing adequate food for their children, it would only be considered neglect if the parents were aware of food assistance programs but did not use them (NCCANI 2002). In sum, flawed and prejudiced assumptions equating drug use or poverty with parental unfitness underlie many official policies related to reporting to child protective services and foster care, often with devastating consequences.

The Legacy: Stereotyping and Paternalism

Examining the negative and unfounded stereotypes associated with being a black woman can help us understand the increasingly punitive and controlling nature of welfare and criminal justice policy. Under slavery, stereotypes about black women abounded. Believing enslaved women to be deceptive and crafty, slave owners denied them privacy and subjected their reproductive lives to close surveillance. Believing that slave women possessed superhuman strength and a high tolerance for pain made it easier to justify subjecting pregnant women and new mothers to arduous physical labor on the plantations and denying them adequate food and rest. Believing they were not as emotionally attached to their children helped justify separating mothers from their children.

Contemporary stereotypes portray black women as careless, promiscuous welfare queens who breed children to get more money (Collins 1990; Roberts 2002). Those who use drugs will "do anything" and are completely indifferent to any harm they may cause to themselves or others (Humphries 1999). Such stereotypes go hand-in-hand with paternalistic efforts to control black women's reproduction. To the uninformed ear, paternalism may sound like a good thing (or at least not like a bad thing). It remains, however, a dehumanizing structural arrangement. By stigmatizing and controlling the behaviors of a subordinate group, paternalistic practices help maintain systems of social, cultural, and economic oppression. Paternalism not only makes it easier to justify punishment, it directs us to punish women "for their own good." Moreover, demonizing women makes it easier to justify separating mothers from their children through incarceration.

Now, as during slavery, black and low-income women "are dealt with as if they are incapable of understanding their own best interests or functioning autonomously without guidance by their social superiors" (Neubeck and Cazenave 2001, 135–136). Legislators' attempts to blame black women for a range of social ills, and their attempts to control black women's fecundity, pregnancies, and child-raising are two sides of the same coin.

Today, public discourse overtly linking race and reproduction is rare (Neubeck and Cazenave 2001). Yet, the peculiar view, originating in slavery, that the government and other official actors have a paternalistic right to control black women's reproduction continues to shape our current policies. Many of our policies are developed by people who by and large do not appreciate the reality of poverty. They reflect middle-class Horatio Alger–like assumptions that all women can pull themselves up by their bootstraps if sufficiently motivated by, for example, financial incentives to not have children, or threats of having their children taken away. Even liberal policies that recognize that poor black families are victims of societal injustice "[use this] victimization as an excuse to intervene in their families instead of a reason to work toward social change" (Roberts 2002, 256).

Paternalistic policies and practices such as family caps, birth control incentives, foster care, and termination of parental rights purport to be race-neutral but in reality are anything but. At one end of the spectrum, low-income black women are viewed as self-centered individuals who can and should carry full responsibility for their actions; at the other end, they are defined as victims of social circumstance who cannot be trusted to make good decisions for themselves. Both positions stereotype poor black women as unable or unwilling to exert some positive influence over their reproductive capacities. Whether inspiring policies of increased surveillance, punishment, mandatory treatment, or termination of parental rights, for the "mother's own good" or in the interest of children, neither position seriously considers that low-income black women may exert some positive influence over their lives and bodies (cf. Flavin 2002).

If we aim to promote the health and well-being of women and children, our purposes would be better served by recognizing all women as allies—not adversaries or incompetents—who share a goal of freely chosen pregnancies that result in healthy women and children. Low-income women should play a greater role in setting the agenda. Advocacy and grassroots organizations should be sought as active allies—not only informing policies, but serving as a bridge between formal agencies of social control and the women and children they purport to serve.

Admittedly, the trust needed for effective alliances may not be readily forthcoming after more than a century of trying to control the most intimate aspects of black women's lives and bodies. Our willingness to blame women even in the face of staggering evidence of structural inequality highlights our refusal to recognize and address institutionalized racism. Unless we acknowledge the racist roots of our current laws and policies, however, we will be condemned to reproduce them.

NOTES

1. The author would like to thank Pierre Diaz, Mary Bosworth, and Miki Akimoto for their incisive comments on an earlier draft.

2. Kapsalis (2002) points out that, although a fistula may make a woman smell of feces and urine, it would not have affected her ability to work. Thus, the "duties" to which Sims refers appear to be related not only to her labor in the field or house, but also to her sexual and reproductive obligations to bear future slaves.

3. In May 2004, a New York family court judge, Marilyn O'Connor, barred a couple from procreating until they could prove they could take care of their offspring. She repeated her actions in December 2004 with a second woman (Dobbin 2005).

4. PRWORA's emphasis on heterosexual marriage as a means of ending women's dependence on governmental assistance raises its own set of troubling issues (see Abramowitz 1996; Mink 1998; and Quadagno 1994).

5. Similar restrictions not only affect poor women on Medicaid, but also deny federally funded abortion to Native Americans, federal employees and their dependents, Peace Corps volunteers, low-income residents of Washington, DC, federal prisoners, military personnel and their dependents, and disabled women who rely on Medicare.

6. On March 21, 2001, the Supreme Court ruled in the South Carolina case of *Ferguson v. City of Charleston* that, contrary to past practice, a public hospital cannot test pregnant women for drug use without their consent and turn the results over to police. Nurses and physicians at a public hospital in Charleston instituted a policy whereby pregnant women were tested for cocaine. Those who tested positive were arrested by the police at the hospital on charges of child abuse (Daniels 2000). Over five years, the Medical University of South Carolina arrested thirty women on these grounds. All but one of the women arrested was black; the exception gave birth to a mixed-race baby. Some were taken to jail during their eighth month of pregnancy; others were arrested in their hospital gowns, still bleeding from childbirth (Paltrow 2001; Flavin 2002).

7. Around one in five victims of child maltreatment were physically abused and one in ten were sexually abused. Around half of all victims of child maltreatment were white, one-quarter (25 percent) were African American, and one-tenth were Hispanic (DHHS 2005a). Of the estimated 523,000 children in foster care in 2003, 35 percent were black/Non-Hispanic, 39 percent were white/Non-Hispanic, and 17 percent were Hispanic (DHHS 2005b).

8. The Personal Responsibility and Work Opportunity Reconciliation Act of 1996 replaced the Aid to Families with Dependent Children (AFDC) program with the Temporary Assistance to Needy Families (TANF) program. When people talk about "welfare," they are referring to TANF.

9. Termination of parental rights severs legal and physical ties between parent and child. As the Legal Services of New Jersey termination of parental rights handbook

explains, "If your parental rights to your child are terminated, you will no longer have the right to visit with the child, speak to him or her on the telephone, communicate with the child by mail, or be told where the child is or what is happening to him or her. Your legal right to your relationship and your family's legal right to its relationship with your child will be permanently and completely ended. You will only be able to have contact with your child if the adoptive parents give you permission" (Shear 2002, no pagination).

WORKS CITED

Abramowitz, Mimi. 1996. *Regulating the lives of women: Social welfare policy from colonial times to the present.* Boston: South End Press.

Allina, Amy. 2002. Cash for birth control: Discriminatory, unethical, ineffective, and bad public policy. *Network News* 27: 5–6.

American Civil Liberties Union (ACLU). 2003. *Public funding for abortion: promoting reproductive freedom for low-income women.* Fact sheet. Available at: http://www.aclu.org/ReproductiveRights/ReproductiveRights.cfm?ID=9039&c=1.

American Psychological Association (APA). 2003. *Making welfare to work really work.* Available at: http://www.apa.org/pi/wpo/welfaretowork.html. Retrieved October 4, 2005.

Anonymous. 2002. More adoptions out of foster care. *State Legislatures* 28: 7.

Armas, Genaro C. 2003. Poverty climbs, incomes slide: Census releases numbers on household finances. Washington, DC: Associated Press, September 26.

Britton, Dana M. 2003. *At work in the iron cage.* New York: New York University Press.

Center for Reproductive Law and Policy (CRLP). 2000. *Punishing women for their behavior during pregnancy.* New York: CRLP, September. Available at: http://www.crlp.org/pub_bp_punwom.html. Retrieved October 1, 2003.

Children's Defense Fund. 2004. *Basic facts on welfare.* Available at: http://www.childrensdefense.org/familyincome/welfare/basicfacts.aspx. Retrieved July 7, 2005.

Collins, Patricia Hill. 1990. *Black feminist thought: Knowledge, consciousness, and the politics of empowerment.* New York: Routledge, Chapman & Hall.

Crary, David. 2003. Love locked away: A civil rights group is helping imprisoned mothers keep custody of their children. *Washington Post*, March 23.

Daniels, Cynthia. 2000. Doctors should not police pregnant women's actions. *San Francisco Chronicle*, November 15.

Dobbin, Ben. 2005. Judge orders another homeless drug addict to have no more children. Associated press state and local wire, January 4.

Family Independence Center v. Renee Gamez. 2003. Amicus curiae brief filed by the ACLU fund of Michigan.

Flavin, Jeanne. 2002. A glass half full? Harm reduction among pregnant women who use cocaine. *Journal of Drug Issues* 32: 973–998.

Frank, Deborah, Marilyn Augustyn, Wanda Knight, Tripler Pell, and Barry Zuckerman. 2001. Growth, development, and behavior in early childhood following prenatal cocaine exposure. *Journal of the American Medical Association* 285: 1613–1625.

General Accounting Office (GAO). 1999. *Foster care: States' early experiences implementing the Adoption and Safe Families Act.* Washington, DC: GAO.

———. 2001. *Welfare reform: More research needed on TANF family caps and other policies for reducing out-of-wedlock births.* Washington, DC: GAO.

Genovese, Eugene. 1976 [1972, 1974]. *Roll, Jordan, roll: The world the slaves made.* New York: Vintage Books.

Green, Rob. 2003. Who will adopt the foster-care children left behind? Fact sheet. Washington, DC: Urban Institute. Available at: http://www.urban.org/url.cfm?ID=310809.

Gutman, Herbert. 1976. *The black family in slavery and freedom, 1750–1925.* New York: Pantheon Books.

Humphries, Drew. 1999. *Crack mothers: Pregnancy, drugs, and the media.* Columbus: Ohio University Press.

Kapsalis, Terri. 2002. Mastering the female pelvis: Race and the tools of reproduction. In *Skin deep, spirit strong: The black female body in American culture,* ed. Kimberly Wallace-Sanders, 263–300. Ann Arbor: University of Michigan Press.

Lester, Barry, Linda LaGasse, and Ronald Seifer. 1998. Cocaine exposure and children: The meaning of subtle effects. *Science* 282: 633–634.

Lindsey, Duncan. 1994. *The welfare of children.* New York: Oxford University Press.

May, Elaine Tyler. 1995. *Barren in the promised land.* Cambridge, MA: Harvard University Press.

McCorkel, Jill A. 2003. Embodied surveillance and the gendering of punishment. *Journal of Contemporary Ethnography* 32, 1: 41–75.

Mellon, James, ed. 1988. *Bullwhip days: The slaves remember.* New York: Grove Press.

Mink, Gwendolyn. 1998. *Welfare's end.* Ithaca, NY: Cornell University Press.

Mumola, Christopher. 2000. *Incarcerated parents and their children.* Washington, DC: Bureau of Justice Statistics.

National Clearinghouse on Child Abuse and Neglect Information (NCCANI). 2002. Current trends in child maltreatment reporting laws. Child Abuse and Neglect State Statutes Series. Washington, DC: NCCANI.

———. 2003. *Reporting child maltreatment in cases involving parental substance abuse.* Washington, DC: NCCANI. Available at: http://www.calib.com/nccanch/pubs/usermanuals/subabuse/report.cfm. Retrieved October 1, 2003.

Neubeck, Kenneth, and Noel Cazenave. 2001. *Welfare racism: Playing the race card against America's poor.* New York: Routledge.

Paltrow, Lynn. 2001. The War on Drugs and the war on abortion. *Southern Law Review* 28: 201–252.

Quadagno, Jill. 1994. *The color of welfare: How racism undermined the War on Poverty.* New York: Oxford University Press.

Raimon, Martha. 2000. Barriers to achieving justice for incarcerated parents. *Fordham Law Journal* 70: 421–426.

Roberts, Dorothy. 1997. *Killing the black body: Race, reproduction, and the meaning of liberty.* New York: Vintage Books.

———. 2002. *Shattered bonds: The color of child welfare.* New York: Basic Civitas Books.

Rose, Nancy. 2000. Scapegoating poor women: An analysis of welfare reform. *Journal of Economic Issues* 34: 143–157.

Roth, Rachel. 2004a. Do prisoners have abortion rights. *Feminist Studies* 30, 2: 353–381.

———. 2004b. "No new babies?" Gender inequality and reproductive control in the criminal justice and prison systems. *Journal of Gender, Social Policy, and the Law* 12, 3: 391–425.

Schwartz, Marie Jenkins. 2000. *Born in bondage: Growing up enslaved in the antebellum South.* Cambridge, MA: Harvard University Press.

Shear, Beatrix W., with Nancy Goldhill, Charlotte Adams, Tom Makin, Donna Hildreth, and Patricia Myers. *Termination of parental rights: A handbook for parents.* Edison: Legal Services of New Jersey. http://www.lsnjlaw.org/english/family/tpr.cfm#preface. Last accessed June 6, 2005.

Sinderbrand, Rebecca. 2003. Eugenics: Clearing the collective conscience. *Newsweek*, June 2, 12.

Smith, John. 1988. Personal narrative. In *Bullwhip days*.

Snell, Tracy, and Danielle Morton. 1994. *Women in prison.* Washington, DC: Bureau of Justice Statistics.

Stein, Theodore. 2000. The Adoption and Safe Families Act: Creating a false dichotomy between parents' and childrens' rights. *Families in Society* 81: 586–592.

U. S. Department of Health and Human Services (DHHS) Administration on Children, Youth, and Families. 2005a. *Child Maltreatment 2003.* Washington, DC: U.S. Government Printing Office.

———. 2005b. *The AFCARS report: Preliminary FY 2003 estimates as of April 2005* (10). Available at: http://www.acf.hhs.gov/programs/cb/stats_research/afcars/tar/report10.htm. Last accessed March 29, 2006.

Vega, Cecilia. 2003. Sterilization offer to addicts reopens ethics issue. *New York Times*, January 6.

Whitner v. South Carolina. 1998. 328 S.C. 1, 492 S.E. 2d 777 (Sup. Ct. 1997), cert. denied, 523 U.S. 1145.

Williams, Rose. 1988. Personal narrative. In *Bullwhip days*.

Yeoman, Barry. 2001. Surgical Strike. *Mother Jones* 26, 21–22.

PART THREE

Immigration

CHAPTER 7

Immigration, Social Control, and Punishment in the Industrial Era

Kitty Calavita

ALEXANDER HAMILTON (1791, 123) warned Congress at the country's founding that, if the United States was going to industrialize, immigration had to be encouraged so as to mitigate "the dearness of labor." The second half of the nineteenth century and the early twentieth century witnessed the success of Hamilton's idea, as immigration played a central role in U.S. industrial development. Throughout this period, immigration involved primarily the movement of a labor force, and policymakers welcomed it as such.

It was not solely that immigrants increased the size of the workforce in industrializing America, although this was an important aspect. Rather, as we will see here, they provided a supply of labor that was cheap, racialized, and gendered in ways that contributed to a variety of social control and punishment mechanisms and that shaped the political economy of the emerging capitalist power. This chapter documents the role of immigration law and policy in reflecting and shoring up these mechanisms, as they alternately encouraged, filtered, stigmatized, and criminalized the immigrant flow. The concept of punishment is considered broadly here to include not only formal legal sanctions, but the extra-legal and informal sanctions that more routinely affected immigrants' everyday lives. There is some disagreement in the literature as to whether the foreign-born were overrepresented or underrepresented in prisons and jails during this period (Nelli 1969; U.S. Congress, Senate 1911; Wickersham Commission 1931). What is less debatable is that they were subjected to a range of economic and social punishments related not to crime per se but to their immigrant status.

The following section provides a brief overview of immigration and immigration policy in the mid- to late-nineteenth century, focusing on the central role of immigrants to the United States as a supply of cheap labor and an instrument with which to control the fledgling labor movement. The racialization of immigrants is then examined, including how the Chinese were demonized as a "scourge" (U.S. Congress, Senate 1877, viii) and barred from immigrating in 1882, and how, later, eastern and southern European immigrants were unfavorably contrasted to the "old immigrants" from northern Europe and restricted with quotas (U.S. Congress, Senate 1911). I then suggest that the Bracero Program beginning in the 1940s provided a back-door source of labor once the front door was largely closed to European immigration; with the demise of the Bracero Program and its institutionalization of discounted labor, immigrants were increasingly illegal and subject to the full panoply of social and economic penalties that that designation implies. Finally, I demonstrate the myriad ways in which not just race ideology, but gender ideologies as well, permeated each phase of immigration policy from the Chinese exclusions to the Bracero Program, simultaneously reflecting and advancing these ideologies and the social control mechanisms to which they contributed. Throughout, I suggest that immigrants were themselves used as a mechanism of social control (for example, as a way to offset "the dearness of labor") and were in turn subject to a range of social and economic punishments as demonized Others.

THE GOLDEN DOOR OPENS

European immigration to the United States in the mid-nineteenth century had much in common with that other movement of workers, the importation of African slaves. As one historian of the American South put it, "The African experience was only a special case in the general immigration experience" (Genovese 1974, 311). Although the parallel should not be overdrawn, as there are fundamental differences between forced and (at least nominally) voluntary migration, both slavery and immigration resulted from the demand for "human power to fuel the new systems of production" (3).

Twenty-five million immigrants entered the United States in the last four decades of the nineteenth century, most remaining in urban centers, but others populating the vast hinterland. By 1880, more than 70 percent of the population in each of the largest cities in the United States consisted of immigrants or their children, and the proportion was not much lower in smaller industrial towns (Gutman 1976, 40). The foreign-born increasingly made up the bulk of the industrial workforce. Samuel Lane Loomis stated in 1887 that "not every foreigner is a workingman, but in the cities at least, it may almost be said that every workingman is a foreigner" (quoted in Gutman 1976, 40). Hand in hand with the increase in immigration, the value of U.S. manufactured products soared, rising from $1.9 billion in 1860 to $11.4 billion in 1900, surpassing the combined totals of England, France, and Germany (Bimba 1927).

Hamilton had been right about wages. The editor of the *Engineering and Mining Journal* (1880, 335) noted approvingly that new unskilled immigrants "appear to be solving the labor question." In fact, employers reduced or stabilized wages in every industry and region in which immigrants were heavily concentrated. During and immediately after the Civil War, immigrant workers were imported for the express purpose of breaking strikes and more generally undermining unions. The *Workingman's Advocate* (1869, 2), a prominent Chicago labor paper, noted the trend: "Ever since the completion of the Atlanta telegraph, it has been the threat of unprincipled employers, in every state where unpleasantness has occurred, to threaten the importation of foreign workmen, and in many instances they have been able to put their threats into execution."

The use of immigrants from private labor exchanges in New York, which set up business across the street from the Castle Garden depot where European immigrants landed, became a major weapon in capital's arsenal against striking miners. Between 1872 and 1875, fourteen mining strikes by the new union, the Miners National Association, were broken with the introduction of Swedish, German, and Italian strikebreakers (Gutman 1976). Coming directly from the New York labor exchanges, the immigrants were brought to the mines under heavy guard, both to protect them and to isolate them from the striking mineworkers. Throughout the rest of the century, miners, railway workers, construction workers—the workers of almost every American industry—watched their strikes defeated by the introduction of newly arrived immigrants guarded by armed militias (Foner 1994).

To prevent the development of class consciousness among the immigrants, they were often kept in isolation. According to the report of a senator in 1884 (*Congressional Record* 1884, 5350), four hundred Italians who had replaced striking Buffalo longshoremen were "fenced in" and "kept by themselves." The president of the Knights of Labor union (*Congressional Record* 1884, 5360) testified before Congress that immigrant workers in Frostburg, Maryland, lived in barracks "fenced in to prevent them from being communicated with by the people whose places they had taken." Workers of differing nationalities and languages were hired to minimize communication among them. A manager of a Pittsburgh mill (Bridge 1902, 81) explained that a tractable workforce was best obtained by a "judiciously mixed" combination of foreigners and "young American country boys."

By the mid-1800s, American labor was vociferously protesting this use of immigrants to stabilize wages and stanch unions (Higham 1977; Calavita 1984). Indeed, immigrants—themselves used as a social control mechanism against labor by employers and policymakers—were at the same time demonized and subject to a wide variety of vigilante and informal punishments. Beginning with the depression of 1837–1843, violent anti-immigrant protests were commonplace, often directed at Catholic immigrants and ostensibly driven by nativist fears of "papism." The Broad Street Riot in Boston in 1837, set off by a confrontation between an Irish funeral procession and local fire-fighters, drew a crowd of over fifteen thousand. Rioters marched through the Irish sections of the city, burning and sacking, and forcing the Irish from their homes. Often the violence was explicitly labor-related. Native and for-eign workers battled repeatedly on the railroads and in the textile mills of Philadelphia in 1844 (*Native American* 1844). Striking weavers in Kensington, Pennsylvania, rioted in the streets in 1842, setting fire to immigrant strike-breakers' unfinished work (Montgomery 1972, 418). The same Kensington weaving district was destroyed by rioting workers in May 1843 as they protested the immigrant competition that had allowed employers to cut wages. In the notorious Kensington Riots of 1844, nativists burned the homes of immigrant weavers. After two days of rioting, three thousand federal troops arrived and put Kensington under martial law (Montgomery 1972, 432). By the 1850s, nearly every industrial center in America had witnessed armed attacks on immigrant workers.

Immigration restriction was a central platform of the Know-Nothing Party of the 1850s, and, as organized labor gained momentum in the early 1880s, protection from "the pauper labor of Europe" was a chief rallying cry (*Philadelphia Times* 1882, 1). Despite the protest and its overlay of racist nativism, immigration remained largely unrestricted. The first federal law addressing immigration was the 1864 *Act to Encourage Immigration* (13 Stat. 385) passed during the Civil War to offset labor shortages and associated wage increases. Among other things, the law established the first Federal Bureau of Immigration, with the purpose of recruiting immigrants and facilitating their transportation. Senator John Sherman reminisced in 1884 that the only argu-ment put forth for the law was the high price of labor (*Congressional Record* 1884, 1785).

Several laws were passed in the 1880s that selectively restricted immigra-tion, including an 1882 law barring convicts, "lunatics," "idiots," and "any other person unable to care for himself or herself without becoming a public charge" (22 Stat. 214), and the largely symbolic Anti-Alien Contract Labor Law of 1885 (23 Stat. 332) barring those who had prearranged labor contracts (Calavita 1983). A series of laws in the 1890s involved mostly rewordings and administrative changes, and added to the list of the excluded those suffering from contagious diseases, polygamists, and anyone who had engaged in acts of "moral turpitude." Following President McKinley's assassination, a 1903 law (32 Stat. 1213) barred "anarchists, or persons who believe in or advocate the overthrow . . . of the government . . . or the assassination of public officials." But these restrictions did nothing to interrupt what Carnegie (1886, 35) called "a golden stream which flows into the country each year." Carnegie applauded the immigrant stream: "Sixty percent of this mass," he said, are "adults between the ages of 15 [and] 40 years of age. These adults [are] surely worth $1500 each—for in former days an efficient slave sold for that sum."

RACIALIZATION, CHINESE "COOLIE LABOR," AND THE "NEW IMMIGRANTS"

In marked contrast to the general welcome afforded European immigrants by policymakers in the late nineteenth century, Chinese immigrants met vilification as "an inferior race" and "a distinct race of people . . . wholly incapable of assimilation" (*Congressional Record* 1882, 1637, 1584). With the Central Pacific Railroad completed in the 1870s, the Chinese immigration that had been pivotal to its construction was declared a "terrible scourge," and in 1882 the Chinese Exclusion Law (22 Stat. 58) was passed. Labor historians disagree about the primary reasons for the enactment of the Chinese exclusion, with some emphasizing the role of anti-Chinese racism in the labor movement (Sandmeyer 1973; Hill 1996; Saxton 1971; Mink 1986; Lyman 2000), and others insisting that Congress itself had fueled the racism and then strategically come to American labor's "rescue" (Gutman 1976; Gyory 1998). Putting aside the question of ultimate causes or primary movers, there is no doubt that racism was a defining feature of the debate.

As they debated the exclusion of Chinese laborers (but not of merchants, who were conveniently deemed "honorable" and "respectful"), metaphors abounded, likening "coolie labor" to "leeches," "hordes of . . . rats," "locusts," and "flies on a bee-gum on a summer's day" (*Congressional Record* 1882, 1545, 1583, 1904, 1642). A few themes were repeated over and over in this race narrative. Among the most ironic, given the exploitation of Chinese workers by employers who paid them less than the prevailing wage, was the proposition that Chinese workers had the biological capacity to subsist on below-subsistence wages, and were thus unfair competitors to American working-men and women. The Senate's special report on Chinese immigration (U.S. Congress, Senate 1877, v) had proclaimed, "They [the Chinese] can subsist where the American would starve. They can work for wages which will not furnish the barest necessities of life to an American." Another recurring theme was the deceitful nature of the Chinese. Time and again, it was contended that the Chinese were natural liars, with "little regard for the sanctity of an oath" (U.S. Congress, Senate 1877, vi); that "the masses of the [Chinese] people do not regard truth" (*Congressional Record* 1882, 1708); and, that "these men have no more moral sense of the obligation of an oath administered in our courts than a brute" (*Congressional Record* 1882, 1903).

Repeated references to African Americans, to the experience of slavery, and to lingering hostilities less than thirty years after the Civil War confirmed that Chinese exclusion was being framed first and foremost as a race issue. With considerable historical revisionism and self-congratulation, senators warned each other not to tackle another "race problem": "Nobody believed then, and nobody believes now who has studied the history of the races and the history of the world, that they [blacks] will ever be equal in all respects to the Caucasian race . . . They were a part of the people here [sic]; we could not send them abroad; and because we treated them with humanity, with righteousness, and with justice, shall we say that we are bound to extend to all the nations of the earth the same rights that we extended to them?" (*Congressional Record* 1882, 1713).

President Chester Arthur signed the Chinese Exclusion Law (22 Stat. 58) on May 6, 1882. In addition to barring the entry of Chinese laborers for a period of ten years, the law reiterated the ineligibility of Chinese (as "nonwhite" persons) to naturalization, an ineligibility that had been affirmed in a San Francisco circuit court decision in 1878 (*In re Ah Yup*, C.C.Cal. 1878). In 1894, Congress barred indefinitely the immigration of Chinese laborers (28 Stat. 1210), an exclusion that was not repealed until 1943. By the turn of the twentieth century, only a few thousand Chinese were admitted annually (Salyer 1995; Lyman 1977). In 1907, Japanese laborers were excluded by a "gentlemen's agreement" in which Japan was persuaded to deny them passports.

Enactment of the Chinese exclusion laws did nothing to appease anti-Chinese sentiment or the willingness of ordinary people to act on it. Iris Chang (2003, 132) describes the climate of vigilantism and the violence perpetrated against the Chinese as nativist vigilantes delivered their racist punishment: "Far from appeasing the fanatics, the new restrictions inflamed them. Having succeeded in barring the majority of new Chinese immigrants from American shores, the anti-Chinese bloc began a campaign to expel the remaining Chinese from the United States. During a period of terror now known as 'the Driving Out,' several Chinese communities in the West were subjected to a level of violence that approached genocide." The violence included raids on Chinatowns in three western cities. In one instance, six hundred Chinese residents of Tacoma, Washington, were rounded up by local citizens and "herded" to a railroad station where they spent the night unsheltered under a violent rainstorm (Chang 2003, 133). Two people died of exposure, one apparently was driven insane, and the others were shipped out of town on the railroad.

At the time that the Chinese exclusion laws were passed, the race thinking that they represented was not broadly extended to European immigrants, who, for a while longer, continued to be thought of by employers and policymakers as "that golden stream." But populist anger at European immigrants continued unabated, and began to increase as the new immigrants began coming from southern and eastern Europe. Italians, particularly Sicilians, were among the most vilified. As Higham (1977, 90–91) tells it, from Baltimore to West Virginia, from Colorado to Boston, in the 1890s Italians were assumed to be criminal and lynched when official justice failed, with local officials sometimes complicit in the lynchings (see also Messerschmidt, this volume).

A decade later, as the new immigrants began to form the backbone of the militant labor movement, even capital's unequivocal appreciation of European immigration began to dissipate. The last two decades of the nineteenth century witnessed the most violent worker protests and capital counteroffensives in U.S. labor history, punctuated by the police firing on unarmed strikers at the McCormick Harvester Plant in Chicago and the Haymarket Square explosion the next day, the Homestead Strike of 1892, and the Pullman Strike of 1894.

In spite of capital's efforts to isolate foreign workers and minimize their assimilation into the labor movement, and in spite of the American Federation of Labor's reluctance to organize them, the new immigrants from southern and eastern Europe soon learned both the meaning of industrial strife and the techniques of class struggle. It is not hard to understand the increased prominence of immigrants at the vanguard of the labor movement. By 1909, new immigrants constituted the majority of the industrial working class, as 60 percent of the men and 47 percent of the women in the twenty largest mining and manufacturing establishments were recent immigrants (U.S. Congress, Senate 1911, 322). Wage reductions and layoffs hit recent immigrants first and hardest, as they almost invariably occupied the least desirable and most unstable positions in each industry. As a Ruthenian priest said in 1907, "My people do not live in America, they live underneath America" (quoted in Leiserson 1971, 128).

With support from the Industrial Workers of the World (IWW) and a number of small independent unions, by 1906 many spontaneous uprisings led by immigrant workers stunned their employers. Foreign workers on streetcars and in the clothing trades, textiles, packing houses, and steel mills launched some of the most successful strikes of the period. The Lawrence Textile Strike in 1912 is a good example of this resistance. In January 1912, Lawrence mill wages were reduced and machines speeded up, whereupon the largely Italian workforce at one mill went out on strike, with the shout "Goddamn it to hell! Let's strike! Strike!" (quoted in Adamic 1963, 166). Within minutes, one thousand workers crowded the street. The strike spread to other mills, and in less than an hour thousands of immigrant textile workers filled the streets of Lawrence. One alarmed observer warned that "the capacity of this great host of recent immigrants . . . for continuous, effective solidarity is one of the revelations of the present strike" (quoted in Hourwich 1912, 392).

Although the New England social elite had for years engaged in racist nativism against immigrants, the change in the source of immigrants to southern and eastern Europe, along with their increasing militancy, bolstered this race thinking. In 1890, the president of the American Economics Association warned his audience of scholars against the invasion of races of "the very lowest stage of degradation" (Walker 1891, 37). Capitalists increasingly explained labor unrest as the product of imported workers with un-American ideas. The National Association of Wool Manufacturers (1912, 139,142) explained away the IWW as "this baleful organization of European origin" created by the "foreign invasion of the anarchists and socialists, criminals and outcasts from other nations."

The introduction of the eugenics movement into the United States and the Binet-Simon scale for determining I.Q. gave this nativist racism additional momentum. In 1912, the U.S. Public Health Service employed Henry Goddard to administer the Binet I.Q. test to landing immigrants at Ellis Island. From this, Goddard (1913, 105–107) concluded that 83 percent of Jews, 80 percent of Hungarians, 79 percent of Italians, and 87 percent of Russians were "feebleminded." This and other similar experiments "scientifically" validated the blame ascribed to recent immigrants for poverty, unemployment, and labor unrest in an otherwise rational and just society (Rafter 1997).

One solution devised for the problem of "feeble-mindedness" was involuntary sterilization, advocated for all "defectives"—not solely the feebleminded, but criminals, alcoholics, and other "ne'er-do-wells." The punitive procedure was first introduced in the prisons of Indiana, and eventually spread to thirty-three states. Justice Oliver Wendell Holmes Jr., a strong proponent of eugenics, put the Constitutional stamp of approval on forced sterilization in 1927 with what he wrote in a landmark U.S. Supreme Court case involving a young woman named Carrie who had been involuntarily sterilized in Virginia and who purportedly had a "feeble-minded" mother and daughter. "Three generations of imbeciles are enough," Justice Holmes infamously declared (*Buck v. Bell*, 274 U.S. 200). Subsequent scholarship reveals that neither Carrie nor her mother or her daughter were mentally impaired or suffered from any mental illness, but these findings were of course too late for this family and for the many immigrants and others among the estimated sixty thousand subjected to the "therapeutic" punishment of involuntary sterilization (Gould 1985; Rafter 1997; see also Flavin, this volume).

Intensive Americanization programs were established in the 1910s in government–industry partnerships, but eventually the effort was abandoned in the face of increasing concerns of racial inferiority and related immigrant radicalism. John Higham (1977, 262) paraphrased an article in the *Saturday Evening Post* following the Red Scare of 1919, "Why try to make Americans out of those who will always be Americanski?" With industrial mechanization during World War I reducing the need for European immigrants, and the Red Scare heightening anti-immigrant fears, Congress began to debate closing the front door.

It was during this same period that the drive for the prohibition of alcohol reached a fever pitch. When Prohibition took effect in 1920, it represented "an act of ceremonial deference toward old middle-class culture" (Gusfield 1986, 8). Related to this "struggle for status" (7–8), the political fight for Prohibition was precipitated by the association of drinking with the "dangerous classes" of immigrants and other members of the urban proletariat, and with the social disorder these classes were now thought to provoke. But, if Prohibition was triggered in part by fears of lawless and disruptive urban immigrants, it in turn had the effect of criminalizing those immigrants further as they were disproportionately ensnared in its legal net. As Higham (1977, 268) put it, "[T]he ban on alcohol hit the immigrants two ways: it increased their conspicuousness as lawbreakers and brought down upon their heads the wrath of a 100 per cent American morality."

As members of Congress debated immigration restrictions within this context, they declared Jews and others from southern and eastern Europe to be "abnormally twisted," "unassimilable," and "filthy un-American" (*Congressional Record* 1920, 172). The Emergency Quota Law of 1921 (42 Stat. 5) limited the number of foreign-born who could be admitted from each country to 3 percent of the number of people of that nationality in the United States according to the census of 1910. The 1924 Quota Law (43 Stat. 153) reverted to the 1890 census, in an explicit effort to reduce further the numbers admitted from southern and eastern Europe. The laws applied primarily to European immigration, as Chinese and Japanese had already been largely barred, and the quotas exempted Western Hemisphere immigrants.

Back-Door Immigration and the Bracero Program

Throughout the Congressional hearings on the Quota Laws, interest was shown in using Mexican labor as a substitute for the European source. It was assumed that the virtue of Mexican immigration was that, while supplying vital workers to labor-intensive and seasonal enterprises such as agriculture, these workers would return to Mexico—or could be made to depart—during hard times or in the off-season (U.S. Congress, Senate 1921, 87). In recognition of Mexicans' important role in southwest agriculture, and as workers for the Southern Pacific and Santa Fe Railroads, they had already been excluded from the literacy test requirement of 1917 (39 Stat. 874).

Immigration had been hailed in the 1890s: "Men, like cows, are expensive to raise and a gift of either should be gladly received" (*New York Journal of Commerce* 1892, 2). Immigration from Mexico was doubly beneficial since it was thought the Mexicans' sojourn in the United States could be made contingent on the continued demand for their labor. The Bracero Program institutionalized these virtues, and injected an element of control over both the workers' entrance and, at least theoretically, their departure. The Bracero Program was in fact a series of programs from 1942 to 1964, usually involving

bilateral agreements between the United States and Mexico for the importation of Mexican farm workers to work for growers and ranchers in the West.
Most of these agreements specified that braceros were to be contracted at
reception centers in Mexico, paid the "prevailing wage," and provided with
housing and meals during their employment period (Calavita 1992).

As part of a package to encourage growers to use braceros instead of their
increasingly undocumented workforce, the Immigration and Naturalization
Service (INS) launched a number of high-profile raids, the most visible of
which was code-named "Operation Wetback" (Ngai 2004). In early summer of
1954, the Border Patrol set up road blocks, boarded trains, and cordoned off
neighborhoods, detaining Mexican immigrants. Police were instructed to arrest
suspects on vagrancy charges and turn them over to Border Patrol agents. The
operation was declared a success by the INS, which boasted of having deported
close to one million Mexican workers and their families (Ngai 2004, 156–157).
But there were widespread allegations of abuse. Reports that Mexicans and
U.S. citizens of Mexican descent had been beaten, harassed, and deported were
so alarming that the term *Operation Wetback* came to be synonymous with
human rights violations and a kind of official vigilantism in the name of immigration control (Garcia 1980; Morgan 1954).

If Operation Wetback was meant as a "stick" to discourage employers from
relying on undocumented immigrants, lax enforcement of bracero contracts
was a "carrot" to entice them to hire braceros (Calavita 1992). Scholarly
research and government reports consistently revealed that employers violated
the terms of contracts, and that wages were depressed and unemployment
increased among local farm workers in areas where the Bracero Program operated (Anderson 1963; Galarza 1956; Galarza 1964; President's Commission on
Migratory Labor 1951). As crop harvesting was increasingly mechanized and as
the Bracero Program was under attack from organized labor and much of the
public, the controversial system was allowed to die in December 1964.

By then, a relationship of symbiosis between Mexican workers and U.S.
growers had become thoroughly entrenched, stoked by formal and informal
government policies. Almost five million Mexican workers had been brought
to the U.S. as braceros; approximately five million undocumented workers
were apprehended in the same period. Undocumented immigration continued to increase with the demise of the Bracero Program, each year exceeding
the previous year's record. By 1986, twenty years after the last braceros left the
fields, apprehensions of undocumented immigrants reached over 1.5 million
per year. With the immigrant flow increasingly illegalized, Mexican immigrants
in particular were positioned as "outlaws in the promised land" (Cockcroft,
1986) and subject to economic penalties in the form of discounted labor,
social penalties in the form of exclusions from civic membership, and

legal sanctions as "impossible subjects" (Ngai 2004; see also Urbina and Smith, this volume).

INTERSECTIONS OF GENDER AND RACE IN IMMIGRATION LAW

Less obvious than the race issues and class-power dynamics that shaped the immigrant experience and immigration policy, the politics of gender is also a central protagonist in this story (Glenn 2002). The prototypical immigrant worker of the late nineteenth and early twentieth centuries was imagined as male ("Men, like cows . . ."), although of course millions of immigrant women passed through Castle Garden, Ellis Island, and other major ports, and joined the burgeoning industrial workforce. The workforce itself was strictly gendered, with women found predominantly in the garment industry, in domestic service, in laundries, and in a variety of other services and light manufacturing. As the "back door" and seasonal work came to replace the front door of permanent European immigration, the immigrant stream at mid-century was increasingly composed of men. The Bracero Program—which admitted only adult male farm workers—institutionalized this gender dynamic and took to its logical conclusion the preference for a labor force with no strings attached, consigning all reproductive functions to the country of origin (Glenn 2002).

Assumptions about the gendered quality of immigration—and the intersection of these gender ideologies with race and class thinking—were particularly conspicuous in the debates that surrounded Chinese exclusion. Race, class, and gender were so entangled during these debates that they often stood in for one another, or bled into and defined one another. Thus, anti-Chinese racism was expressed in terms of repulsion for "the coolie class" (*Congressional Record* 1892, 3480), and merchants were extolled as a race apart. Chinese immigrant women (generally assumed to be prostitutes) bore the full brunt of the intermingling of notions of race, class, and gender. So encompassing was the stereotype of Chinese immigrant women as prostitutes that Congress presumed it had addressed Chinese women's immigration with the Page Act of 1875 barring prostitutes (18 Stat. 477), and made no mention of women in the exclusion laws.

When the subject of women did come up during the debates, it was in the context of making the case for Chinese racial and moral inferiority. In the House of Representatives, it was proclaimed, "There are 4,000 Chinese women in the State [of California]. There are from 1,200 to 2,000 in the city [of San Francisco], and they are all prostitutes or concubines, or second wives" (*Congressional Record* 1882, 1903); "Out of the four or five thousand Chinese females in California there are not six who pretend to be good women" (1936); "Few [Chinese women] come here except from Chinese brothels, or raised for prostitution in China, which is a business there" (1903); and, "Their women are imported as slaves and are brought here and held here as slaves" (1903). Condemning Chinese men for not bringing their families with them, a failure instanced as an indication of their moral depravity, one senator reported, "His associations are with harlots of his own race" (1545).

It should be noted here that a number of Chinese women *were* brought to the United States as prostitutes, with many sold into virtual slavery, although there is wide disagreement about the proportion of Chinese women thus engaged (Chang 2003, 80–85; Cheng Hirata 1979; Ling 1998, 193). Far less debatable is the question of their discriminatory treatment by law enforcement. At a time when prostitution per se was not generally illegal, there were laws directed at Chinese prostitution, such as the 1866 California law, "An Act for the Suppression of Chinese Houses of Ill Fame," which stated that Chinese prostitution was a "public nuisance" and targeted Chinese brothels for various forms of official harassment (Chan 1991, 99). Another California law, in 1870, made it illegal to land Asian women at any California port unless it could be proven that they were "of correct habits and good character" (quoted in Chan 1991, 98). Although the specific reference to Asian women was deleted in 1874, this California law and the federal Page Act of 1875 were used primarily against Chinese women, many of whom spent days, often months, at the infamous Angel Island detention facility in San Francisco Bay before being admitted or sent back to China. Although systematic records are scarce, it appears that suicides in these rudimentary detention facilities, where women were separated from their husbands and male children and kept isolated for months at a time, were not uncommon (Ling 1998, 29–39).

Since the debates surrounding the Chinese Exclusion Law of 1882 had given no indication of whether the wives of Chinese merchants were to be allowed entry, or whether other Chinese women were to be considered laborers and excluded, it fell to enforcement officials and the courts to make such determinations and ultimately to shape policy. In virtually all cases, it was decided that "the wife must be regarded as taking the status of the husband" (*In re Ah Moy*, 21 Federal Reporter 785; *In re Ah Quan*, 21 Federal Reporter 182). In most cases, this meant that the wives of laborers were barred, while the wives of merchants—assuming they could validate their marital status— were admitted.

The derivative status of wives was the defining feature not just of their ability to immigrate, as in the Chinese case, but also of their citizenship. The Naturalization Act of 1855 (10 Stat. 604) established the concept of dependent citizenship for women when it automatically conferred U.S. citizenship on foreign-born women who married U.S. citizens (unless the woman was racially precluded from naturalizing). Although this law protected these women from deportation and gave them inheritance rights, it deprived them of their native citizenship without their consent and affirmed the dependent status of wives (Bredbenner 1998). The full implications of the gendered ideologies underlying this law became clear in 1907 when the Expatriation Act (34 Stat. 1228) withdrew citizenship from American women who married foreigners. For American suffragists who had capitalized on the increasing xenophobia of the period to argue that if naturalized immigrant men could vote, *they* certainly should be able to, the Expatriation Act—steeped in its own xenophobia and patriotic rhetoric—was a stark warning of the costs of that strategy.

The Expatriation Act powerfully demonstrated the interconnections among and between race, gender, immigration, and social control, as suffragists paid the price for their anti-immigrant strategies in their effort to win the vote. Another illustration came in 1922, when the Cable Act (42 Stat. 1021) revoked the policy of automatically granting immigrant women citizenship upon marrying an American. This revisiting of the wisdom of giving immigrant women automatic citizenship followed on the heels of the Nineteenth Amendment giving women the right to vote. As Candice Lewis Bredbenner (1998, 43) explains, "Derivative citizenship could no longer function exclusively as the agent of marital solidarity and patriarchal power if it also served as married women's pathway to achieving an autonomous political voice." The history of naturalization policies, and the cross-cutting of gender and race issues throughout, highlight not only their myriad intersections, but the shared destinies of those who find themselves on the wrong side of these intersections, and the high price to be paid for ignoring that common fate (see Bosworth, this volume).

CONCLUSION

It is often observed that immigration acts as a mirror that "clarifies that which is latent. . . . In the functioning of the social order, it unmasks that which is masked to reveal what many prefer to ignore" (Sayad 1996, 10). Immigration policy shapes the social order not only by affecting the size and nature of the population, but also by reinforcing prevailing ideologies and shoring up the social relations in which they are embedded. Nineteenth- and early-twentieth-century immigration policymakers and captains of industry were quite explicit in their intent to use immigration law as an instrument of social control and engineering, and the mirror held up to their musings reveals much about the social order they intended to shape.

Andrew Carnegie (1886, 35) compared immigrants to "efficient slave(s)"; the editor of the *Engineering and Mining Journal* (1880, 335) told his readers that immigration was the solution to workers' wage demands; and the first immigration agency established by Congress was designed to stir up immigration from Europe in an effort to stabilize wages during the Civil War. If the use of new immigrants as a method of controlling labor demands was explicit, so too was the racialization that often went hand in hand with their poverty. First the Chinese and later Italians, Jews, Poles, and others from southern and eastern Europe were vilified as "brutes" and eventually restricted: in the case of the Chinese, after they were no longer needed for railroad construction; in the case of Europeans, once they came to be seen as themselves the labor problem. As Mexican immigrant labor substituted for the European source, the racialization of immigration was perpetuated and enhanced by its increasing illegalization.

The gender dynamics of immigration and immigration policy are arguably less transparent than these class-power and race dimensions, having more often gone unnoticed by policymakers and thus unspoken. But gendered and raced assumptions about Chinese women as prostitutes, about Mexican men as farm workers, or relating to the derivative status of wives, have had their own powerful impacts on the shape of immigration and the "functioning of the social order." Part and parcel of this shaping of the social order and its ideological infrastructure were a wide variety of formal and informal punishments exacted by state actors, therapeutic professionals, employers, and vigilantes, including forced sterilizations, anti-immigrant pogroms, protracted isolation in detention facilities, and, above all, discounted labor. As the other chapters in this book demonstrate, these gender, race, and class dynamics permeate not only immigration policy and the punitive practices surrounding it, but a host of other domestic policies, as well as the selective dismantling of borders that comprises contemporary globalization and that takes us "back to the future" as outsourcing employers scour the globe for cheap labor.

WORKS CITED

Adamic, Louis. 1963. *Dynamite: The story of class violence in America.* Gloucester, MA: Peter Smith.

Anderson, Henry. 1963. *Fields of bondage: The Mexican contract labor system in industrialized agriculture.* Mimeograph. Berkeley, CA.

Bimba, Anthony. 1927. *The history of the American working class.* New York: International Publishers.

Bredbenner, Candice Lewis. 1998. *A nationality of her own: Women, marriage, and the law of citizenship.* Berkeley and Los Angeles: University of California Press.

Bridge, James Howard. 1902. *The inside story of the Carnegie steel company: A romance of millions.* New York: Arno Press.

Calavita, Kitty. 1983. The Anti-Alien Contract Labor Law of 1885 and "employer sanctions" in the 1980s. *Research in law, deviance, and social control* 5: 51–82.

———. 1984. *U.S. immigration law and the control of labor, 1820–1924.* London: Academic Press.

———. 1992. *Inside the state: The bracero program, immigration, and the INS.* New York: Routledge.

Carnegie, Andrew. 1886. *Triumphant democracy, or fifty years' march of the Republic.* New York: Charles Scribner's Sons.

Chan, Sucheng. 1991. The exclusion of Chinese women, 1870–1943. In *Entry denied: Exclusion and the Chinese community in America, 1882–1943*, ed. Sucheng Chan. Philadelphia, PA: Temple University Press.

Chang, Iris. 2003. *The Chinese in America: A narrative history*. New York: Penguin Books.

Cheng Hirata, Lucie. 1979. Free, indentured, enslaved: Chinese prostitutes in nineteenth-century America. *Signs* 5: 3–29.

Cockcroft, James D. 1986. *Outlaws in the promised land: Mexican immigrant workers and America's future*. New York: Grove Press.

Congressional Record. 1882. 47th Congress, 1st Session. Washington, DC.

———. 1884. 48th Congress, 1st Session. Washington, DC.

———. 1892. 52nd Congress, 1st Session. Washington, DC.

———. 1920. 66th Congress, 3rd Session. Washington, DC.

Engineering and Mining Journal. 1880. May 15: 335.

Foner, Philip S. 1994. *History of the labor movement in the United States*. New York: International Publishers.

Galarza, Ernesto. 1956. *Strangers in our fields*. Washington, DC: Joint U.S.–Mexico Trade Union Committee.

———. 1964. *Merchants of labor: The Mexican bracero story*. Santa Barbara, CA: McNally and Loftin.

Garcia, Juan Ramon. 1980. *Operation wetback: The mass deportation of Mexican undocumented workers in 1954*. Westport, CT: Greenwood Press.

Genovese, Eugene D. 1974. *Roll, Jordan, roll: The world the slaves made*. New York: Pantheon.

Glenn, Evelyn Nakano. 2002. *Unequal freedom: How race and gender shaped American citizenship and labor*. Cambridge, MA: Harvard University Press.

Goddard, Henry H. 1913. The Binet tests in relation to immigration. *Journal of Psycho-Asthenics* 18: 105–107.

Gould, Stephen Jay. 1985. *The flamingo's smile: Reflections in natural history*. New York: W.W. Norton and Company.

Gusfield, Joseph R. 1986. *Symbolic crusade: Status politics and the American temperance movement*. 2nd edition. Urbana: University of Illinois Press.

Gutman, Herbert. 1976. *Work, culture, and society in industrializing America: Essays in American working-class and social history*. New York: Alfred A. Knopf.

Gyory, Andrew. 1998. *Closing the gate: Race, politics, and the Chinese Exclusion Act*. Chapel Hill: University of North Carolina Press.

Hamilton, Alexander. 1791. Report on manufactures. Comp. in *American State Papers, Finance (Washington, DC: Gales and Seaton, 1832)*.

Higham, John. 1977. *Strangers in the land: Patterns of American nativism, 1860–1925*. New York: Atheneum.

Hill, Herbert. 1996. The problem of race in American labor history. *Reviews in American History* 24: 189–208.

Hourwich, Isaac A. 1912. *Immigration and labor: The economic aspects of European immigration to the United States*. New York: G. P. Putnam and Sons.

Leiserson, William M. 1971. *Adjusting immigrant and industry*. Montclair, NJ: Paterson Smith.

Ling, Huping. 1998. *Surviving on the gold mountain: A history of Chinese American women and their lives*. Albany: State University of New York Press.

Lyman, Stanford. 1977. *The Asian in North America*. Santa Barbara, CA: ABC-CLIO.

———. 2000. The "Chinese question" and American labor historians. *New Politics* 7: 113–148.

Mink, Gwendolyn. 1986. *Old labor and new immigrants in American political development: Union, party, and state, 1875–1920*. Ithaca, NY: Cornell University Press.

Montgomery, David. 1972. The shuttle and the cross: Weavers and artisans in the Kensington Riots of 1844. *Journal of social history* 5: 411–446.

Morgan, Patricia. 1954. *Shame of a nation: A documented story of police-state furor against Mexican-Americans in the U.S.A.* Los Angeles, CA: Los Angeles Committee for the Protection of the Foreign Born.

National Association of Wool Manufacturers. 1912. *Bulletin* 42: 139–142. *Native American.* 1844. July 16.

Nelli, Humbert. 1969. Italians and crime in Chicago: The formative years, 1890–1920. *American Journal of Sociology* 74: 373–391.

New York Journal of Commerce. 1892. December 13: 2.

Ngai, Mae. 2004. *Impossible subjects: Illegal aliens and the making of modern America.* Princeton, NJ: Princeton University Press.

Philadelphia Times. 1882. June 18.

President's Commission on Migratory Labor. 1951. *Migratory labor in American agriculture.* Report of the President's Commission on Migratory Labor. Washington, DC: U.S. Government Printing Office.

Rafter, Nicole Hahn. 1997. *Creating born criminals.* Champaign: University of Illinois Press.

Salyer, Lucy E. 1995. *Laws harsh as tigers: Chinese immigrants and the shaping of modern immigration law.* Chapel Hill: University of North Carolina Press.

Sandmeyer, Elmer Clarence. 1973. *The anti-Chinese movement in California.* Urbana: University of Illinois Press.

Sayad, Abdelmalek. 1996. La doppia pena del migrante: Riflessioni sul "pensiero di stato." *Aut aut* 275: 8–16.

Saxton, Alexander. 1971. *The indispensable enemy: Labor and the anti-Chinese movement in California.* Berkeley and Los Angeles: University of California Press.

U.S. Congress. Senate. 1877. *Report of the joint special committee to investigate Chinese immigration.* Senate Report No. 689. 44th Congress, 2nd Session.

———. 1911. *Report of the Dillingham Commission.* Senate Document No. 747. 61st Congress, 3rd Session.

———. 1921. *Hearings: Emergency immigration legislation.* 66th Congress, 3rd Session.

Walker, Francis A. 1891. The tide of economic thought. *Publications of the American Economic Association* 6: 37.

Wickersham Commission. 1931. *Report of the National Commission on Law Observance and Enforcement: Crime and the foreign-born.* Washington, DC: U.S. Government Printing Office.

Workingman's Advocate. 1869. December 25: 2.

U.S. STATUTES AT LARGE

The Naturalization Act of 1855. 10 Stat. 604 (1855).

Act to Encourage Immigration. 13 Stat. 385 (1864).

The Page Law. 18 Stat. 477 (1875).

The Chinese Exclusion Act. 22 Stat. 58 (1882).

The Immigration Act. 22 Stat. 214 (1882).

Anti-Alien Contract Labor Law. 23 Stat. 332 (1885).

Chinese Exclusion Act. 28 Stat. 1210 (1894).

The Immigration Act of 1903. 32 Stat. 1213 (1903).

The Expatriation Act of 1907. 34 Stat. 1228 (1907).

The Immigration Act of 1917. 39 Stat. 874 (1917).

The Emergency Quota Law of 1921. 42 Stat. 5 (1921).

The Cable Act. 42 Stat. 1021 (1922).

The 1924 Quota Law. 43 Stat. 153 (1924).

COURT CASES

Buck v. Bell, 274 U.S. 200.

In re Ah Moy, 21 Federal Reporter 785.

In re Ah Quan, Federal Reporter 182.

In re Ah Yup, C.C. Cal 1878.

CHAPTER 8

Identity, Citizenship,
and Punishment

Mary Bosworth

Each age and society re-creates its "Others." Far from a static thing then, identity of self or of "other" is a much worked-over historical, social, intellectual, and political process that takes place as a contest involving individuals and institutions in all societies.

—Edward Said, *Orientalism* (1995)

NONCITIZENS ARE ONE OF THE fastest growing populations in United States penal facilities.[1] They are held in state and federal prisons and in local jails. They are also placed in institutions run by the U.S. Bureau of Immigration and Customs Enforcement (ICE), formerly known as the U.S. Immigration and Naturalization Service (INS), and in private facilities contracted to ICE.[2]

A series of acts passed over the last ten years indicates that the capacity of the state to incarcerate immigrants, refugees, and other foreigners has been vastly enhanced. These laws include the Illegal Immigration Reform and Responsibility Act of 1996 (IIRIRA), the Antiterrorism and Effective Death Penalty Act of 1996 (AEDPA), and, most recently, the USA Patriot Act of 2001.[3] Although different in scope and focus, each act has included mandatory detention as a response to issues associated with noncitizens.

Given the overcrowded nature of most prisons in the United States, not to mention their apparent failure to solve the social problems for which they are already utilized, it seems important to investigate why confinement has become the tool to which the government is now turning with such enthusiasm to deal with unwanted immigrants. After all, for some time now criminologists have been criticizing the policy of mass imprisonment so willfully pursued throughout the United States. Depending on their political allegiance, commentators point out the sheer cost of incarcerating so many, the racial disparities that have been incurred, the strains placed on individual facilities, the growing reliance on the private sector to assume some of the burden of running the ever-increasing numbers of facilities, and, of course, the general ineffectiveness of imprisoning so many. Commonly, critics single out the war on drugs as the main cause of the current prison population explosion. Changes in sentencing policies introduced in the 1980s and 1990s also greatly reduced judicial discretion and brought in longer mandatory minimum sentences (Garland 2001; Tonry 2004; Jacobson 2005).

In light of the controversy that mass imprisonment has provoked, it seems perplexing that institutions of confinement should so easily have become a primary tool in the management of foreigners. To a large extent, just as the war on drugs has effectively constructed addiction as a crime rather than a public health problem calling for counseling or treatment, the current tendency toward incarcerating noncitizens only makes sense if it can be argued that these people are either criminal or pose some substantial risk to the safety and well-being of society. Yet, what risks do such people pose? To what extent is the "danger" of the foreigner operating at a symbolic or metaphorical level? What, precisely, is the prison or detention center being employed to do?

By enhancing the capacity of the state to incarcerate foreigners, recent legislation appears to have conflated the distinct categories of immigrant, criminal, asylum seeker, and terrorist. For example, although usually detention is applied only as a punishment for illegal activity, recent legislation has enshrined its use as "preventative" in a number of different circumstances to do with noncitizens (Cole 2002). Thus, incarceration has become the standard response for asylum seekers who arrive with or without proper documentation. As a result, law-abiding people seeking to escape torture and oppression in their countries of origin are increasingly likely to be placed in a county jail or in an ICE detention center while their claims are being processed in the United States. Similarly, people who have committed what are otherwise civil offenses regarding their immigration status—by failing to renew their visa, or by working while in the United States on holiday—can be treated in this manner (detained), as if they had violated criminal law, as by stealing property or committing some kind of violent offense. The uniform nature of the response to such a variety of activities suggests not just a terrific failure of imagination on behalf of the U.S. government and its representatives, but also that the prison may be playing a more complex and subtle role in managing the actual and symbolic border of U.S. society.

Borders define who may come and who may go. In the language of recent social theory, they are both inclusive and exclusive sites that sort the deserving and the undeserving (Young 1999). They set out who belongs, and who is an outsider. In the process, they help us (the majority, or those in power) to know ourselves (Bhaba 1990; Bhaba 1994). We are the ones able to cross. We are the ones who determine who can come in. Conceiving of the prison as a border places issues of identity at the center of an analysis of punishment at the same time as it reveals the significance of issues of race and gender in the policies surrounding immigration.

THE PRISON AS THE BORDER

In the war against terror, and in the everyday monitoring of immigration, nations police their borders. Immigration officers check passports and visas at all entry points, whether airports, road crossings, or harbors. The borders, it is thought, are weak. They are the means by which outsiders may enter. However, they cannot simply be closed, since traffic, of course, goes both ways; the border also provides a means of exit, and, in this process, too, sorts the legitimate from the illegal. One cannot go to France on holiday, or to Mexico, without leaving the boundaries of the United States. Once people leave they may not return unless they are U.S. citizens or possess some proxy for this, such as permanent residence status or a visa. As they are departing, their documentation is checked, as well, to verify whether they have overstayed their visa. Those who have, risk detention prior to removal, as well as a ten-year ban on reentry to the United States. Although totalitarian regimes typically restrict their citizens' ability to leave their nation's borders, these days most countries are more concerned with regulating who wants to enter.

This desire to reduce, monitor, and police who comes into the country is often justified by a number of practical concerns, most in some way based on economic factors. Thus, immigration laws dictate how many foreigners may participate in a host nation's workforce, as well as who is eligible for welfare, housing, and education. Since the terrorist attacks in New York City and Washington, DC, of September 11, 2001, these same laws have been presented as key elements in the ongoing task of reducing risk in the United States from external threats and from dangers posed by specific communities already in residence.

Yet it would be a mistake to view such policies and practices as operating simply in response to straightforwardly utilitarian concerns. Instead, these laws, and the boundaries they maintain, operate on a powerful symbolic level that often creates an environment of fear and mistrust. By stating who may enter and where, they differentiate the center from the margin, and distinguish the "One" (citizen) from the "Other" (foreigner). In doing so, they follow Edward Said's (1995, 332) vision of identity formation, in which he argues that the construction of identity "involves establishing opposites and 'others' whose actuality is always subject to the continuous interpretation and re-interpretation of their differences from 'us.'"

Those who seek to cross barriers from the outside are, by their nature, foreign. They are, in other words, different. They are unknown and perhaps unknowable. Even though at certain moments such diversity is celebrated—just think of the nationality-based parades like Columbus Day and Saint Patrick's Day throughout the year—more commonly such difference is a cause for concern. According to cultural studies theorists Edward Said (1995) and Julia Kristeva (1988), we usually fear and sometimes hate those who are from elsewhere. Why? Because, with their cultural, historical, and personal expectations and experiences, foreigners and immigrants propose alternative frameworks of doing and being. Moreover, by crossing borders, particularly if without proper documentation or permission, they suggest that the barrier may be a figment of our imagination; it may be no more than a line in the sand.[4] It cannot, in other words, and despite the best-laid plans of the state, protect us, nor differentiate "us" from "them." Foreigners, after all, are always already in our midst.

Prisons, too, may be conceived of as borderlands. Certainly they have many barriers. They are, by nature, places of exclusion and seclusion wherein we confine those judged undeserving of liberty, sympathy, treatment, or trust. They are also meant to protect society from those individuals who pose risks within it. People cannot pass through them without control, supervision, and surveillance; rather, they have to do something specific to enter. Either a person must work for the state as a corrections officer, or he or she must commit a crime. Visitors, whether family, friends or lawyers, are allowed only temporary entry and only if they can provide the proper paperwork and identification. Everyone is also required to attain a regulated goal before they may be let out. Their sentence must come to an end; perhaps they may be granted parole or, if judged to pose no threat to society, may be given permission to work in or to visit the community. Perhaps the person leaving is just clocking out, and will return for another shift the next day.

As at other border crossings, those who pass through prisons are monitored as they arrive and leave. Information and documentation are gathered on each inmate, and nobody is allowed to come or go without permission. As scholars have observed since Foucault, a range of daily practice, much of it dependent on new technologies, from closed circuit video monitoring at entries and exits to prison officer logs and daily timetables, are used to monitor and manage offenders, in a bid to reduce the potential risk they pose to the public (Jones 2000). Other similarities can also be identified: like foreigners, criminals are generally feared. They also define categories of deserving (law-abiding) and undeserving (criminal) members of society. In the United States, a high proportion are drawn from communities of color, particularly from Mexico (see Urbina and Smith, and Díaz-Cotto, this volume).

Such likenesses that exist on a symbolic level between these two groups have become increasingly manifest in practice, as more and more immigrants and refugees are enclosed with regular U.S. offenders. In the intermingling of ideas about crime, deviance, and foreigners, the prison (or detention center) is playing a crucial role. The border, it seems, passes through society's very center to the penal institutions hidden within.

MASS IMPRISONMENT

Traditionally, immigration has been controlled by the law, the labor markets, and law enforcement officials. Often, these elements work together. Thus, partly in response to concerns over cheap day laborers flooding California in the early 1990s, the Clinton government introduced changes to immigration law, which in turn were implemented by an expanded number of INS officials and border patrols. Prior to these changes, immigrants caught at the border, particularly at the border with Mexico, were usually merely denied entry and forcibly returned. These days, however, they are routinely taken into custody. As a result, the numbers of foreigners held in detention has been growing rapidly since the mid-1990s.

Information about precise numbers of confined noncitizens is a little confusing, as figures are available in forms that differ over a number of years and come from a range of jurisdictions. Although, in principle, almost all noncitizens subject to detention are ultimately processed by and become the responsibility of ICE, in practical terms they may not always be known to the immigration services unless identified or reported as such by the agency holding them. So-called criminal aliens, for example, who are serving sentences in state or federal prisons, may not always be known to the immigration services and thus subject to the Institutional Removal Program, whereby at the end of their sentence they are detained prior to deportation. Also, separate jurisdictions count noncitizens in differing ways. Thus, New York, unlike other states, includes all who were originally born outside the country, irrespective of their actual citizenship status, in the state's statistics on foreigners behind bars. Taking into account these caveats, we may nevertheless say that on June 30, 2002, the year for which the most recent figures are available, 88,776 noncitizens were in the custody of state or federal correctional authorities. At the time, this figure represented nearly 7 percent of all state and federal inmates. As a comparison, this proportion is roughly equivalent to the total number of women prisoners held in the United States (Harrison and Karberg 2004, 5).

In the federal system alone, noncitizens made up 25 percent of the total prison population, accounting for 33,873 incarcerated individuals. Most (over 80 percent) were held in only five states: California (19,418), New York (8,306), Texas (8,002), Florida (4,526), and Arizona (3,412) (Harrison and Karberg 2003, 5). Within this federal population, the numbers of prisoners doing time for immigration offenses (as distinct from criminal offenses) grew from 1,593 in 1985 to 13,676 in 2000, an escalation of 859 percent. At the same time, the average length of sentence served by this particular subset of noncitizens grew from about four months to twenty-one months (Scalia and Litras 2002).

According to ICE, at the end of 2002 there were 21,065 detainees being held specifically under ICE jurisdiction by the Office of Detention and Removal (DRO). The DRO holds "unauthorized aliens" while their cases are being heard to determine whether they can stay in the United States, as well as those who are awaiting removal. Such people may be housed in one of fifteen detention facilities around the country, eight directly operated by ICE and the rest contracted out to private companies. Others are housed in various state and local jails that the DRO pays for as needed. Still more are held in one of the two joint federal facilities at Oakdale, Louisiana, and Eloy, Arizona. Oakdale, for example, holds primarily men of Cuban nationality, some of whom are in legal limbo as Cuba refuses to take them back and the United States will not release them.

Over half of those individuals reported by the DRO in 2002 were held in federal and state prisons and local jails, while about one-third were held in ICE-operated facilities (5,087) and almost 10 percent were in private facilities under exclusive contract to ICE (1,936). Not quite 50 percent (10,763) of the detainees had been convicted of criminal offenses, and 1,725 had pending criminal cases. Almost equal numbers of detainees had been convicted of violent offenses (31.6 percent) and drug offenses (31.4 percent); these constituted the largest groups under ICE jurisdiction, and were followed by persons convicted of property offenses (14.7 percent) and crimes against public order (12.6 percent).

In interpreting these figures, connections can be made between the treatment of noncitizens and the broader war on drugs that is usually singled out to comment on the practice of mass imprisonment. Overall, combining federal, state, and ICE statistics, drug offenses constitute the major criminal offense for which noncitizens are imprisoned, despite the relatively minor role that many play. Numerous foreign women, for example, have been imprisoned for drug smuggling (see Díaz-Cotto, this volume). In states like New York, these so-called drug mules often receive harsh mandatory minimum sentences for their first offense, even though the laws were originally intended to punish drug kingpins. As with drug offenders, foreigners confined for criminal offenses, immigration law violations, actual or suspected terrorism, or while their asylum case is pending, tend to be overwhelmingly drawn from communities considered nonwhite. The largest group of immigrants in—or indeed outside of—detention centers in the United States is Mexican. The next most common countries of origin, at least in the federal system, are Colombia, the Dominican Republic, and Nigeria (Scalia 1996). These countries are all also, with the possible exception of the Dominican Republic, nations targeted by United States foreign policy related to the war on drugs.

The range of activities for which noncitizens are incarcerated suggests that foreigners may be peculiarly vulnerable to confinement and to other forms of state punishment. In comparison to many other nations, the United States has traditionally boasted a fairly open immigration policy in which all who could work and contribute to the construction of the new society were welcome. Yet limits have always existed. In other words, though the "war on terror" is clearly influencing current practice, the history of immigration to the United States is filled with examples of mass imprisonment, harsh policing, and unfair treatment. Likewise, for some years, critics have argued that INS policies, like criminal justice ones, tend to target certain groups more than others. In short, the current crop of legislation governing the treatment of refugees, asylum seekers, immigration offenders, and criminal aliens are part of a long history of population management. However, the harshness of recent legislation, in addition to the zeal with which it is currently being enforced, deserves special attention. It is to this topic that the next sections are devoted.

THE LAW

For the purpose of the law, noncitizens are broken down into three distinct groups: refugees and asylum seekers, immigrants, and nonimmigrants or tourists. Numerous laws govern the rights and treatment of these types of noncitizens in the United States. The history of these laws reveals that the numbers of whites allowed to cross the border legitimately has been continually reduced, while there has been a fairly uniform level of hostility toward persons of color from any location (see Calavita, this volume). Although certain nationalities identified as nonwhites, such as the Chinese and the Japanese, were welcomed for a time, such individuals usually faced much harsher rules than did contemporaneous immigrants from Europe. Historically, at any rate, immigrants permitted to work still faced numerous barriers when they wanted to become citizens, buy property, or marry white Americans. Nor were they welcome in periods of economic uncertainty, when it was feared they might usurp the jobs of U.S. citizens. Today as then, even those who become citizens are often subject to what Thomas Joo (2002, 13–15) and others have labeled the "permanence" of foreignness.

The Immigration Act of 1924 established the first clearly articulated laws of U.S. citizenship and immigration; the Immigration and Nationality Act of 1952 consolidated previous legislation into one coordinated statute. Revised many times by Congress since it was first introduced—extensively in 1990 and then again by the more recent acts of 1996 and in 2001—the Immigration and Nationality Act continues to set out the parameters of who may or may not enter the country, as well as what such persons are entitled to when they arrive. In the 1924 act, certain quotas of citizens from areas designated Western and from those designated non-Western were allowed to enter the United

States each year. These days, U.S. law instead, like that of other countries, gives preference to skilled immigrants who can fill certain employment needs.

In terms of incarceration, the Illegal Immigration Reform and Immigrant Responsibility Act of 1996 and the 2001 USA Patriot Act have been particularly momentous. Both of these acts established confinement as the fall-back position when dealing with foreigners. Foreigners, it seems, are presumed guilty, or, at the very least, thought to pose significant risk, until they can prove otherwise. The nature of the risk they pose, however, is far from clear. Under some circumstances it would appear to be economic, despite the research suggesting that immigrants stimulate economic growth, by taking on jobs others shun, by striving to succeed, and by providing a new consumer base. At other times, as with the Cuban refugees in the 1980 Mariel boat lift, the concern, as expressed, seems a fear of criminal past and future illegal activity. Once again, research shows otherwise, indicating that migrants break fewer laws than do citizens. Since 2001, of course, foreigners—or at least certain kinds of non-Americans—are increasingly being represented as potential security threats, even though the numbers of known terrorists either caught at the border or found in the United States remains almost nil.

ILLEGAL IMMIGRATION REFORM AND IMMIGRANT RESPONSIBILITY ACT OF 1996 (IIRIRA)

Well before the current war against terror, the United States had begun to use detention as a primary means of dealing with certain foreigners. The Immigration Act of 1990, for example, which modified much of the Immigration and Nationality Act of 1952, enabled the INS to detain aliens pending a decision on whether or not they were to be deported. However, until the passage of the Patriot Act in 2001, it was Title III of the Illegal Immigration Reform and Immigrant Responsibility Act of 1996—implemented in 1997—that most radically expanded the use of detention as a means of managing noncitizens. In addition to changing the way asylum seekers were dealt with at the border, Section 321 of IIRIRA introduced a number of new offenses for which permanent resident aliens and those on work or tourist visas could lose their residency and be deported. Legal resident aliens, or those in possession of a "green card," who are convicted of crimes known as aggravated felonies, must now be detained prior to removal proceedings even if they are ultimately found eligible to stay in the country. Despite the ominous label given to such crimes, "aggravated felonies" includes a range of activity including acts as minor as simple drug possession. Similarly, asylum seekers are routinely detained during the time it takes for immigration officials to ascertain the veracity of their claim. Anyone found to have overstayed a visa, or caught attempting to enter without one, is also held. All immigrants and asylum seekers have to be detained prior to deportation or removal.

IIRIRA was part of a general hardening of views toward immigrants that occurred against the backdrop of a deepening punitive sentiment that also targeted offenders and the poor. At the same time, economic and work-based restrictions on employers and the state began to loosen. Just two years before the 1996 act, for example, President Clinton signed into law the Violent Crime Control Act, which not only put more police on the streets and lengthened sentences, but also introduced a series of new federal capital offenses. That same year, the North American Free Trade Agreement (NAFTA) came into being, and, at the same time, the INS launched Operation Gatekeeper in San Diego and the state of California approved Proposition 187, which denied health, welfare, housing, and education to illegal immigrants and their children. In 1996 Clinton signed into law the Antiterrorism and Effective Death Penalty Act (AEDPA) and the Personal Responsibility and Work Opportunity Reconciliation Act (PRWORA). While AEDPA began the process of criminalizing activities that the USA Patriot Act continues, PRWORA not only denied benefits to illegal immigrants and their children, but also threw thousands of American citizens, predominantly women, off the welfare rolls and back to "work"—or homelessness or starvation. PRWORA makes drug offenders ineligible for public housing, and permits a tenant to be evicted if a family member or guest uses drugs.

Although the links among these acts may not always be clear, together they created an environment where immigration, poverty, and criminality become equally feared, despised, and regulated. One result of this interconnection, according to a recent report by the Lawyers Committee for Human Rights (2002), is that women's ability to gain asylum in United States has been considerably undermined. IIRIRA, it seems, has been particularly disastrous for women. The summarily expedited removal process, established by Section 302 of this act, gives immigration officials at the borders, rather than trained immigration judges, the power to remove persons in as little as twenty-four hours and no later than seven days, if their claim is judged unconvincing. This change of policy has given enormous discretion to people not always best able to evaluate the veracity of an individual's bid for refugee status. Crimes endured by women seeking asylum, such as organized rape, domestic violence, or genital mutilation, are not easily spoken of.[5] Such crimes also occupy an ambiguous status in the legislation and its definition of "reasonable fear of persecution or torture," as witnessed, even before IIRIRA, by the difficulties faced in 1994 by Fauziya Kasinga, who fled her home in Togo to avoid female genital mutilation. Although she was ultimately allowed to remain in the United States, Kasinga had to endure many years of detention. And with IIRIRA, even if women are found to have a "credible fear of persecution," the act dictates that they must "be detained for further consideration of the application for asylum." Finally, evidence suggests that those who somehow make it into the United States on a more general visa often do not meet the new deadline created by IIRIRA that bars asylum claims not filed within one year of a refugee's arrival.

THE USA PATRIOT ACT

The USA Patriot Act that was signed into law six weeks after the September 11, 2001, attacks on the Pentagon and the World Trade Center, and recently re-ratified by Congress, has vastly increased the U.S. government's capacity to monitor and detain noncitizens; it has also expanded the FBI's ability to watch U.S. citizens. At a hefty 342 pages, the Patriot Act is an imposing document that is not always easily comprehensible to a nonlawyer. An examination of just two parts of it reveals a complex relationship between punishment and citizenship. First, Section 215, which enables the FBI to monitor foreigners without establishing probable cause, means that noncitizens are no longer protected by the Constitutional rights afforded others. Indeed, this section of the act has increased the FBI's ability to monitor anyone residing in the United States, but citizens retain a few more civil rights than do foreigners. Second, Section 412 has broadened the capacity of the state to hold noncitizens suspected of terrorism for lengthy periods of time, without legal assistance and without charge.

Section 215

Section 215 of the USA Patriot Act has received considerable attention in the United States, in part because it may be used against citizens as well as foreigners. This is the part of the act that lets the government obtain "any tangible things (including books, records, papers, documents and other items) for an investigation to protect against international terrorism or clandestine intelligence, provided that such investigation of a United States person is not conducted *solely* on the basis of activities protected by the first amendment to the Constitution" (emphasis added). The FBI does not have to establish probable cause or have any reason to look through peoples' possessions. Foreigners, in particular, can be investigated simply for exercising what were previously understood to be their First Amendment rights of freedom of speech and association—by, for example, logging onto specific websites that the government may be monitoring. Prisoners are the only other group of people in the United States whose First and Fourth Amendment rights are similarly curtailed.

According to the ACLU, this section of the Patriot Act "was *specifically intended* to authorize the FBI to obtain information about innocent people—people who are not engaged in criminal activity or espionage" (Beeson and Jaffer 2003, 8). Such a purpose sits uneasily with Constitutional safeguards and common assumptions about the importance of protecting privacy that

Americans traditionally hold so dear. This provision is commonly compared to the Palmer Raids and McCarthyism, and is thought to open the window for gross misconduct by the FBI by giving it, and the attorney general in particular, almost unlimited power. The situation worsens, according to the ACLU, once it is realized that "Of course, not all innocent people are likely to be equally affected. As it has done in the past, the FBI is once again targeting ethnic, political, and religious minority communities disproportionately" (Beeson and Jaffer 2003, 8). If indeed such forms of identity underpin FBI suspicion, a point somewhat difficult to prove given the secret nature of much FBI activity under the Patriot Act, this fact would illustrate the myriad ways in which immigration and ideas of risk are, and always have been, racialized.

Section 412

Like Section 215, Section 412 has meant that noncitizens are no longer protected by the U.S. Constitution. It has also given substantial powers to the attorney general. With no more than the attorney general's unreviewed certification that he or she has reasonable grounds to believe that a noncitizen "engaged in terrorist activities or other activities that threaten national security," the noncitizen may be detained by ICE for up to seven days without charge (Chang 2002, 64). If the person certified by the attorney general as a "terrorist" has committed any immigration violations, however minor and unrelated to terrorism, he or she may be detained for as long as immigration proceedings take, with renewed certification from the attorney general every six months. Once again, the Fourth Amendment standard of probable cause is no longer required. In addition, unlike other legal matters, where the defendant has the right to know the evidence against him or her, a noncitizen certified as a terrorist need never be informed of the information held by ICE and the attorney general.

CONCLUSION

Since September 11, 2001, "security" increasingly has been constructed as both an internal and external problem in most countries (Zedner 2003). Risk, in other words, does not purely emanate from elsewhere; it is around us all the time. Under such circumstances, it becomes imperative to know who the enemy is, at the very moment that this is hardest to determine. In other words, identity has become one measure of security: anyone diverging from the norm (nonwhite, wearing a head scarf or a turban, speaking a foreign language, etc.) is a potential threat. Yet, because the risks are both internal and external, how to identify the "other" has also been complicated. The "other," it seems, indeed "is never outside or beyond us" (Bhabha 1990, 4).

Whereas sentencing practices epitomized by the war on drugs have effectively stigmatized United States communities of color and linked the identities of "black" and "criminal" in popular imagination, more recently attention is being turned to new groups of people in and outside the country as potential threats to safety and order. For example, between September 11 and November 4, 2001, twelve hundred Arab and Arab American men were arrested and detained. Not one of these men, who were held often for many months without contact with their families or lawyers, were charged with anything to do with the terrorist attacks of 9/11. Instead, a number were convicted of fairly minor immigration offenses and some low-level crimes. Almost all were either exonerated and allowed to remain in the United States, or were deported (Human Rights Watch 2003; Chang 2002).

From September 11, 2002, until the system was suspended on December 1, 2003, the U.S. Justice Department set up the National Security Entry-Exit Registration System (NSEERS), requiring citizens from a range of primarily Muslim states or those with Muslim majorities to register with officials in the United States or risk deportation. This large-scale initiative proved highly controversial and difficult to enforce, and was subsequently shelved, but not before the initiation of deportation proceedings against thirteen thousand people, all of whom would have been subject to mandatory detention (U.S. Committee for Refugees 2004).[6]

NSEERS has since been replaced by three new schemes, each of which broadens the surveillance of foreigners even further. First, the United States has recently introduced fingerprinting at all entry points for nearly all foreign nationals seeking entry, as well as passport scans for all foreigners not in possession of a "green card" upon leaving. In addition, nonimmigrant aliens subject to the original NSEERS registration may be required to further registration and interviews at the discretion of the Department of Homeland Security (DHS). Finally, a new monitoring program specifically targeting students, called the Student and Exchange Visitor Information System (SEVIS), has been set up, under which nonimmigrant aliens must notify the DHS of any change of address or change of educational institution, and through which they can be called in for further registration and interview under NSEERS.

The creation of new fears and anxieties, along with the perpetuation of some old ones, seems to be effectively reentrenching the practice of confinement at the precise moment that the legitimacy of the prison has been assailed on a number of other parameters. The expense and apparent failure of the war on drugs in the United States is finally being noted outside academia, as states struggle to maintain the vast infrastructure of penal facilities that sprang up throughout the 1980s and 1990s (Jacobson 2005). Increasingly, some states, like California, are experimenting with diversion of first- and second-time drug offenders. Others, like New York, are rolling back parts of their harshest mandatory minimum sentences.

Although it is unlikely that the numbers of foreigners will ever rise to that of the U.S. citizens incarcerated for drug offenses, their population is significantly large as to fill some beds that might otherwise be left empty. Moreover, due to the similarities in race, gender, and class of the noncitizens with drug offenders, their incarceration continues a well-worn path. Not only are immigration centers disproportionately full of men of color (Welch 1996; see also Welch, this volume), but, as mentioned above, women are being disadvantaged and prevented from entering the United States by the new legislation. Finally, the links that exist between the state and the private sector in the management of noncitizens, as embodied in the private companies that run some ICE facilities, continue to intermingle punishment and capital in alarmingly familiar ways (Greene 2001).

In this activity, the prison and detention center seem to have acquired new vibrancy and enhanced legitimacy. In addition to the "surrogate ghetto" role identified by scholars like Loïc Wacquant (2000), prisons are also now the new borderlands, protecting us not merely from trouble within United States society, but also from trouble from without. Given their track record and the distinct nature of individuals who are being grouped together by the new immigration legislation, the obvious question that remains is what the long-term effects will be of this new form of mass imprisonment.

NOTES

1. I would like to thank Michal Bosworth, Jeanne Flavin, and Anthony Gerbino for their helpful comments on an earlier draft of this chapter. I would also like to thank the Crime Research Centre at the University of Western Australia for inviting me to present a paper based on an earlier version of this chapter.

2. In 2003, the old immigration and naturalization service was absorbed into the new ministry for Homeland Security and divided into two separate agencies. The Bureau of Citizenship and Immigration Service now deals with visas and other everyday issues facing foreigners in the United States, while, according to its mission statement, the Bureau of Immigration and Customs Enforcement (ICE) "is responsible for identifying and shutting down vulnerabilities in the nation's border, economic, transportation and infrastructure security." (U.S. Immigration and Customs Enforcement 2005.)

3. This act's full name is "Uniting and Strengthening America by Providing Tools Required to Intercept and Obstruct Terrorism (USA Patriot Act) Act of 2001."

4. In fact, the United States responded to this possibility in the 1990s, as so many other nations have before and since, by walling off sections of its border—in this case, the border with Mexico. Given the extensive size of this border, a complete barrier was not possible, raising the question: what practical purpose does a partially built wall serve?

5. In partial recognition of this problem, the Violence against Women Act of 1994 and 2000 included provisions for allowing battered women whose immigration status was contingent on their husband, to file independently for the right to remain in the United States.

6. In an attempt to avoid such detention and deportation, many people who had missed the opportunity to apply for refugee status in the United States within one

year of their arrival tried to find asylum in Canada. The U.S. Committee for Refugees reports that four times as many Pakistanis made claims in the first three months of 2003, at the height of NSEERS, as in the second quarter of the year. Few were successful, however, as Canada sent most back to the United States (U.S. Committee for Refugees, 2004).

Works Cited

Beeson, Ann, and Jameel Jaffer. 2003. *Unpatriotic acts: The FBI's power to rifle through your records and personal belongings without telling you.* New York: American Civil Liberties Union.

Bhabha, Homi K., ed. 1990. *Nation and narration.* London: Routledge.

———. 1994. *The location of culture.* London: Routledge.

Chang, Nancy. 2002. *Silencing political dissent: How post–September 11 antiterrorism measures threaten our civil liberties.* New York: Seven Stories Press.

Cole, David. 2002. In aid of removal: Due process limits on immigration detention. *Emory Law Journal* 51: 1003–1039.

Garland, David. 2001. *The Culture of control: Crime and social order in contemporary society.* Oxford: Clarendon Press.

Greene, Judith. 2001. Bailing out private jails. *The American Prospect* 12: 23–27.

Harrison, Paige M., and Jennifer C. Harberg. 2004. *Prison and jail inmates at midyear 2003.* Bureau of Justice Statistics Bulletin. Washington, DC: U.S. Department of Justice. NCJ 203947.

Human Rights Watch. 2003. *World report, 2003.* New York: Human Rights Watch.

Jacobson, Michael. 2005. *Downsizing prisons: How to reduce crime and end mass incarceration.* New York: New York University Press.

Jones, Richard. 2000. Digital rule: Punishment, control, and technology. *Punishment and Society* 2: 5–22.

Joo, Thomas W. 2002. Presumed disloyal: Executive power, judicial deference, and the construction of race before and after September 11. *Columbia Human Rights Law Review* 34: 1–48.

Kristeva, Julia. 1988. *Étrangers à nous-mêmes.* Paris: Fayard.

Lawyers Committee for Human Rights. 2002. *Refugee women at risk: Unfair U.S. laws hurt asylum seekers.* New York: Lawyers Committee for Human Rights.

Said, Edward. 1995. *Orientalism: Western conceptions of the Orient.* London: Penguin.

Scalia, John. 1996. *Noncitizens in the federal criminal justice system, 1984–1994.* Bureau of Justice Statistics Special Report. Washington, DC: U.S. Department of Justice. NCJ 160934.

Scalia, John, and Marika F. X. Litras. 2002. *Immigration offenders in the federal criminal justice system, 2000.* Bureau of Justice Statistics Special Report. Washington, DC: U.S. Department of Justice. NCJ 191745.

Tonry, Michael. 2004. *Thinking about crime: Sense and sensibility in American penal culture.* New York: Oxford University Press.

U.S. Committee for Refugees. 2004. *World refugee survey.* Washington, DC: U.S. Committee for Refugees. Available at: www.refugee.org/wrs04.

U.S. Immigration and Customs Enforcement, 2005. *ICE Mission.* Available at http://www.ice.gov/graphics/about/index.htm. Retrieved June 20, 2005.

Wacquant, Loïc. 2000. The new "peculiar institution": On the prison as surrogate ghetto. *Theoretical Criminology* 4: 377–387.

Welch, Michael. 1996. The immigration crisis: Detention as an emerging mechanism of social control. *Social Justice* 23: 169–185.

Young, Jock. 1999. *The exclusive society*. London: Sage.

Zedner, Lucia. 2003. The concept of security: An agenda for comparative analysis. *Legal Studies* 23: 153–176.

LEGISLATION

Antiterrorism and Effective Death Penalty Act of 1996 (AEDPA). Public Law No. 104–132, 110. Stat. 1214 (1996).

Illegal Immigration Reform and Responsibility Act of 1996 (IIRIRA). Public Law No. 104–208, div. C., 110. Stat. 3009–546 (1996).

Immigration Act of 1924, Ch. 190. 43. Stat. 153.

Immigration and Nationality Act of 1952. Public Law 86–129.

Immigration and Nationality Act of 1990. Public Law 101–649.

Personal Responsibility and Work Opportunity Reconciliation Act, 1996 (PRWORA). Public Law 104–193.

USA Patriot Act of 2001. Public Law 107–56.

Violent Crime Control and Law Enforcement Act of 1994. Public Law 103–322, §10001 et seq. [42 U.S.C. §14171].

CHAPTER 9

Immigration Lockdown before and after 9/11

ETHNIC CONSTRUCTIONS AND THEIR CONSEQUENCES

Michael Welch

ALTHOUGH RECENT OBSERVATIONS on the government's crackdown on illegal immigrants in a post-9/11 society suggest that this is a new phenomenon, punitive immigration policies were in full swing before the events of September 11th, 2001 (see Calavita and Bosworth, this volume). Law enforcement sweeps and mass detentions in the wake of 9/11 represent a continuation and expansion of tactics developed in the mid-1990s during a wave of moral panic over illegal immigrants (Welch 2005a; Welch 2003a; Welch 2003b; Welch 2002a). This chapter connects the periods before and after the terrorist attacks on the World Trade Center and Pentagon by pointing to social constructions aimed at criminalizing certain ethnic minorities. Moreover, attention is turned to the consequences of these ethnic constructions, especially in the realm of harsh immigration policies and practices.

The emergence of detention as a key mechanism of social control adopted by the INS (Immigration and Naturalization Service, currently known as the Bureau of Immigration and Customs Enforcement, or ICE) remains the central focus of this chapter. The first section tracks major policy developments in the 1990s, citing numerous ethical and practical problems associated with detention. In the second portion, these issues are discussed further, in the context of the war on terror. The discussion begins by examining the immigrant problem as a socially constructed phenomenon involving moral panic.

CONSTRUCTING THE IMMIGRANT PROBLEM

As a sociological perspective, social constructionism adds tremendously to our understanding of the process by which the immigration issue surfaced in the

1990s. During that period, the so-called problem of immigration emerged, as nativists and those advocating restrictions on immigration warned that non-white immigrants posed a threat to America's Eurocentric culture, its economy, and its public safety. Demands in the form of tougher immigration laws and policies were then put forth as an attempt to thwart the perceived threat. At the same time, the media offered heightened attention to nativist campaigns, often stoking negative stereotypes of immigrants. Public opinion, influenced by political rhetoric and extensive media coverage, added support to the notion that immigration was a serious social problem requiring more coercive measures of social control, most notably detention and deportation. In the end, moral panic over immigrants had taken hold, leading to a disaster mentality in which ethnic outsiders were depicted as dangers to American society (see Cohen 2003; Goode and Ben-Yehuda 1994; Bosworth, this volume).

Fueling anti-immigrant hostility, nativists and restrictionists have commonly resorted to criminalizing immigrants by casting them as predatory villains, drug dealers, and even terrorists (Beck 1996; Brimelow 1995; Buchanan 1996). Compounding matters, stereotypes have a potent effect on America's psyche, as the general public often is willing uncritically to accept inaccurate versions of tragic events. For example, in 1995, the bombing of a federal building in Oklahoma City contributed to growing fears about terrorists and fueled suspicion of Arab immigrants. In the aftermath of the blast, the *New York Post* editorialized: "Knowing that the car bomb indicates Middle Eastern terrorists at work, it's safe to assume that their goal is to promote free-floating fear and a measure of anarchy, thereby disrupting American life" (Naureckas 1995, 6). Similarly, *New York Times* columnist A. M. Rosenthal wrote: "Whatever we are doing to destroy Mideast terrorism, the chief terrorist threat against Americans has not been working" (Glassner 1999, xiii). Eventually, investigators determined that the bombing was not the handiwork of Arab terrorists but that of Timothy McVeigh, a white U.S. citizen and former military serviceman; nevertheless, Muslims had been stereotyped as terrorists and threats to American national security (Council on American-Islamic Relations 1995).

In another example, Peter Brimelow's *Alien Nation* delivers a blow to immigrants by associating them with a number of criminal events in the early 1990s:

> In January 1993, a Pakistani applicant for political asylum opens fire on employees entering CIA headquarters, killing two and wounding three! In February 1993, a gang of Middle Easterners (most illegally overstaying after entering on non-immigrant visas; one banned as terrorist but admitted on a tourist visa in error) blow up New York's Word Trade Center, killing six and injuring more than 1,000!! In December 1993, a Jamaican immigrant (admitted as a student but stayed) opens fire on commuters on

New York's Long Island Rail Road, killing six and wounding 19!!! WHAT'S GOING ON??!!? (Brimelow 1995, 6).

Other opponents of immigration weighed in on the crime issue. Dan Stein, of the restrictionist group FAIR (Federation for American Immigration Reform), announced: "A series of jarring incidents in 1993 gave the public the unmistakable impression that immigrants are not all honest and hard-working. Some are here to commit crimes" (Stein 1994, 27; also see Tanton and Lutton 1994; Tanton and Lutton 1993). In another remark demonstrating intolerance of illegal aliens, William Colby, former Central Intelligence Agency (CIA) director, boldly stated: "The most obvious threat for the U.S. is the fact that . . . there are going to be 120 million Mexicans by the end of the century . . . [The Border Patrol] will not have enough bullets to stop them" (quoted in Acuna 1996, 115). Whereas Roy Beck, in his book *The Case against Immigration* (1996), relies on rhetoric less inflammatory than that of Colby, Brimelow, and other nativist crusaders, there are numerous passages in which immigrants are blamed for lawlessness, such as "One of the most insidious costs of federal high-immigration policies is the increase in social tensions and crime" (Beck 1996, 215). Adding to his case against immigration, Beck writes: "Numerous organized crime syndicates headquartered in the new immi-grants' home countries have gained solid beachheads of operations" (17). Again, fears of crime and of immigrants are nearly indistinguishable, thus fuel-ing greater public anxiety (see Bosworth, this volume). Amid greater public outcry, legislators push for more of the three P's: penalties, police, and prisons.

THE PUNITIVE RESPONSE

The moral panic over immigrants that developed in the early- to mid-1990s pressured the public and political institutions to reevaluate immigration policies. Whereas previous immigration laws were formulated according to such concerns as labor skills and family reunification, legislation passed in 1996 issued a forceful criminal justice mandate driven by moral panic and an undifferentiated fear of crime, terrorism, foreigners, and people of color. The *Illegal Immigration Reform and Immigrant Responsibility Act of 1996* (IIRIRA) increased criminal penalties for immigration-related offenses and provided measures designed to enhance INS presence and enforcement at the border (see Bosworth, this volume). Under the new statute, the INS instituted an expedited removal process that allows agents to deport immediately persons arriving to the United States without proper documents; moreover, the INS obtained the authority to bar illegal immigrants from reentering the United States for as long as ten years.

Scholars of moral panic remind us that pseudo-disasters commonly pre-cipitate new laws placing additional restrictions on existing freedoms, liberties, and due process (Cohen 2003; Goode and Ben-Yehuda 1994). The 1996 immigration and antiterrorism laws did just this, an especially shocking transition considering that for many years the immigration review process was becoming progressively fairer. In fact, INS hearing judges had been attending to individual circumstances while the courts reviewed the officers' decisions, acting as final arbiters of whether particular cases met Constitutional muster. The new statutes undermine such due process, issuing the INS unparalleled powers and limiting judicial review of deportation and detention decisions made by immigration judges. The laws authorized the INS to use secret evidence to detain and deport suspected terrorists, and expanded the scope of crimes considered aggravated felonies and thus grounds for deportation. Underscoring its coercive and punitive nature, the new law was made retroactive, meaning any person convicted of a crime now reclassified as an aggravated felony could be deported, regardless how old the conviction. The INS also had the newly created power to denaturalize nonnative-born U.S. citizens convicted of certain crimes, and to indefinitely detain deportable aliens even when there was virtually no chance their former countries would allow their return. Because the United States has no official diplomatic ties with Cuba, Iran, Iraq, Laos, and Vietnam, former satellites of the Soviet Union, or Gaza, there are no means for repatriation of their citizens. As a result, detainees from these countries, along with those persons who are not citizens of any country, having given up or been stripped of their birth citizenship when they immigrated to this country, remain in detention indefinitely (ACLU 2000).

PROBLEMS BEHIND BARS

The political and punitive response to moral panic over immigrants, embodied in the 1996 statutes, produced a greater reliance on detention. That policy shift, however, also generated an array of institutional problems that continue to worry human rights organizations. Traditionally, penologists have described prisons as total institutions, because they force inmates to lose contact with the outside world, especially their families, who would otherwise serve as a vital source of support (Goffman 1961). Nowadays, though, outside supermaximum secure facilities, contemporary correctional facilities have departed from their past, becoming less-than-total institutions allowing inmates to have much more contact with the free world (Farrington 1992). The exception to that trend is immigration detention, in which detainees remain exceedingly isolated from their families, their lawyers, and the courts (Human Rights Watch 1998).

Whereas confining immigration detainees in local jails located hundreds of miles from their families and legal counsel adds to their misery, being frequently transferred deepens their hardship. In an attempt to accommodate the logistics of court appearances, immigration case status, and availability (and cost) of bed space, the government often shuttles detainees from facility to facility and from state to state. Decisions to transfer detainees, however, rarely consider the locations of families and lawyers; in many instances, neither families nor attorneys are notified when detainees are transferred. Many such transfers contradict Principle 20 of the U.N. Body of Principles, which states: "if a detained or imprisoned person so requests, he shall if possible, be kept in a place of detention or imprisonment reasonably near his usual place of residence." Principle 20 was established for an obvious reason: so that detainees might receive crucial support from families and legal counsel. Moreover, many families have difficulty financing long-distance travel and accommodations.

Due to the enormous impact that the 1996 legislation has had on immigration detention policies, the INS has grown faster than its ability to keep track of its booming detainee population. Consequently, it is not uncommon for the government to lose its detainees. In one incident, an asylum seeker was denied his appeal in federal court when he did not appear. Later, the INS realized that he was still in its custody but it had failed to locate him in time for his hearing. In a similar case, a lawyer for a group of detainees suing over dangerous jail conditions wrote to the INS, desperately trying to find a member of the group who had been transferred from a Pennsylvania jail. Justice Department lawyers reported that the detainee had been deported. Government officials eventually notified immigration lawyers that he had not been deported but moved to another jail within the vast detention network (Tulsky 2000a; Welch 2002; Welch 2000).

Compounding their problems, many detainees drift through the convoluted hearing process without the aid of an attorney. Even though they have the right to a lawyer (although not at government expense), many go unrepresented because they cannot afford to pay legal fees; many are simply not lucky enough to draw the interest of a pro bono organization that will prepare their case without charge. While behind bars, detainees are subjected to harsh conditions of confinement. In many cases, this means deplorable living conditions, language barriers, and inadequate medical and mental health care. These problems are compounded by a larger indifference to the basic dignity of detainees. At the Liberty County (Texas) Jail, a female detainee complained, "The jail took away my shoes because they were a different color. I walk around barefoot. The jail does not give us underwear or a bra—even when we have our period. I just have to sit around when I am using a Maxi pad" (Human Rights Watch 1998, 60).

PHYSICAL AND SEXUAL ABUSE

Criticism over the warehousing of INS detainees sharply intensifies as undocumented immigrants and asylum seekers fall victim to physical or sexual abuse, a problem more likely to occur in local jails (Casimir 2001;

Dow 2001; Sullivan 2000). Indeed, fear of victimization is pervasive among INS detainees: "Here, our lives are in constant danger where there is no classification of inmates. I'm mixed with murderers, sexual molesters, armed robbers, and the mentally disturbed," said one asylum seeker held in the Ayovelles (Louisiana) Parish Prison (Human Rights Watch 1998, 51). For the truly unfortunate detainees, their fears are realized. Immigration detainees at the Pike County (Pennsylvania) Jail have persistently complained of excessive disciplinary sanctions and physical abuse by guards. Ramòn Medina reported being placed in "the hole" (solitary confinement) after telling correctional officers that he was going to file a complaint against them. According to Medina, he was brought to the solitary confinement cell with his hands and feet handcuffed and was hit and kicked in the head and arms by four correctional officers. Medina said that one of the officers, Brian Bain, took off his uniform and yelled at Medina, "[W]e can do this as men," before proceeding to beat him with the three other officers present. "I was hit in the eye and head and am in a lot of pain. I can't sleep at night. I also have a bone sticking out of my left hand" (Human Rights Watch 1998, 83). While in "the hole," Medina was kept naked without a mattress, using toilet paper to keep warm. Medina issued a complaint against Officer Bain, who was subsequently dismissed from the jail. A Pike County Jail official explained that Officer Bain was dismissed due to "burnout"; previously, jail administration officials had twice ordered him to undergo counseling.

Similar problems persist in detention centers operated by the government. Among its most troubled facilities is the Krome Detention Center in Miami, which gained national publicity beginning in the early 1990s when three educational specialists were dismissed after reporting incidents of physical and sexual abuse (LeMoyne 1990). During that controversy, INS officials at Krome denied allegations of violence and human rights abuses. Constance K. Weiss, an INS administrator at Krome, begged the question: "Why would we want to run a place where we beat the hell out of people?" To that question, refugee advocates replied in a two-part answer: "To discourage other potential refugees and because it is easy to get away with. Detained immigrants are a powerless group . . . without recourse to normal political or legal channels" (Rohter 1992, E-18).

Human rights advocates were astonished to find that, despite national headlines, an FBI investigation, and several lawsuits against staff members, ten years later abuse against INS detainees continues (Human Rights Watch 1998; Dow 1998). Having learned that some of the INS officers implicated in abuse incidents in 2000 also were identified in her report ten years earlier, Cheryl Little, executive director of the Florida Immigrant Advocacy Center, said, "We feel so helpless. How can this be happening in the United States of America?" (Sullivan 2000, EV10).

In 2000, ninety female detainees held at Krome were transferred to a county-operated jail (a move intended to protect them), as federal agents continued their investigation of sexual abuse at the facility (Chardy 2000a; see also Miller, this volume). Authorities had already charged Lemar Smith, a corrections officer, with sexually assaulting a male-to-female transsexual detainee. The victim, an asylum seeker from Mexico, said she was raped in an isolation cell a second time after she reported the initial assault to three INS supervisors. At least a dozen detention officers were removed from duty at Krome or reassigned to jobs amid a widening sex and bribery scandal (Sullivan 2000). Indeed, the problems at Krome highlighted the fact that the INS was struggling to protect its detainees not just at local jails, but at the facilities operated by it directly or through contracts with private corporations. Unfortunately, research and first-hand accounts suggest that such problems continue (Dow 2004).

Human rights advocates applauded the move to protect the women, but also expressed concern about moving the detainees to a county jail. Attorneys for the detainees recommended that the women be released into the community or supervised at shelters. However, Robert A. Wallis, the INS district director, insisted that the agency would transfer the women "to a full service, state of the art facility that would ensure those detainees the most safe, secure and humane detention conditions possible" (Tulsky 2000b, EV2). Cheryl Little expressed concern over the transfer: "No question about it: it's a jail. It would be highly inappropriate to move the women to local county jails. None of the women at Krome are serving criminal sentences" (Chardy 2000a, EV2). Others commented on the controversy. Wendy Young of the Women's Commission for Refugee Women and Children, which issued a blistering report on the conditions of women at the INS detention center, added: "County prisons and hotels are not acceptable alternatives to Krome. Conditions are harsh and very punitive. INS detainees are second-class citizens at county jails because they don't get their constitutional rights like the other inmates" (Chardy 2000a, EV3; Women's Commission for Refugee Women and Children 2000; Women's Commission for Refugee Women and Children 1998). Acknowledging the ironies of immigration control inherent in immigration detention policy, Young remarked, "Where else in the United States do you jail the people who were sexually abused rather than the people who committed the abuse?" (Tulsky 2000b, EV1). Cheryl Little agreed, stating: "Clearly, we didn't want females at Krome exposed to abusive officers. But in trying to solve one problem, they created another. They are, in some ways, punishing the victims" (Tulsky 2000b, EV2).

Tragically, the INS plan to protect the detainees by transferring them to a county jail failed. Two days after being admitted to a Miami-Dade County jail, a number of the women allegedly were "flashed" by a male inmate. In a separate incident that same day, another female inmate was allegedly sexually assaulted by a male prisoner, triggering an internal investigation at the facility. Critics of INS detention practices were infuriated, noting that the women were supposed to be segregated from male inmates and supervised only by female officers. "The irony is not lost on these women. The women were supposedly transferred for their own protection, and they're telling me they're every bit as vulnerable as they were at Krome. The women are being unduly punished and victimized," said Cheryl Little (Ross 2001, EV1; Chardy 2000b).

Since the passage of the reformed immigration laws in 1996, the government stepped up its reliance on detention, but due to limited capacity at its own processing centers, the agency has had to send its detainees to county jails, federal prisons, and private lockups where neglect and abuse of immigration detainees is commonplace. Recognizing the need to reform the INS, Commissioner Doris Meissner, as one of her final acts before resigning in 2000, ordered agency officials to exercise more discretion in the use of detention (and removal), and, equally important, she introduced new standards for confinement. Meissner seemed genuinely interested in softening the impact of the 1996 immigration laws. Under new detention standards then being phased in at local jails, the rights of INS detainees (e.g., access to counsel and the courts, as well as an end to the practice of strip searches before and after visits from attorneys) were emphasized, along with improved institutional services (e.g., food, health care, access to telephones) (INS 2000). A year later, not only were reform efforts stalled but in many cases detention became harsher. The events surrounding September 11th figure prominently in the expansion of a coercive detention policy as it was bolstered further by the *USA Patriot Act* of 2001.

WAR ON TERROR

In response to the attacks of September 11th, the FBI and the INS embarked on a sweeping investigation that involved apprehending thousands of persons suspected of having information about terrorist activity. Although the dragnet was frequently haphazard and random, Middle Eastern males (and those who appeared Middle Eastern) became profiled in the course of the investigation. In its report, *Presumption of Guilt: Human Rights Abuses of Post–September 11th Detainees* (2002), Human Rights Watch discovered a growing use of profiling on the basis of nationality, religion, and gender. Being a male Muslim noncitizen from certain countries became a sufficient basis for suspicion. The cases suggest that where Muslim men from certain countries were involved, law enforcement agents presumed some sort of a connection with, or knowledge of, terrorism until investigations could subsequently prove otherwise. The questioning led to the arrest and detention of as many as 1,200 noncitizens, although the precise number is unknown due to the Justice Department's unwillingness to divulge such information. Of those arrested, 752 were charged, not with terror-related crimes but with immigration violations (e.g., overstaying a visa) (Welch 2006).

Ethnic Profiling

Despite objections from civil liberties and human rights organizations, the Department of Justice expanded its use of profiling in the war on terror by introducing a special registration program in December 2002. The program, intended to produce vital information about terrorist activity, required registration by certain nonimmigrant male visitors over the age of sixteen who entered the United States before September 30, 2002. Specifically, special registration applied to all such males from countries that, according to the U.S. government, have links to terrorism, including twelve North African and Middle Eastern countries plus North Korea, and affected more than eighty-two thousand students, tourists, businessmen, and their relatives. Those who attended special registration were required to complete a personal information form, then fingerprinted, photographed, and interviewed by the FBI. In the first few months of special registration, the Justice Department had failed to discover any links to terrorism, raising questions of its effectiveness. Initially, about one thousand people were detained but only fifteen were charged with any criminal violation and none was charged with a terrorism-related crime. Most detained were in violation of immigration laws, most commonly of overstaying a visa in hope of finding a job and eventually adjusting his status to legal resident (Gourevitch 2003, EV2; Welch 2005a).

One of the most controversial incidents occurred in Los Angeles, where more than four hundred foreign nationals who appeared for registration were handcuffed and detained. Soheila Jonoubi, a Los Angeles-based attorney representing several of the men, said that the detainees spent the next several days (and in some cases weeks) in custody. Many were strip-searched, verbally accosted, deprived of food and water, bedding, and adequate clothing, and denied information as to why they were being detained. The Justice Department reported that the men were detained because their visas had expired; after completing background checks, all but twenty were released. Still, many of those detained held legal immigration status and were waiting to receive work permits that had been delayed by the INS due to a backlog in processing a high volume of applications (Talvi 2003a; Talvi 2003b).

Whereas the registration of more than eighty-two thousand failed to uncover any major links to terrorism, the Justice Department has moved forward with plans to deport as many as thirteen thousand Arab and Muslim men whose legal immigration status had expired. Many had hoped for leniency since they had cooperated fully with the program. Detentions coupled with deportations have sent shock waves through immigrant communities across the nation, producing unprecedented levels of fear. Many Middle Eastern men and their families (many of whom are U.S. citizens) have fled the country, particularly to Canada where they intend to apply for political asylum (Cardwell 2003).

Even government agencies have weighed into the debate over the utility of the special registration program. The General Accounting Office (2003) issued a report that left many questions unanswered as to the value of the project. This study included interviews with officers, many of whom expressed doubts over the usefulness of registration in the campaign against terrorism. Still, the Justice Department defended the special registration program. "To date, the program has not been a complete waste of effort," replied Jorge Martinez, who points out that it has led to the arrest of "a wife beater, narcotics dealer, and very serious violent offenders" (Gourevitch 2003, EV6). To which, critic Alex Gourevitch countered: "But that isn't exactly the same as catching terrorists. And if what we really want is to catch wife beaters, narcotics dealers, and violent offenders, the Justice Department should simply require everyone in America to show up and register" (2003, EV6).

In a major development in June 2003, President Bush announced guidelines barring federal agents from relying on race or ethnicity in their investigations. One exception to that policy is terrorism, however, allowing agents to use race and ethnicity in investigations aimed at identifying terrorist threats. Officials in the immigration service would continue to require visitors from Middle Eastern nations to undergo registration and special scrutiny. Civil rights groups swiftly denounced the policy, since it perpetuates stereotyping and provides authorities with legal justification to single out Arabs, Muslims, and other who may fall under suspicion. The initiative also falls short of what Bush claimed to do about racial profiling. In a February 2001 national address, Bush declared that racial profiling was "wrong, and we will end it in America" (Lichtblau 2003a, A1). Ibrahim Hooper of the Council on American-Islamic Relations also complained about the policy, especially in light of a recent investigation by the inspector general at the Department of Justice documenting evidence of abusive tactics in the war on terror (Lichtblau 2003a; Lichtblau 2000b). Indeed, since Bush's 2001 pronouncement, a series of national polls and research have indicated an ongoing desire among many Americans to curtail some liberties of Muslim Americans (Nisbert and Shanahan 2004).

Evidence of Abuse

In a timely report, Glenn A. Fine, the inspector general at the Department of Justice, confirmed suspicions that the government's approach to the war on terror was plagued with serious problems. The report concluded that the government's round up of hundreds of illegal immigrants in the aftermath of 9/11 was a mistake, since it forced many people with no connection to terrorism to languish behind bars in unduly harsh conditions. The inspector general found that even some of the lawyers in the Justice Department had expressed concerns about the legality of its tactics, only to be overridden by senior administrators. Suggesting that the Justice Department had cast too wide a net in the fight against terrorism, the report was critical of FBI officials, particularly in New York City, who made little attempt to distinguish between immigrants who had possible ties to terrorism and those swept up by chance in the investigation (U.S. Department of Justice 2003a; U.S Department of Justice 2003b; see Lichtblau 2003a).

The report shows that a total of 762 illegal immigrants were detained in the weeks and months after the attacks on the Pentagon and the World Trade Center. Most of the 762 immigrants have now been deported, and none have been charged as terrorists. The report validated complaints that the 84 detainees housed at the Metropolitan Detention Center in Brooklyn faced a pattern of physical and verbal abuse from some corrections officers and were subjected to unduly harsh detention policies, including a highly restrictive, twenty-three-hour lockdown. Detainees also were handcuffed and placed in leg irons and heavy chains any time they moved outside their cells. Compounding their isolation, detainees were limited to a single phone call per week and, due to a communication blackout, families of some inmates in the Brooklyn facility were told their relatives were not housed there. The report faulted the Justice Department for not processing suspects more rapidly, a procedure that would have determined who should remain in detention while releasing others (see Lichtblau 2003a; Liptak 2003).

Several other groups released reports that, like the inspector general's investigation, have documented serious violations of civil liberties and human rights (American Civil Liberties Union 2001; Amnesty International 2003; Human Rights Watch 2005; 2003; 2002; Lawyers Committee for Human Rights 2003). In addition to problems posed by profiling, as embodied in the government's special registration program, these organizations argued, the government had engaged in arbitrary detention, abuse of detainees, and a host of other procedural infractions. Moreover, civil liberties attorneys remain critical of the government for misusing immigration law to circumvent its obligations under the criminal justice system. According to them, the Department of Justice has established new immigration policies and procedures that undermine previously existing safeguards against arbitrary detention by the government. These problems are exacerbated by the official secrecy whereby the Department of Justice refuses to disclose information concerning the persons being detained.

CONCLUSION

In the 1920s, W. I. Thomas (1923) pointed out that what people believe to be real, will be real in its consequences. Since then sociologists have concentrated on the importance of popular perceptions and their effects on society

(Best 1999; Glassner 1999). Moral panic is indicative of turbulent societal reaction to social problems, particularly those producing a disaster mentality in which there is a widespread belief that society is endangered. As a result, there is a sense of urgency to do something immediately or else society will suffer graver consequences later—a sense compelling social policy to undergo significant transformation in a rash attempt to diffuse the putative threat. These social constructions provoke intense public hostility and condemnation aimed at a particular group; correspondingly, they strengthen the social control apparatus with more criminal justice legislation that produces more penalties, police, and prisons (see Bosworth and Miller, this volume).

Altogether, IIRIRA (1996), the Antiterrorism and Effective Death Penalty Act (1996), and the USA Patriot Act (2001) continue to produce a host of violations against civil liberties and human rights. Moreover, the enforcement of these statutes is patterned along predictable lines of race and ethnicity that criminalize immigrants of color. Similarly, antiterrorist tactics are driven by stereotypes depicting Middle Eastern people as threats to national security. As Anthony D. Romero of the ACLU observes, "The war on terror has quickly turned into a war on immigrants" (Liptak 2003, A18).

In closing, civil liberties organizations oppose the government's claim that, to fight effectively the war on terror, citizens must surrender some of their freedoms. That reasoning marks a false paradigm insofar as national security is not predicated on diminishing civil liberties. Mass detention produced by the special registration program is dysfunctional and ineffective. Former executive director of the ACLU, Ira Glasser, reminds us: "No one can be made safe by arresting the wrong people. In focusing on [the wrong targets], the government certainly violated their civil rights but, more important to most Americans, abandoned public safety as well" (Glasser 2003, WK12). As has often been noted, public and political leaders need to be cautious not to overreact to the tragic events of September 11th (Cole 2003; Cole and Dempsey 2002). Drawing on lessons from social constructionism and moral panic, it remains important to contain fear of terrorism and anxiety over national security so as to not undermine fair and just treatment of immigrants, refugees, and asylum seekers (Welch 2004; Welch and Schuster 2005a, Welch and Schuster 2005b).

WORKS CITED

Note: In this listing, EV refers to electronic version of a publication.

Acuna, Rodolfo. 1996. *Anything but Mexican: Chicanos in contemporary Los Angeles*. New York: Verso.

American Civil Liberties Union (ACLU). 1997. *The rights of immigrants*. Located at: www.aclu.org.

———. 2000. *ACLU joins Fix '96 campaign for justice for immigrants*. Located at: www.aclu.org.

————. 2001. *Know your rights: What to do if you're stopped by the police, the FBI, the INS, or the Customs Service.* Located at: www.aclu.org.

Amnesty International. 2003. *Annual report.* New York: Amnesty International.

Beck, Roy. 1996. *The case against immigration: The moral, economic, social, and environmental reasons for reducing immigration back to traditional levels.* New York: Norton.

Best, Joel. 1999. *Random violence: How we talk about new crimes and new victims.* Berkeley and Los Angeles: University of California Press.

Brimelow, Peter. 1995. *Alien nation: Common sense about America's immigration disaster.* New York: Random House.

Buchanan, Patrick J. 1996. Speech delivered at the Heritage Foundation, Washington, DC, January 29. Federal Document Clearing House.

Cardwell, Diane. 2003. Muslims face deportation, but say U.S. is their home. *New York Times,* June 13, A22.

Casimir, Leslie. 2001. Asylum seekers are treated like criminals in the U.S. *New York Daily News,* February 16, EV1–4.

Chardy, Alfonso. 2000a. Krome women to be moved. *Miami Herald,* December 12, EV1–3.

————. 2000b. Jailed INS detainees cut off, advocates say. *Miami Herald,* December 26, EV1–3.

Cohen, Stanley. 2003. *Folk devils and moral panics: The creation of the mods and rockers.* 3rd edition. London: Routledge.

Cole, David. 2003. *Enemy aliens: Double standards and Constitutional freedoms in the war on terrorism.* New York: The New Press.

Cole, David, and James X. Dempsey. 2002. *Terrorism and the Constitution: Sacrificing civil liberties in the name of national security.* New York: The New Press.

Council on American-Islamic Relations. 1995. *A special report on anti-Muslim stereotyping, harassment, and hate crimes: Following the bombing of Oklahoma City's Murrah Federal Building.* Washington, DC: CAIR.

Dow, Mark. 1998. Our daily ordeal is going unnoticed: Cries for help from Krome. *Haiti Progress,* August 12–18, EV1–10.

————. 2001. We know what INS is hiding. *Miami Herald,* November 11, EV1–3.

————. 2004. *American gulag: Inside U.S. immigration prisons.* Berkeley and Los Angeles: University of California Press.

Farrington, Keith. 1992. The modern prison as total institution? Public perception versus objective reality. *Crime and Delinquency* 38, 1: 6–26.

General Accounting Office. 2003. *Better management oversight and internal controls needed to ensure accuracy of terrorism-related statistics.* Washington, DC: General Accounting Office.

Glasser, Ira. 2003. Arrests after 9/11: Are we safer? *New York Times,* June 8, WK12.

Glassner, Barry. 1999. *Culture of fear: Why Americans are afraid of the wrong things.* New York: Basic Books.

Goffman, Erving. 1961. *Asylums: Essays on the social situation of mental patients and other inmates.* Garden City, NY: Anchor.

Goode, Erich, and Nachman Ben-Yehuda. 1994. *Moral panics: The social construction of deviance.* Cambridge, MA: Blackwell.

Gourevitch, Alex. 2003. Detention disorder: Ashcroft's clumsy round-up of foreigners lurches forward. *The American Prospect,* January, EV1–7.

Human Rights Watch. 1998. *Locked away: Immigration detainees in jails in the U.S.* New York: Human Rights Watch.

————. 2002. *Presumption of guilt: Human rights abuses of post–September 11th detainees.* New York: Human Rights Watch.

————. 2003. *World report 2003: Events of 2002.* New York: Human Rights Watch.

————. 2005. *Guantánamo: Three years of lawlessness.* January 11. http://hrw.org/english/docs/2005/01/11/usdom9990_txt.htm. Last retrieved: June 6, 2005.

Immigration and Naturalization Service (INS). 2000. INS to adopt new detention standards to be implemented at all facilities housing INS detainees. Press release, November 13.

Lawyers Committee for Human Rights. 2003. *Imbalance of powers: How changes to U.S. law and policy since 9/11 erode human rights and civil liberties.* New York: Lawyers Committee for Human Rights.

LeMoyne, James. 1990. Florida center holding aliens is under inquiry: Additional complaints made of abuse. *New York Times,* May 16, A16.

Lichtblau, Eric. 2003a.U.S. report faults the roundup of illegal immigrants after 9/11: Many with no ties to terror languished in jail. *New York Times,* June 3, A1, A18.

————. 2003b. Terror cases rise, but most are small-scale, study says. *New York Times,* February 14, A16.

Liptak, Adam. 2003. For jailed immigrants a presumption of guilt. *New York Times,* June 3, A18.

Naureckas, Jim. 1995. The Jihad that wasn't. *Extra,* July, 6–10, 20.

Nisbert, Erik, and James Shanahan. 2004. MSRG special report: Restrictions on civil liberties, views of Islam, and Muslim Americans. Media and Society Research Group, Cornell University, Ithaca, NY. Available at www.comm.cornell.edu/msrg/report1.a.p11.

Rohter, Larry. 1992. "Processing" for Haitians is time in a rural prison. *New York Times,* June 21, E18.

Ross, K. 2001. Sexual abuse fears reach beyond Krome. *Miami Herald,* January 7, EV1–2.

Stein, D. 1994. Population, migration, and America: Is immigration a threat to national security? A speech to the National War College Class of 1995, August 24.

Sullivan, Julie. 2000. Prison conditions severe even for jails. *The Oregonian,* December 9, EV1–10.

Sullivan, Julie, and Brent Walth. 2000. Ex-lawmaker watches reforms exceed intent. *The Oregonian,* December 9, EV 1–3.

Talvi, Silja. 2003a. Round up: INS "special registration" ends in mass arrests. *In These Times,* February 17, 3.

————. 2003b. It takes a nation of detention facilities to hold us back: Moral panic and the disaster mentality of immigration policy. Located at: www.lipmagazine.org. January 15, EV1–8.

Tanton, John, and Wayne Lutton. 1993. Immigration and criminality in the U.S.A. *Journal of Social, Political, and Economic Studies,* Summer: 210–226.

————. 1994. *The immigration invasion.* Petoskey, MI: Social Contract Press.

Thomas, W. I. 1923. *The unadjusted girl.* Boston, MA: Little, Brown.

Tulsky, Frederic N. 2000a. Asylum seekers face tougher U.S. laws, attitudes. *San Jose Mercury News,* December 10, EV1–9.

————. 2000b. Detained immigrants who allege sex abuse are transferred to jail. *San Jose Mercury News,* December 13, EV1–2.

U.S. Department of Justice. Office of the Inspector General. 2003a. *Supplemental report on September 11 detainees' allegations of abuse at the Metropolitan Detention Center in Brooklyn, New York.* December. Washington, DC: U.S. Government Printing Office.

————. 2003b. *The September 11 detainees: A review of the treatment of aliens held on immigration charges in connection with the investigation of the September 11 attacks.* June. Washington, DC: U.S. Government Printing Office.

Welch, Michael. 1996. The immigration crisis: Detention as an emerging mechanism of social control. *Social Justice* 23: 169–184.

————. 2000. The role of the Immigration and Naturalization Service in the prison industrial complex. *Social Justice* 27: 73–88.

————. 2002a. *Detained: Immigration laws and the expanding INS jail complex.* Philadelphia: Temple University Press.

————. 2002b. Detention in INS jails: Bureaucracy, brutality, and a booming business. In *Turnstile justice: Issues in American corrections,* 2nd edition, ed. Rosemary L. Gido and Ted Alleman. Englewood Cliffs, NJ: Prentice Hall.

————. 2003a. Ironies of social control and the criminalization of immigrants. *Crime, Law, and Social Change* 39: 319–337.

————. 2003b. The trampling of human rights in the war on terror: Implications to the sociology of denial. *Critical Criminology* 12, 2: 1–20.

————. 2004. Quiet constructions in the war on terror: Subjecting asylum seekers to unnecessary detention. *Social Justice: A Journal of Crime, Conflict, and World Order* 31, 1–2: 113–129.

————. 2005a. Profiling and detention in the war on terror: Human rights predicaments for the criminal justice apparatus. In *Visions for change: Crime and justice in the twenty-first century,* 3rd edition, ed. Roslyn Muraskin and Albert R. Roberts. Englewood Cliffs, NJ: Prentice Hall.

————. 2005b. *Ironies of imprisonment.* Thousand Oaks, CA: Sage Publications.

————. 2006. *Scapegoats of September 11th: Hate crimes and state crimes in the war on terror.* New Brunswick, NJ: Rutgers University Press.

Welch, Michael, and Liza Schuster. 2005a. Detention of asylum seekers in the UK and US: Deciphering noisy and quiet constructions. *Punishment and Society: An International Journal of Penology* 7, 4: 397–417.

————. 2005b. Detention of asylum seekers in the US, UK, France, Germany, and Italy: A critical view of the globalizing culture of control. *Criminal Justice: The International Journal of Policy and Practice* 5, 4: 331–355.

Women's Commission for Refugee Women and Children. 2000. *Behind locked doors— Abuse of refugee women at the Krome Detention Center.* New York: Women's Commission for Refugee Women and Children.

————. 1998. *Forgotten prisoners: A follow-up report on refugee women incarcerated in York County, Pennsylvania.* New York: Women's Commission for Refugee Women and Children.

PART FOUR

Globalization

CHAPTER 10

The Carceral Contract

FROM DOMESTIC TO GLOBAL GOVERNANCE

Lisa E. Sanchez

FOR SOME TIME NOW, the United States has engaged domestically in a form of "spatial governmentality" (Sanchez 1998; 2002) defined by the production of a rightless, stateless, criminal subject—a *suspect-subject of terror.* As part of this strategy, states have developed laws and tactics of preventative risk management along with detailed racial and spatial strategies of governance and punishment. Since September 11, 2001, the United States has expanded such practices and ideas into the international arena through the "war on terror."

In this chapter, I compare American gang suppression laws that define the criminal subject as a "street terrorist," with discourses from the war on terrorism that refer to the "international terrorist" or "illegal combatant." In doing so, I suggest that increasingly the United States is relying on a form of risk-based governmentality that is embodied domestically in preventative, community policing and internationally in the doctrine of the pre-emptive strike. Definitions and the existence of subjects of crime are central both to prevention and pre-emption. Neither could proceed without a rightless, stateless subject—a *homo sacer* (Agamben 1998). Such a figure is defined as an imminent threat, always already criminal precisely because crime prevention and security require that people be arrested prior to—that is, in the absence of—any crime or harmful act being committed.

GOVERNING THROUGH CRIME AND POPULATION

Around a decade ago, Jonathan Simon proposed that advanced industrial societies were "governed through crime" (Simon 1997). He wrote that the over developed societies of the West and North Atlantic were "experiencing not a crisis of crime and punishment but a crisis of governance that has led [them] to prioritize crime and punishment as the preferred contexts of governance" (173).

As examples, Simon cited vast increases in incarceration, a multiplication of laws, enhanced penalties, mandatory minimum sentences for nonviolent and drug offenses, changes in the statute of limitations for appeals on criminal convictions, and an enmeshment of incarceration and supervision in which relatively minor probation violations frequently resulted in reincarceration. Focusing most closely on the U.S. context, he pointed to the resurgence of punitive views among the general public, and the obsessive attention to crime in the media and in the political agendas and campaigns of Congress, state legislators, and presidential candidates. The reinvigoration of "governance by rule and sanction," he wrote, reveals crime and punishment as the "preferred metaphor[s] for all forms of social anxiety" (173). To put it plainly, by the late 1980s, understanding, measuring, and talking about crime had become a cultural pastime.

To understand the effect of the move from governance by a diffuse array of sociolegal relationships and institutions to one increasingly centered on criminal justice and on the fear and prevention of crime, one need not look far. The logic of crime prevention is embedded in modern architecture and urban planning. The architecture of fear is exemplified in planned and gated communities, in privately policed shopping malls, and in the use of security cameras in stores and around the perimeters of businesses. Similarly, urban planning strategies, public space ordinances, and law enforcement practices designed to eliminate "disorder"—the "broken windows" approach popularized by James Q. Wilson and George Kelling (1982)—tell the story of how we govern through crime. The body becomes an object of governance as it ventures into the workplace, public institutions, and public spaces. The imposition of drug testing by private corporations and government employers, and of pregnant women in public hospitals, illustrates the extent to which the criminal law has become part and parcel of the American consciousness and private life. Similarly, as members of residential communities that involve us in the policing of our neighbors, we are the unsuspecting subjects and objects of governance. Consider for example "neighborhood watch" programs, homeowner's insurance policies that provide financial incentives to people who purchase security devices, nuisance suits, and tenant tort actions. In each of these instances, we see the boundaries between civil and criminal law and between public and private space blurred. People are subjected to the surveillance of a wider cadre of officials and self-appointed, quasi-legal agents, and are liable to the criminal law in a way that would not have been possible before the 1980s.

But the new way of governance is not only about crime, and the concomitant technologies of surveillance and governance by crime control and crime risk management are not distributed equally across the population. Racial profiling, public space housing sweeps, police surveillance cameras, drug- and prostitution-free zones, gang suppression laws, and anti-gang-loitering ordinances remind us that the U.S. obsession is also fundamentally about race. At the same time as we see the public and private life spaces of ethno-racial communities become increasingly subject to surveillance, removal, and exclusion in the post–civil rights era, we are reminded of similar exclusions in the pre–civil rights era wherein racial segregation, police brutality, and racial violence reigned firm. The Black Codes, the internment of Japanese Americans, and the Native American removal projects come to mind (see Young and Spencer, Messerschmidt, Banks, and Calavita, this volume).

Although this culture of governance has developed in part through discourses of crime, it is also constituted in a related array of strategies and tactics whose development was accelerated during the past quarter-century by the rise of neoliberalism and from anxieties about increased international migration, trade, and cultural exchange. Such factors have all been attributed to what has variously been called the "era of globalization" and the "age of migration."

Of course, despite an acceleration of these strategies and technologies in recent years, government through population segmentation and racial spatial ordering has a long history. Michel Foucault (1991) used the term "governmental rationality" or "governmentality" to describe the tactics, technologies, and institutions that developed in the late eighteenth century. In Western states at that time, a logic of administrative justice focused on the health and wealth of the population, in contradistinction to prior forms of social organization that were established and justified on the basis of obedience to the law of a divine or earthly sovereign. The family became the primary political economic unit, with population as the new site of governance. Likewise, Foucault and others document a shift in focus from individual deviance to the health of populations, and the use of population segments and geographic tactics for organizing and managing populations. Indeed, though some scholars question the sequential logic of Foucault's argument whereby governmentality would seem to replace sovereignty (Agamben 1998; Merry 1998; Butler 2004), Foucault's work usefully reveals the historically contingent nature of population as an eighteenth-century fiction designed to assist economists and government leaders in the management and reorganization of economic-residential units for capital and liberal democratic governance.

Although governance by population has existed since at least the 1700s, the perfection of methods and means of geographic management and social control reached a high point in the late 1980s, and has continued to escalate into the new millennium. This move was not uncomplicated. In the United States, the decline of the welfare state in the late 1970s was greeted with a resurgence of the ideology of personal choice and responsibility. Under neoliberalism, all social relationships, including those between citizen and state, take on the logic of a contract wherein personal freedom is contingent on compliance with a rapidly multiplying array of imposed regulations and quasi-legal relationships. Whereas the welfare state sought to govern through large social groups, advanced liberal societies give the appearance of government through "the regulated and accountable choices of autonomous agents—citizens, consumers, parents, employees, managers, investors—[and] through intensifying and acting upon their allegiance to particular 'communities'" (Rose 1996, 42).

At the same time that citizens of advanced capitalism appear both less dependent and less beholden to a paternalistic state, demographic classification systems, such as the census, health and insurance records, criminal histories, and regional and national crime data have become more detailed and more extensive. While the rhetoric of liberal legality highlights individual choice and freedom, the distribution and aggregation of citizens into population segments based on personal characteristics and experiences belies the individual powers of rights-bearing citizens by extending the possibilities of surveillance and by channeling people into a web of governable, interlocking categories and relationships. Neoliberal governance thus depends upon the proliferation of small-scale regulatory effects that reach across territories and permeate the interstices of everyday life. "At once totalizing and individualizing," such strategies congeal in political formations that can govern "all and each" with stealthy precision (Gordon 1991, 3; Foucault 1991).

GANGS AS DOMESTIC SUBJECTS OF TERROR

How is it that presumably objective categories and measurements of science, and seemingly rational uses of government, underpin and legitimate regimes of racial profiling, punishment, and removal? To answer this question, we must examine more closely what criminologists mean by "crime causation" and "prevention," as well as their correlates, "crime risk" and "criminal propensity." We must, in other words, seek to understand how race becomes incorporated as if an independent variable into notions of crime risk and prevention at the level of law-making and enforcement practice.

As part of late-twentieth-century risk management, U.S. states and municipalities began to encode a series of laws designed to eliminate disorder and to enable the police to engage in preventative community policing efforts. The racial content of these practices is most clearly visible in anti-gang laws that were ushered in across a number of states at this time (Strosnider 2002). Included among the array of legal measures taken against so-called gang members in localities in the U.S. that continue today are: (1) state statutes defining new "gang-related" crimes, and statutes redefining existing crimes as "gang-related"; (2) city ordinances and other measures enabling police, prosecutors, and citizens to enjoin and arrest those identified as gang members from activities not ordinarily considered crime (e.g., standing, walking, or bicycling in a public place, or carrying spray cans, marking pens, or baseball bats); (3) provisions enabling the transfer of juveniles accused of gang affiliation or gang-related activity to adult court; (4) law enforcement policies that convene special enforcement teams—gang suppression units—for the sole purpose of targeting and enforcing existing laws against presumed gang members.

These laws became widespread across the United States in the 1980s and 1990s, by 2002 existing in twenty-eight states and the District of Columbia (Strosnider 2002). The state of California and the city of Chicago provide particularly salient examples of how gang suppression laws operate as racial spatial governmentality. Chicago, in particular, led the way in rearticulating and reinvigorating the status offense in the form of the "anti-gang-loitering ordinance." The state of California, in encoding the most expansive gang suppression legislation of any of the fifty states (including provisions in all four of the abovementioned categories) under the 1988 Street Terrorism Enforcement and Prevent (STEP) Act and Proposition 21 (2000), pioneered and promoted many risk-prevention technologies and community policing strategies.

The 1992 Chicago Gang Congregation Ordinance, the subject of the famous *Morales* case taken up first by the Illinois State Supreme Court in October 1997, then by the U.S. Supreme Court in 1999, gave police exceptionally broad powers to disperse suspected gang members from public spaces. Specifically, it enabled police to disperse gang members from city areas where two or more known or suspected gang members were found standing together, and to arrest people for failure to disperse (Roberts 2001). The Chicago law called for "aggressive action . . . to preserve city streets and other public places," and carries a penalty of arrest and a fine or six months jail time (Chicago, Ill., Municipal Code 8–4–1–015, 1992). In just three years, police issued more than 89,000 dispersal orders and made more than 42,000 arrests (Strosnider 2002, 102).

The language and enforcement of Chicago's Gang Congregation Ordinance revealed clearly the tacit assumption of race as a causal factor in crime simply because crime statistics showed people of color to be more frequently arrested and convicted of crime. This, of course, confused causation and correlation, and relied on politically charged data—national and local (i.e., internal police department) crime statistics—highly sensitive to skewed policing and reporting practices. The ordinance also conflated propensity and causation. The assumption that a person is more likely to commit crime (i.e., has a propensity for crime) because of his or her membership in a racial or ethnic group overrepresented in arrest and conviction data too often equates to racial profiling and racially targeted policing and arrest practices.

Although anti-gang-loitering ordinances supposedly prohibit crime by specifically targeting what are called "criminal gang members," they are applied precisely in *the absence of any activity that is otherwise actionable under criminal or civil law*. The very text of the Chicago law made this clear: the law targeted gang members who "try to avoid arrest by committing no offense punishable under existing law" (Chicago, Ill., Municipal Code 8–4–1–015; *Chicago v. Morales*, 177 Ill.2d 440 687 N.W. 2d 53 [1997]). The problematic nature of this approach becomes clearer when the actual picture of illicit activity among so-called criminal gang members is taken into account. Even among those who self-identify as gang members or who are listed as gang-affiliated in police records, the extent to which they break the law is vastly exaggerated. Some estimate that only 10 percent of those affiliated with a gang are involved in serious criminal activity (Klein 1995). With respect to the specific data on gang-related offenses, the Chicago police reported a total of 1,127 gang-related aggravated batteries, as compared to 5,251 gang-loitering arrests, in 1993 shortly after the gang-loitering ordinance had gone into effect. A year later, when enforcement of the law was in full force, aggravated batteries had remained constant at 1,172, but gang-loitering arrests had increased nearly 200 percent to 22,056 (*Chicago v. Morales* 1997, fn. 7).

In 1997, the Illinois Supreme Court reasoned that a criminal statute must meet two basic criteria to satisfy the vagueness doctrine. It must first be "sufficiently definite so that it gives persons of ordinary intelligence a reasonable opportunity to distinguish between lawful and unlawful conduct . . . [and it must] adequately define the criminal offense in such a manner that does not encourage arbitrary and discriminatory enforcement."

The *Morales* decision implies but does not directly establish the racial discrimination (in this case, the criminalization of status based on race) of gang suppression legislation. Not only did the court argue that the law does not "discourage arbitrary or discriminatory enforcement" (*City Chicago v. Morales* 1997), the decision further stipulated that "gang membership may not be established solely because an individual is wearing clothing available for sale to the general public." One justice, for example, questioned police admissions that they viewed baseball hats bearing the Chicago Bulls insignia as "gang attire." Underlying the racially charged and otherwise empty content of the law, the Illinois Supreme Court observed that "gang-loitering ordinance[s] are drafted in an intentionally vague manner so that persons who are undesirable in the eyes of police and prosecutors can be convicted even though they are not chargeable with any other particular offense" (*City Chicago v. Morales* 1997). Underlining this problem, the court decided that "[p]ersons suspected of being in criminal street gangs are deprived of the personal liberty of being able to freely walk the streets and associate with friends, regardless of whether they are actually gang members or have committed any crime." Quoting a lower court judge, the decision concludes with a reference to longstanding provisions against using the criminal law to criminalize one's status as a person of color, as was done under the Black Codes over a century earlier: the police cannot just "lock [people] up just for being who [they] are."

In 1997, the U.S. Supreme Court upheld the Illinois Supreme Court's decision, ruling the ordinance unconstitutional, finding it impermissibly vague and in violation of the due process of law (*City of Chicago v. Morales, 527 U.S. 41 [1999]*). Just one year later, the city of Chicago passed a new gang loitering ordinance that successfully circumvented the void-for-vagueness provision of *Morales* by specifying "hot spots" of gang activity for enforcement (Chicago, Ill., Mun. Code § 8–4–015[a][2000]). These hot spots, of course, are concentrated in communities of color, and have thus intensified the effects of racial profiling on people of color. By the year 2001, the law had not considerably diminished violent crime. But in conjunction with Chicago's public housing sweep laws, it had contributed significantly to the dismantling of residential housing projects and relocation of poor Latinos/as and African Americans to the now decaying suburbs, while removing numerous people to prisons or correctional supervision. By 2002, Chicago's famous Cabrini Green and Robert Taylor Homes had been leveled. With the last of the inner-city housing projects demolished, the physical evidence of instrumental support for the poor, and the only remaining symbol of a former era of more reasoned social service policies (however misguided their particular application in Chicago public housing may have been), has been destroyed. At the same time, developers are rebuilding these same neighborhoods for middle- and upper-middle class residence and consumption, and the University of Illinois is constructing accommodation too expensive for faculty and staff to afford in the immediate vicinity of the University of Illinois at Chicago, where housing projects once stood.

Gang-loitering ordinances aim to manage populations in place by channeling people into specific regions and activities—in this case, into prisons and less valuable, more rundown residential neighborhoods—and by disciplining the movements of racialized bodies in public space. Chicago's ordinance reflects a logic of risk management prevention, which always already attaches a presumed propensity to commit crime to those individuals named in the law. As a result, the enforcement of the laws are justified on the assumption that mere membership in the group—i.e., being a young man or woman of color, coded "gang"—equates to criminality and poses an imminent threat.

In addition, gang-loitering ordinances represent what I call a "carceral contract"—a regime of confinement and example of "forced consent" (Sanchez 2004a; Sanchez 2004b). Recall that the law gives the police powers to disperse suspected gang members from public space. In other words, no crime has been committed until the police approach someone with an order to disperse. It is only after this demand is made that any law has been violated—that is, the "failure to disperse on demand." The law is constituted as a two-step process that criminalizes the second step only after making invisible the first action by the state—namely, an unjustified intrusion. It is this first step that introduces opportunities for discrimination and abuse, forcing its own violation, in a manner akin to search and seizure laws. The second step in the process, however excessive, nevertheless appears to be applied equally and without reference to race or ethnicity.

Although it is easy enough to argue that the law, in fact, is not applied equally, the key point is that the second step of arrest and punishment is not possible without the first. It is the precise moment when police contact that would have previously been impossible suddenly occurs, that racially discriminatory enforcement practices, as well as violations of Constitutional rights to due process, equal protection of laws, freedom of association and travel, arise. Only certain people are likely to be arrested under the ordinance. Those who are deemed a threat according to the subjective assessments of police officers enforcing what is already a racially coded law are targeted by the law; specifying gang hot spots only enhances this effect. In addition, although detailed accounts of the way the law is actually enforced are few and far between, some suggest that there really is no second step in the process. Rather, suspected gang members are approached and arrested for violation of the anti-gang-loitering ordinances before ever having the opportunity to disperse and without knowing what law they have violated or what is required of them (Roberts 2001).

It is important to note that the violation of Constitutional rights and the discriminatory effects of anti-gang-loitering ordinances are well masked in what appears as something akin to a contractual agreement. The approach and request to disperse would appear quite a civil procedure, but the suspect-subject has no real right to refuse. It appears, like an offer, as an element of civil contract, but failure to agree with the terms results in arrest under criminal law. In this way, the elements and practices of civil law are appropriated and manipulated to give the law and its enforcement the appearance of civility, while rationalizing a law that amounts to a status offense. The law transfers all legal responsibility onto the target of the imposed contract—he must be at fault, since he failed to comply with the demands of an officer of the law. Further, it relieves the state and its agents of all accountability, while justifying what really is an abuse of force/enforcement, an abuse of state power. This kind of "carceral contract" is not universally imposed on all citizens who occupy the public space. Rather, it is extended only to those who, by their appearance, are perceived to pose a threat to social order. In the case of gang-loitering ordinances, the "contract" is imposed strictly upon racialized subjects because only racially marked individuals and communities are counted (e.g., in police statistics, national crime databases, and youth gang surveys) as gang members.

In California, similarly discriminatory laws had been encoded under the 1988 "Street Terrorism Enforcement and Prevention (STEP) Act" and under Proposition 21 (2000). In this case, however, rather than simply encoding one sweeping ordinance, as Chicago did, the STEP Act criminalized conduct, and enabled local jurisdictions to write ordinances and injunctions, to target so-called gang members and to enforce gang suppression laws in four broad categories that targeted gang members. It added laws to the penal code, defining new gang-related crime and enhanced penalties for existing crimes if in their commission they could be deemed "gang-related," i.e., committed by a gang member. The law also enabled citizens and prosecutors to write laws enjoining gang members from activities that could not otherwise be considered crime by using a strategy usually applied under civil law (the civil injunction) but applying it to activities generally considered civil (e.g., walking, standing, carrying pens) but to which were attached criminal penalties. Finally, the STEP Act enabled transfer of juveniles accused of gang-related activity to adult court and enabled police to organize gang suppression units, like the infamous Los Angeles CRASH team. An acronym for "Community Resources against Street Hoodlums," this unit became notorious for abuses that included planting evidence and shooting so-called gang members after they had been handcuffed.

Officers of gang units look for crime before any evidence or complaint is brought forward. They do not to look for it just anywhere, however, rather only among those individuals labeled gang members and in those neighborhoods where the so-called gang members have been said to reside. Thus, even aside from the contempt of certain members of the CRASH team and other officers of California gang units who abused the law and, under it, youth of color, the law in many ways invited abuse, even structuring it into the job, through the requirement that gang unit officers justify their work based on arrest and clearance rates.

Although the stated purpose of gang-loitering ordinances and gang suppression legislation was to reduce gang violence, these seem to have had little effect in reducing violent crime. In Los Angeles, for example, gang homicide rates nearly doubled in the five years after the STEP act was encoded (Klein 1995). In addition to granting a means for police officers to make contact and arrest people for all kinds of activities not otherwise legally actionable, the law provided for enhanced penalties on anyone who could be construed as having associations with a gang. As a result, it had substantial effect on the California prison population and rising incarceration and reincarceration rates of African Americans and Latinos in California.

What is explicit in California's Street Terrorism and Enforcement Act is implicit in all gang congregation, gang suppression, nuisance, drug-free- and prostitution-free-zone laws—that is, the equation of darkness and terror. These laws constitute a late-twentieth-century trend toward terror, while at the same time hunting down terrorists. In the process, the laws serve to connect the domestic and the global suspect-subject of regulatory governance, and thus foreshadow a now obvious relationship between "gang" and "terror," "gang member" and "terrorist," through darkness—that is, through the category of race. The domestic subject of terror and the global subject of terror are one and the same: both are dark, both are outside the boundaries of society, and both are monstrous.

The Global Suspect-Subject of Terror

In the flurry of counter-terrorist activity after 9/11, President Bush ordered the detention of two men for their alleged ties to al-Qaeda. The first, Yaser Esam Hamdi, was a Louisiana-born citizen of Saudi descent; the second, José Padilla, was a Chicago-born Latino said to be a former Chicago gang member, prisoner, and convert to Islam who went by the name Abdullah Al Muhajir. Deeming both men "enemy combatants," Bush condemned them to indefinite military detention (Gearan 2004). In May 2004, at the same time that the Supreme Court began to deliberate on the legality of the detention of Hamdi and Padilla, news began to erupt of American military police abusing Iraqi prisoners and photographing them in pornographic poses in Abu Ghraib prison near Baghdad (Abou El-Magd 2004; see Miller, this volume). By the end of the month, new complaints about other centers of confinement in the U.S.-led war on terrorism, in Afghanistan and Guantanamo Bay, Cuba, appeared.

Taken together, these events suggest that parallel languages and strategies of war and regulation are reconfiguring global and domestic relations. The decision to label Hamdi, Padilla, and all those shipped to Guantánamo and Abu Ghraib as illegal combatants rather than as prisoners of war or criminal offenders is, like the gang suppression laws, already a type of conviction, insofar as it effectively strips citizens and foreigners of their rights. Such individuals then become particularly vulnerable to, and are thought to deserve, harsh treatment, since they are both legally and socially deemed outside the law. They also figuratively and actually disappear from sight, placed in high-security penal establishments like Abu Ghraib that, in the name of security, are themselves operated outside the law.

From the beginning, the U.S.-led war on terrorism has been carefully crafted around several significant absences. Most dramatically, there has been little representation of dead or injured bodies. Recall that the attack on Iraq was presented to the American public as a fireworks show featuring "shock and awe," "precision-guided missiles," and "surgical strikes." It was over seemingly as quickly as it had begun, in eighteen days. There were eighteen days of bombing, costing thousands of Iraqi civilians and soldiers their lives, and then the Bush administration declared the "end of major combat operations." The date was May 2, 2003, and it was followed by almost an entire year of near-total silence, at least in most of the U.S. press, about the war and the loss of life in the region.

Such a view of war mirrors the process of sterilization described by Elaine Scarry (1987) in *The Body in Pain*, wherein injured and dismembered bodies both escape and exceed depiction, and technologies and strategies of war are renamed for easier consumption. In official reportage of the Vietnam War, for example, state and military leaders used the "body count" as a mark of success, so that soldiers and civilians who lost their lives in the war became evidence of U.S. might. Similarly, bombs were given cute names like Daisy Cutter and Pink Rose to mask the death and destruction they caused. In Afghanistan and Iraq somewhat more complex forces are at work as, post-Vietnam, the public needed some persuasion. Thus, in an appeal to patriotism, combat operations were known as Operation Enduring Freedom and Operation Iraqi Freedom, and the body count became a thing of the past. In apparent acquiescence to President Bush's statement that the American people "don't need to see," the media failed to report on the numbers of Iraqis, Americans, and coalition forces dying in the region. Protest at the domestic level seemed, along with bodies, to disappear shortly thereafter.

A second significant absence in the war on terrorism has been a constructed absence of leadership and statehood. This has been the case not so much among coalition forces, whose leadership is clear, if removed. Rather, it has been the absence of leadership among the so-called enemy, embodied most obviously, under two slightly different strategies, by two absent figures, Saddam Hussein and Osama bin Laden. While Saddam Hussein was caught and subjected on television to a dental examination and delousing before disappearing from public view (to solitary confinement at an undisclosed location), Osama bin Laden is still missing, and is said always to be at large somewhere in the border zone between Afghanistan and Pakistan. In removing leaders and leadership (here, the ejection of the Taliban also becomes significant), coalition leaders and the press have effectively represented Afghani and Iraqi territory as nations without states, and the people of those territories as living in a nation without a state. The construction of the two men as missing, transient, and nomadic enables both the construction of the leaders (and by extension, their followers) as border figures who are stateless and monstrous and undeserving of rights under national or international law, and the construction of the nations as stateless—i.e., without leadership or political organization, also without rights, even without existence on the international map. Such stateless nations without leaders are then easily portrayed as territories of unclear borders, in a state of disorder, chaos, emergency—in a state of jeopardy, open for "democracy" and "development."

The orchestrated absence of leadership and state in the war on terrorism also has accomplished another important task. It has enabled the coalition to avoid the appearance of involvement in a national, ethnic, or religious war: what is being fought is not a state or country, a people, or a religious group. Each of these actions would be a violation of the Geneva Convention. Rather, the coalition is said to be fighting a practice or idea, a "network" of stateless (read: rightless) individuals. Thus, not only has the removal of leaders, along with the destruction of infrastructure, politics, and social networks during the initial bombing in both countries, constituted an absence of leadership, it also has constituted an absence of state, ethnicity, and religion.

Still, the most significant *absence* in the war on terrorism has been the proclaimed absence, since May 2, 2003, of combat operations—that is, of actions of war itself. Although the media silence has not been complete (since networks reported some of the fighting and deaths in Fallujah, there was a flurry of interest in photographs of coffins of U.S. soldiers returning from Iraq, and certain stations list the names of U.S. soldiers as they die in the war), the representation of U.S.-coalition troops executing combat operations—i.e., fighting, killing people, dying, and making war—has been almost entirely absent. Consequently, for most Americans, as well as for many citizens of the coalition, it seems the declaration in May of 2003 of the Bush and Blair administrations of the "end of major combat operations" actually signaled the end of the war.

This "absence" of combat (really, of war itself) has served two critical functions for the war on terrorism and for the postmillennial model of imperialism that constructs and polices the "terrorist" as global criminal. First, it constituted any and all combat after May 2003 as an "uprising" or "insurgence" and thus all soldiers and civilians resisting coalition combat, occupation, and so-called aid as "insurgents" and "enemy combatants." Second, despite some criticisms leveled by nations like France and Spain, it has effectively wiped from much of the Western/Northern register of consciousness the use of mass incarceration as a technology of war and neocolonial occupation in Iraq and Afghanistan. In the wake of the scandal at Abu Ghraib prison outside of Baghdad, Iraq, most people remained unconcerned, until a much later date, about the manner in which practices of removal and confinement are being used to execute the so-called transition to democracy in Iraq, and the fact that prisoners of war are not, as we understood them in a former era, a relatively few isolated soldiers held in prison camps. Rather, the prison is being used as an institution of containment and threat to silence Iraqi protests against the occupation, a technology of twenty-first-century conquest and empire. If the war and the war camp—the prison—has been largely invisible to American and coalition citizens, what has emerged clearly and become central to U.S./U.K. knowledge about the war is the image (and category) of the "insurgent" and "the terrorist," and the contrasting images of the righteous American/coalition soldier, giving "humanitarian aid" and engaging in "democratizing efforts."

Taken together with the constructed absence of leadership and state, the insurgent/enemy combatant became the same as the international (or the domestic, "street") terrorist. Denied, primarily through a twist of rhetoric, the subject position of citizen of a state, soldier, or lawful resister, Iraqis and any Afghanis who fought against the coalition forces after 9/11 were constructed as stateless, rightless rogues, monstrous border figures. They belonged to no one and no community, lurking on the borders between nation-states, living like animals in the darkness underground, as Saddam Hussein was shown to have done, or lurking in caves on the borders between nation-states, as bin Laden is said to be doing. From this perspective, the movement of Afghanis and Iraqis from members of national and local communities to suspected terrorist to enemy combatant to war prisoner can take place seamlessly and with little protest from outside. From inside Iraq and Afghanistan, protest is significantly diminished by the mere threat of receiving similar treatment. Such a view also conveniently constructs the executioners of war—the American and coalition soldiers, and the military and political leaders of the coalition forces—as unwarlike, as "peace keepers," as international citizens providing "humanitarian aid": in other words, as civil.

Although we are not necessarily used to seeing similarity across borders, the links between the rhetoric and strategies of war against the domestic, "street" terrorist and against the global "international" terrorist are manifold. The enemy combatant and the insurgent *are* the criminal gang member. Both insurgent and gang member differ from earlier, more explicitly racialized terms to construct the "enemy." The war in Vietnam, for example, explicitly targeted the Viet Cong, a clearly marked ethnic group with a national and political identity. Although many Americans believed that the Viet Cong represented a communist threat, they were able eventually to see that the war in Vietnam involved killing human beings and destroying communities. In contrast, the insurgent or enemy combatant, and especially the international terrorist, ostensibly could be anyone. He belongs not to any one group; he is a nomad, a stateless criminal. Denied membership in any legitimate state, community, or national or ethnic group, he is understood in relation to a network of criminals of varied origin and ethnicity.

In fact, however, he is not just anyone. Just as the vast majority of "street terrorists" arrested and apprehended are young men of color plus a few women of predominantly Latino/a, African American, and Southeast Asian heritage from (and of) impoverished neighborhoods, international terrorists are predominantly young Muslim men from the Persian Gulf region, South and Southeast Asia, and Muslim countries in Africa. It really is no mystery: they are young men of color of the global South who follow the teachings of Islam.

The tropes of terrorism being circulated in the current war are far-reaching, perhaps even more important than the failures and successes of the military. These tropes constitute the global suspect-subject without rights, as a category of racial subjects who are always already criminal, always already outside the boundaries of law and society. Although it remains to be seen whether the international community will continue to tolerate, tacitly accept, or fail to challenge the political and military actions of coalition forces and leaders, for the time being the coalition is proceeding to capture, detain, and incarcerate men and women in Iraq, Afghanistan, Guantánamo Bay, and in the United States (the detention of Hamdzi, Padilla, and several others whose detentions have been less public) as if they were stateless criminals without rights.

The use of mass confinement in the global context, made possible in part by the carceral contract and the deployment of strategies of racial spatial governmentality, is central to the reconstruction of the imperial project as one of managerial regulation. The "order to disperse," as used against gang members in the United States, and as implied in Iraq by the occupation, killing, incarceration and torture of thousands of Iraqis—that is, of young Muslim men of the global South—is central to the carceral contract. This arrangement extracts compliance through domination, and strips citizens of their rights through criminalizing activities that cannot otherwise be considered crime, or strategies that would be considered normal and legitimate responses to occupation under the terms of international war. This line of attack would not be possible without the parallel categories "criminal gang member" or "street terrorist," and "international terrorist," "insurgent," or "enemy combatant." At the same time, these strategies mask the violence of the state and nation-state by altering the time sequence and making invisible the violent intrusion of the soldier or police officer onto the body of the Other. That moment is always the moment of contact. In the gang-loitering ordinance, it is the approach before the order to disperse, an order that is by definition without cause or warrant, as is presumably required in something like a traffic stop or residential search; in the war on terrorism, the moment so far has been defined by the occupation. Yet of course these moments of contact—this approach, and this invasion and occupation—are made invisible under the construction of resistance either as the "refusal to obey an order to disperse" or when the "resistance to occupation" is construed as "insurgence" and "enemy combat." In each instance, it is the refusal to be stripped of rights and citizenship status that lands a person in prison or in the morgue; it is the refusal to "agree" to be imprisoned for contesting activities that are unconstitutional or in violation of international law. In each such case, there can be seen to be a case of "forced consent," a "carceral contract," violation of which results in confinement, injury, or death.

CONCLUSION

To return to where we began, in the domestic sphere, late-twentieth-century strategies of risk management, and the rise of so-called preventative, community policing have created a *domestic suspect-subject of terror*—the young person of color, the "criminal gang member." Forging a whole new category of racialized subjects, constituted as *criminal-* and *suspect-subjects*, these policies deny the rights of citizenship to large sections of the population. Laws, which appear on their surface to be about minor violations and misdemeanors, criminalize activities—e.g., walking, standing, riding bicycles, carrying pens—that no citizen could be prevented from doing. In the process, they formulate a racialized subject without rights, and the transformation, through the racially coded category "gang," of subjectivity from citizen to non-rights-bearing subject, suspect, criminal.

The ideological and discursive construction of the gang member as street terrorist that is apparent in the California gang suppression law, the Street Terrorism and Enforcement (STEP) Act presents gang members as universally vicious and dangerous. Likewise, the STEP Act draws upon the currency of international terrorism to justify enhanced penalties against gang members and to authorize and legitimate laws that could not have been successfully passed if broadly construed as laws applicable to any person—that is, to any *citizen*. Although a concern with gangs has existed at least since the early part of the twentieth century, early-century gang members, such as the Italian mafia, actually saw their day in court as rights-bearing citizens. The making of the late-twentieth-century gang member as a racialized subject without rights, an alien outsider, a monster in need not of correction, but of utter removal, thus marks a turn away from earlier constructions and treatments of gangs like the Mafia, the Ku Klux Klan, or the Hells' Angels.

The contemporary discourse and vocabulary of terrorism not only constructs the gang member anew as a suspect-subject of terror, and thus contributes to the ongoing construction and recalibration of American racial formation (Omi and Winant 1986), but it also reconstitutes (through its opposite: the entitled self-governing citizen-subject, the standard normal citizen, coded white, male, middle-class), the unself-governing—i.e., deficient but correctable—subject. In other words, the creation of a domestic subject without rights in the form of the criminal gang member, domestic terrorist outsider not only embodies the terms of its own monstrosity (Foucault 1994; Puar and Rai 2002); it helps to constitute a parallel population of the poor, people of color, women, who, in contrast to their monster terrorist brothers and sisters, are not fully entitled to or deserving of the rights of citizenship but are allowed to strive toward citizenship.

The policing techniques used in the late twentieth century and the present strategies used in war intertwine to create the global suspect-subject as one without rights. The signaling of anomie and transience in the discourse of social disorganization as a lack of community (domestic) and statelessness as a lack of state (international), and the positioning of street terrorists and international terrorists as stateless and without community, facilitate these processes. The roles of the carceral contract, of governmentality, and of confinement are significant in this process. In this sense, the discourses and technologies of war and crime become inseparable components of postmillennial neoimperialism, dealing centrally in risk and threat, and banking on the currency of terror and fear. The new strategies of war and confinement are the new tools of empire.

WORKS CITED

Abou El-Magd, Nadia. 2004. Photos of naked Iraqi prisoners outrage Arabs. *Los Angeles Times*, May 2.

Agamben, Giorgio. 1998. *Homo sacer: Sovereignty and bare life*. Stanford, CA: Stanford University Press.

Butler, Judith. 2004. *Precarious life: The powers of mourning and violence*. London: Verso Press.

Foucault, Michel. 1991. Governmentality. In *The Foucault effect*, ed. Graham Burchell, Gordon Colin, and Peter Miller. Chicago, IL: University of Chicago Press.

———. 1994. The Abnormals. In *Michel Foucault: Ethics, subjectivity and truth: Essential works of Foucault*, ed. Paul Rabinow. New York: The New Press.

Gearan, Anne. 2004. U.S. seeks appeal on "dirty bomb" suspect. *Chicago Tribune*, January 17, 11.

Gordon, Colin. 1991. Governmental rationality: An introduction. In *The Foucault effect: Studies in governmentality*, ed. Graham Burchell, Gordon Colin, and Peter Miller. Chicago, IL: University of Chicago Press.

Klein, Malcolm W. 1995. *The American street gang*. New York: Oxford University Press.

Merry, Sally Engel. 1998. The Kapu on women going out to ships: Spatial governmentality on the fringes of empire. Paper presented at the annual meeting of the Law and Society Association, June 4–7, Aspen, CO.

Omi, Michael, and Howard Winant. 1986. *Racial formation in the United States*. New York: Routledge.

Puar, Jaspir, and Amit Rai. 2002. Monster, terrorist, fag: The war on terrorism and the production of docile patriots. *Social Text, September 11: An Anniversary Issue*.

Roberts, Dorothy. 2001. Foreword: Race, vagueness, and the social meaning of order maintenance. *Journal of Criminology and Criminal Law* 89: 775–836.

Rose, Nicholas. 1996. Governing "advanced" liberal democracies. In *Foucault and political reason*, ed. Andrew Barry, Thomas Osborne, and Nikolas Rose, 37-64. Chicago, IL: University of Chicago Press.

Sanchez, Lisa E. 1998. Boundaries of legitimacy: Sex, violence, citizenship, and community in a local sex economy. *Law and Social Inquiry* 22: 543–580.

———. 2002. Enclosure acts and exclusionary practices: Neighborhood associations, community police, and the expulsion of the sexual outlaw. In *Between law and culture: Locating sociolegal studies*, ed. David Goldberg and Michael Musheno, 122–140. Minneapolis: University of Minnesota Press.

———. 2004a. The death of violence. Paper presented at the University of California at San Diego Center for the Study of Race and Ethnicity colloquium, March 15, San Diego, CA.

————. 2004b. Signature and the use of "forced consent" in the criminal law. Paper presented at the annual Law and Society Association, May 27–30, Chicago, IL.

Scarry, Elaine. 1987. *The body in pain: The making and unmaking of the world.* Oxford: Oxford University Press.

Simon, Jonathan. 1997. Governing through crime. In *The crime conundrum*, ed. Lawrence Friedman and George Fischer, 171–190. Boulder, CO: Westview Press.

Strosnider, Kim. 2002. Anti-gang ordinances after *City of Chicago v. Morales*: The intersection of race, vagueness doctrine, and equal protection in the criminal law. *American Criminal Law Review* 39: 101–146.

Wilson, James Q., and George Kelling. 1982. Broken windows: Police and neighborhood safety. *Atlantic Monthly* 249, 29–38.

LEGISLATION

California Street Terrorism Enforcement and Prevention (STEP) Act. 1988. California Penal Code §§186.20–186.33.

Chicago Gang Congregation Ordinance. Chicago, Ill., Mun. Code §8–4–015 (1992).

Chicago Gang Loitering Ordinance. Chicago, Ill., Mun. Code §8–4–015(a) (2000).

Proposition 21 (West Cal. Legis. Serv., Proposition 21 [2000]).

COURT CASES

City of Chicago v. Morales, 527 U.S. 41 (1999).

Chicago v. Morales, 177 Ill. 2d 440, 687 N.E. 2d 53 (1997).

CHAPTER 11

Latina Imprisonment and
the War on Drugs

Juanita Díaz-Cotto

THE NUMBER OF LATINAS(OS) in the prisons and jails of the
United States and Latin America[1] has increased substantially during the past
two decades as a direct result of the globalization of the United States' war on
drugs (Dorn et al. 1996; U.S. Office of National Drug Control Policy 1997;
United Nations 1977; United Nations 1987; United Nations 1991). The war
on drugs is a series of national and international political, social, and economic
policies aimed at reducing the production, processing, trafficking, and consumption of "illicit drugs," such as marijuana, heroin, cocaine, and, increasingly, methamphetamines. Although Latinas have been severely impacted by
antidrug policies, few studies have focused on Latinas or even acknowledged
their plight.[2] By considering diverse sources of information on Latinas imprisoned in the United States, Latin America, and Europe, this chapter will provide a deeper understanding of how the globalization of the war on drugs has
affected them and their communities.

LATINAS(OS) IN THE UNITED STATES
AND CRIMINAL JUSTICE

The United States has the highest incarceration rate in the world. At year end
2004, over 2.1 million people were held in the nation's local, state, and federal
facilities (Harrison and Beck 2005). This does not include the approximately
168,000 people held in private jails and prisons (Harrison and Beck 2004). Even
though national crime rates have steadily decreased since the 1990s, the incarcerated population continues to grow (Lichtblau 2000; Sentencing Project 2003).[3]

The increasing number of convictions under drug-related and mandatory
sentencing laws are among the leading causes for the expansion of the overall
prisoner population (Jacobson 2005). Elsewhere I discuss how war on drug
policies target Latinas(os) for arrest and incarceration (Díaz-Cotto 2004;
Díaz-Cotto 2006) by highlighting the role Latin American countries and

individuals play in "illicit drug" enterprises, while masking the role of United States consumers, private corporations, and government agencies in such ventures.[4] Suffice it to say here that Latinas(os) have been among the most severely affected by the war on drugs because criminal justice policies overemphasize drug-related crimes, because Latinas(os) tend to be overrepresented among drug-related arrests, and because drug-related crimes are punished more severely than many other offenses.

Although in 2000, Latinas(os) as a whole comprised only 12 percent of the United States population (United States Department of Commerce 2001, 1), they comprised 16 percent of all prisoners under state and federal jurisdiction (U.S. Department of Justice 2001, 11). In states like New York and California, the overrepresentation of Latinas(os) within the jail and/or prison population has become even more noticeable, with Latinas(os) comprising around one-third of these states' overall prisoner population (California Department of Corrections 2005; New York State Department of Correctional Services [NYSDOCS] 2001).

Additional factors contribute to the overrepresentation of Latinas(os) in arrest, sentencing, and imprisonment rates (Díaz-Cotto 2000). For example, the Latina(o) population is disproportionately young and poor and thus particularly vulnerable to being arrested and incarcerated. Language barriers, discriminatory law enforcement and immigration policies, inadequate legal representation, and ignorance concerning the inner workings of the criminal justice system also contribute to Latina(o) overrepresentation within criminal justice processes (see Urbina and Smith, this volume). Moreover, during sentencing, Latinas(o) are less likely to be offered alternatives-to-incarceration programs than are African Americans or whites.

Latinas(os) also have been harshly affected by discriminatory sentencing policies, tougher parole board decisions, and federal and state drug-related and mandatory sentencing laws.[5] The last of these reduce defendants' plea bargaining ability, make imprisonment mandatory for some offenses, and increase sentence length for others. Ironically, these laws have had their most adverse impact on those convicted for nonviolent property (e.g., theft, burglary) and drug-related crimes, primarily possession and "under the influence" (Correctional Association of New York [CANY] 1992; CANY 1999; Díaz-Cotto 2006; Human Rights Watch 1997a; Human Rights Watch 2000). Finally, the lack of supportive services provided to Latinas(os) during and after imprisonment has led to their high recidivism rates.

LATINAS(OS) IN THE UNITED STATES AND THE WAR ON DRUGS

Men have historically composed the overwhelming number of those incarcerated in the United States, including 90 percent of all state prisoners sentenced for drug offenses (Harrison and Beck 2003). During the 1980s and 1990s, however, the number of women arrested for drug-related crimes increased significantly. By the end of the 1990s, nearly one in three women state prisoners was sentenced for a drug offense (Harrison and Beck 2003; Maguire and Pastore 2005).

This increase has been more pronounced in states such as New York and California, both ardent supporters of drug-related and mandatory sentencing laws. For example, around 60 percent of the women, but only 32 percent of the men, imprisoned in New York in 1996 were being held for drug offenses (Human Rights Watch 1997a, 13). In California, 26 percent of male prisoners, compared to 43 percent of women prisoners, were being held for drug-related offenses on December 31, 1999 (CDC 2000, Table 13). Additionally, a 1994 Department of Justice study revealed that women in federal prisons convicted of low-level drug offenses received sentences similar to men sentenced for more serious drug offenses (Mauer and Huling 1995).

Several studies have also revealed that, when racial and ethnic factors are taken into account, Latinas(os) and African Americans are more likely to be arrested and incarcerated for drug offenses even when whites are just as likely (Pettiway 1987) or more likely (Isikoff 1991; Meddis 1989) to use the same drugs. Coramae Richey Mann's 1990 study of New York, California, and Florida found that Latinas were 28.8 percent of women arrested for drug offenses in New York but 41.2 percent of women imprisoned for such offenses (Mann 1995, 128).[6] In California, Latinas composed only 18.7 percent of women arrested but 26.1 percent of women imprisoned for drug violations (Mann 1995).

When studying the impact of gender and ethnicity on imprisonment rates, we find that Latinas in New York were more likely than Latinos to be imprisoned for drug offenses. Thus, at the end of 1987, approximately 62 percent of Latinas but only 36 percent of Latinos were imprisoned for drug offenses. By year end 2001, nearly 40 percent of Latinos but 61 percent of Latinas were imprisoned for drug-related crimes (NYSDOCS 2002, 87).

The overrepresentation of Latinas imprisoned, compared with Latinos, for drug-related crimes could be the result of greater drug addiction among Latinas. In fact, a number of Latina addicts and former addicts interviewed by the author in California during the end of the 1990s thought this to be the case. However, they offered additional explanations for the growth in the imprisonment of Latinas, including Latinos' increasing reluctance to take full responsibility for joint crimes committed with Latinas, and Latinos' increasing willingness to try to convince Latinas to take full responsibility for such crimes. In this manner, Latinos sought to avoid the long prison sentences that would have resulted from their greater involvement with the criminal justice system and the stipulations imposed by drug-related and mandatory sentencing laws.

Latinas also were more affected than Latinos by the profiling of women of color from Africa, South America, and the Caribbean as drug couriers. Such profiling by criminal justice personnel and the mass media (CANY 1992) made them more vulnerable to being stopped and searched for drugs at airports—even though the typical drug courier tends to be a man (CANY 1992). Latinas also were more likely than Latinos to be used as "decoys" by drug dealers who sought to detract attention from other passengers on a flight who were transporting even larger quantities of drugs (Dorado 1998).

Further, Latinas did not generally play the roles in drug trafficking networks that would give them access to the sort of information most sought by law enforcement officials and district attorneys. Hence, they did not have the same power as Latinos to conduct favorable plea bargaining negotiations that would allow them to secure release from custody or, at least, a lesser sentence (CANY 1999). Many who were given the opportunity to plea bargain tended to plead guilty even when innocent of some or all of the charges, to receive a lower sentence than would be possible if they were found guilty by a jury. Those who chose trial over plea bargaining generally received longer sentences, as a result of their inability to hire competent defense attorneys. Others, who refused to inform on crime partners out of either loyalty or fear, were frequently given harsher sentences when district attorneys and judges had the ability to affect the decision. In all cases, non-English-speaking Latinas were among the most vulnerable.

The discriminatory treatment Latinas, particularly Spanish-monolingual women, encountered from predominantly white law enforcement officers, attorneys, and court personnel was continued by the predominantly white civilian and security staff in penal institutions (Díaz-Cotto 1996; Díaz-Cotto 2006). Once imprisoned, Latinas, like their non-Latina peers, also had to contend with overcrowded and unsanitary living conditions, medical neglect, and economic exploitation by private and public penal administrators. The lack of educational and vocational programs hindered their ability to adequately support themselves and their families upon their release. These conditions were exacerbated by verbal, physical, and/or sexual assault at the hands of penal staff, discriminatory treatment based on sexual orientation, and cleavages among prisoners based on racial, ethnic, and class distinctions (Díaz-Cotto 1996; Díaz-Cotto 2006; Human Rights Watch 1996; Ross 1998; Watterson 1996).

Further, Latina prisoners, most of them single heads of households, had to contend with separation from their children and other family members and the emotional and psychological trauma such separation entailed (Henriques 1982). Families on the outside also had to grapple with the economic hardship imposed by the incarceration of the family's main breadwinner. Equally important was that the incarceration of a parent, coupled with discriminatory treatment and/or lack of adequate support from social welfare agencies, criminal justice personnel, and other social institutions, led to the eventual institutionalization of many Latina(o) children and juveniles (Gabel and Johnston 1995). These experiences of Latinas with the criminal justice system in the United States are shared by Latinas in Latin America and Europe.

The War on Drugs and Women in Latin America

Women in Latin America have been severely impacted by the exportation of the United States war on drugs to Latin America, beginning with the militarization of the United States–Mexico border in 1981 (Dunn 1996; U.S. Congress 1990). The involvement of the United States and Latin American military in the drug war was designed to help law enforcement agencies to both curb illegal drug trade and quash Latin American revolutionary movements (Alonso 1997), considered equal threats to national and international security.[7]

The violation of civil and human rights in the United States that has accompanied such policies has been documented extensively by civil and human rights organizations (Amnesty International 1998; Human Rights Watch 1995b; Human Rights Watch 1997b; see also Miller, Bosworth, and Welch in this volume). Such policies have led to a growth in the number of foreign nationals detained in jails, prisons, and ICE detention facilities. Once incarcerated, foreign nationals can be held for indefinite periods of time in severely overcrowded facilities and unsanitary conditions while awaiting trial or deportation. Although many of those detained are subjected to physical abuse, women are also exposed to sexual harassment and abuse.

The militarization of the war on drugs coincided with the United States pressuring Latin American countries to pass drug-related and mandatory sentencing laws. As in the United States, such policies in Latin America have led to increasing corruption among those responsible for enforcing the laws, and to the weakening of civil society as the military and other security agencies increasingly encroach on areas previously considered the domain of civil authorities (Leone and Anrig 2003; Lichtblau 2003). Moreover, in Latin America, the war on drugs also has led to an increase in human rights violations, the growth in the number of those arrested and incarcerated, and the construction of more public and private jails and prisons.

Women in Mexico

In Mexico, the war on drugs has resulted in more women being arrested and detained both for low-level drug trafficking and for drug use. Evidence shows that even many of those arrested for non-drug offenses have been falsely charged with drug trafficking and held in preventive detention until they pay the bribes demanded by police or military officers (United Press International 1992). Others have been able to secure their release only after bribing other actors within the criminal justice system (Azaola and Yacamán 1996).

Although some have had their lives and the lives of detained relatives threatened if they refuse to sign confessions or otherwise comply with the aims of criminal justice personnel, others, who refused to comply, have been tortured or have had their children tortured in retaliation (Azaola and Yacamán 1996). Like Latinas in the United States, once incarcerated, women in Mexico are often physically and sexually abused.

A study conducted by the Women's Studies Program of El Colegio de Mexico during the early 1990s revealed that 50 to 64 percent of women imprisoned in Mexico were held for "delitos contra la salud," or crimes involving the trafficking or use of drugs (Azaola and Yacamán 1996, 400). Nonetheless, most women transported only small packages of drugs. Ironically, a number of those addicted to drugs had become addicts while imprisoned. Like many Latinas in the United States, a significant number of Mexican drug users, once addicted, resorted to prostitution to support their drug habit and sometimes that of partners. Also, like their sisters in the United States, addicted Mexican women were repeatedly arrested and incarcerated, because of both their addiction and the illegal actions they took to support their habit.

In Mexico and the United States, prisons are often overcrowded and unsanitary institutions where women are subjected to unrelenting verbal, physical, and/or sexual abuse. In both countries, prison policies that prioritized the needs of male prisoners meant that men had greater access than women to the few available vocational, educational, and work programs provided by prison personnel and civilian volunteers. Like those in the United States, Mexican prison authorities exploited women's labor, restricting prisoners mainly to nonpaid work assignments in traditional women's tasks such as cooking, sewing, cleaning, and laundry. Thus, once released, they continued to be poorly equipped to support themselves and their families adequately. Having little or no formal education, those working outside the home tended to be employed in the service sector before and after incarceration. Most were between eighteen and thirty-five years old (Azaola and Yacamán 1996).

WOMEN IN BOLIVIA

Coca leaf has been grown and consumed safely by Latin American indigenous people for over three thousand years (Laserna 1997). It is used as food, medicine, tea, and in social ceremonies and religious rituals (Rossi 1996). Due to the importance of the crop, Bolivia, like other Latin American nations, initially resisted United States' demands to expand and militarize the war on drugs (Atkins 1998). However, in 1988, the Bolivian government responded to United States threats to impose economic sanctions (Jelsma and Ronken

1998) and intervene militarily, by passing Law 1008, or the Law to Regulate Coca and Controlled Substances.

Law 1008 expanded the definition of trafficking, and violates fundamental due process rights guaranteed detainees under both local and international agreements (Andean Information Network 1996; United Nations 1989). It restricts the right to a defense, freedom from self-incrimination, and access to an impartial judge, a speedy trial, bail, and parole (Andean Information Network 1996).

Along with pressuring passage of Law 1008, the United States has financed, equipped, and trained Bolivian police and military forces (Human Rights Watch 1995a) in both drug interdiction and counterinsurgency tactics. DEA agents joined local forces in carrying out searches, arrests, kidnappings, interrogations, tortures, and the bombing of roads, villages, and housing complexes (Centro de Documentación e Información–Bolivia 1994; de Achá 1996; Human Rights Watch 1995a). Agents have frequently threatened or physically abused family members to force confessions from detainees. Agents have also extorted bribes from family members to secure the release of loved ones from prison (Andean Information Network 1996).

Within this context, there has been an alarming growth in the number of Bolivian women, men, and minors who have been arrested, physically and sexually abused, and/or killed (de Achá 1996; Agreda et al. 1996; Andean Information Network 1996). Hundreds have been framed by police and military personnel and/or forced to confess to crimes under the threat or actual use of physical force, including torture. Many have been detained for up to three years before the adjudication of guilt or innocence. This has occurred even when there was little or no evidence against them. Under these circumstances, it was not uncommon for many to plead guilty, even when innocent, to avoid further abuse and long prison sentences.

In 1994, preventive detention was used in 65 percent of the cases involving presumed violations of Law 1008, though most defendants were charged with low-level, nonviolent crimes (Atkins 1998, 108–109). For example, women primarily helped their families produce coca paste, and transported small quantities of chemical precursors or coca paste (Andean Information Network 1996; de Achá 1998). For those found guilty, prison sentences varied from one to thirty years, depending on whether the individual was convicted of planting, manufacturing, or trafficking drugs, and on whether the person was "found guilty of having sold drugs to someone who becomes intoxicated to the point of death" (Laserna 1997, 150). Fines, court fees, and the confiscation of property accompanied prison sentences. Bolivian attempts to reform the law have been blocked by the United States (Human Rights Watch 1995a).

The enforcement of Law 1008 has also led not only to the growth in the number of women, men, and minors "detained in local police and military stations" as well as in jails and prisons, but also to prison overcrowding and the construction of new prisons subsidized by the United States (Pinto Quintanilla 1999). Of the five thousand prisoners held in Bolivia in 1993, most were held for violation of Law 1008 (Andean Information Network 1997, 9). Minors (between fifteen and twenty years old) composed around 16 percent of those imprisoned for drug-related crimes. They tended to work as sentries or couriers (Laserna 1997). As in the United States, women were more likely than men to be imprisoned for drug offenses. Thus, in 1993, approximately one-quarter of the men but 40 percent of the women were in prison for drug-related crimes (Laserna 1997, 116). By 1997, women made up 16 percent of those imprisoned in Bolivia. Most were single heads of households between twenty and thirty-five years of age. Many had received little or no formal education (de Achá 1998). Like Latinas in the United States, once incarcerated they tended to be abandoned by male partners.

The San Sebastian Women's Prison, like its counterpart for men, is located in downtown Cochabamba. Cochabamba itself is located in the Department of Cochabamba, which contains the Chapare province, where most of the country's coca is grown and where cocaine base is produced. Because the province is at the center of the country's war on drugs, the prison population in Cochabamba is expected to continue to increase.

The San Sebastian Women's Prison was constructed in 1887 for 60 prisoners. By 1991, it held 160 women (Andean Information Network 1997, 11). In 1995, approximately 200 children were living with their parents in the San Sebastian women and men's prisons (Andean Information Network 1997, 11). The children ranged from a few months old to fourteen years of age (de Achá 1998, 135). Although some children lived full-time with their parents in prison, others lived there part-time. Some lived with relatives, friends, or in outside institutions (Andean Information Network 1997). Those who lived in the prison could attend schools or other centers created to serve them during the day. A few of the children and teenagers had the luck to find menial jobs.

According to Gloria Rose Marie de Achá, over 60 percent of the women imprisoned in Bolivia at the end of the 1990s were held for violation of Law 1008 (de Achá 1998, 130). Ninety percent of those held in Cochabamba's San Sebastian Women's Prison, however, were being held for drug trafficking (de Achá 1998, 130–131). Most of the prisoners were migrants, with 70 percent coming from rural areas. Most spoke Quechua (sometimes Aymara) as their first language, and many knew little or no Spanish (de Achá 1998). Even most of those who could speak Spanish had little understanding of the inner workings of the criminal justice system and its procedures. As a result, they could not provide an adequate defense.

In 2000, I toured the San Sebastian Women's Prison, observing firsthand the overcrowded and unsanitary living conditions in which prisoners and their children lived. I saw the hallways and small cells sometimes shared by up to eight people (Andean Information Network 1997). Additional cells, constructed by prisoners themselves out of cardboard or adobe, dangerously increased the size of the building from its original two stories to four. Cells were rented or purchased by prisoners from the government.[8] Prisoners also rented the floor space in the courtyard where over 250 women and their children were forced to sleep due to the lack of cell space. The courtyard also contained sinks where prisoners washed laundry for outsiders in exchange for a small fee. There too, women cooked and prisoners and children socialized and received visitors throughout the day.

Like their male counterparts, women prisoners were responsible for buying food, clothing, toiletries, and other basic necessities for themselves and their children. In 1996, the government allotted prisoners 1.5 bolivianos per day every two months, or $9.00 per month, to meet their basic needs and pay the cost of their cells and of the cleaning and maintenance of the toilets (Andean Information Network 1997). By March 2000, when I visited the prison, the daily allotment had been increased to two bolivianos per day. Even this small amount of money arrived months late.

Although male prisoners were allowed to work in carpentry, cobbling, restaurants, and stores within the prison walls (Andean Information Network 1997; de Achá 1998), sexism restricted women to home-related occupations such as washing and ironing clothes and making and selling food, clothing, jewelry, stuffed animals, and craft products (Andean Information Network 1997; de Achá 1998). In view of these restrictions, it is not surprising that the average monthly wage for women was much lower than that for men.[9] A few women with more resources set up grocery stores inside their cells and sold goods to other prisoners. These women, generally from urban areas, were also able to hire other, generally rural, women to clean their clothes, their cells, and the bathrooms.

Similarly, while male prisoners could live with their wives and children in the men's prison, husbands or partners were rarely allowed to sleep at the women's institution. Men would frequently sneak into the women's prison and stay overnight, but women could be penalized if any man were found in their cells (de Achá 1998). In some cases, women prisoners have been forced to use birth control methods, such as the IUD, to participate in conjugal visits (de Achá 1998).

In view of these conditions, both female and male prisoners organized to meet their basic needs and maintain order within the institutions (Andean Information Network 1997; de Achá 1998; Pinto Quintanilla 1999). These prison organizations existed parallel to those of coca-growing farmers and other sectors of the population on the outside (Agreda et al. 1996). Once released from prison, Bolivian women, like their male counterparts, found themselves displaced, unemployed, and forced to migrate to other parts of the country. Some returned to growing coca for the illegal market as a way to support themselves.

LATINAS IN EUROPE AND THE WAR ON DRUGS

María Cristina Dorado's 1996/1997 study of Latin American women imprisoned in England, Spain, and Germany revealed that Colombian women formed the overwhelming number of Latinas detained for drug trafficking in these countries (Dorado 1998). Latinas in European airports, like those in United States airports, were first stopped for questioning because they came from Latin American countries listed as producers or distributors of illegal drugs, and/or because they fit some stereotype of "drug courier" (Dorado 1998).

The women's initial detention was characterized by isolation and long periods of interrogation. If found to have swallowed balloons filled with drugs, they were subjected to repeated physical examinations and x-rays, given laxatives, and denied showers, adequate meals, and even changes of clothing. In some cases, their hands and feet were shackled to their hospital beds while they slept. Such treatment continued until they had expelled all the balloons. As a result, they suffered much pain and physical discomfort.

Latina drug couriers were often unaware of the type, amount, or value of drugs they were carrying into Europe or the United States. Dorado's (1998) research revealed that 60 percent of the women in her sample were imprisoned for transporting less than a kilo of coke (86). Like their counterparts in the United States, few Latinas arrested in Europe were able to provide an adequate legal defense, due to language barriers, to the lack of competent legal representation, and to lack of knowledge of the criminal justice system (CANY 1992; Dorado 1998). Although international conventions (e.g., European Convention on Human Rights, Vienna Convention) agree that in cases concerning drug trafficking, short-term imprisonment should be used only as a last resort, and that sentences should be uniform across countries, Latinas in Europe were quickly sentenced, the length of penalty depending on the city, the court, and the country involved (Ambos 1996; Dorado 1998). In England, for example, Latinas served longer sentences than did other women imprisoned for similar crimes (Green 1996).

As in the United States, most Latina drug couriers arrested in Europe were single heads of households motivated to transport drugs for economic reasons. Some who initially refused to act as couriers had had their lives and those of family members threatened. Others had been tricked into transporting the drugs by relatives, friends, or acquaintances (Dorado 1998). Most of Dorado's sample were urban Colombian women, ranging from twenty-six to forty years of age and with low educational levels (80). Once sentenced, Latina prisoners, particularly Spanish-monolingual women in Europe and the United States, were alienated from non–Latina prisoners and staff by cultural and/or language barriers. The great distance separating them from their families in Latin America further increased their isolation.

CONCLUSION

Policies pursued by the United States and by Latin American governments have led to the militarization of the war on drugs, the weakening of civil society, and a sharp increase in the number of human rights violations by both law enforcement and military forces. These have been accompanied by the increasing incarceration of Latinas(os) and/or their children, and the building of more penal institutions. Within this context, Latinas have continued to be incarcerated for low-level, nonviolent, drug-related and/or economic crimes. Although, for some Latinas, economic and drug-related crimes were primarily motivated by addiction to drugs and the need to support a drug habit, for most Latinas the main motivation was economic—that is, the need to support themselves and their families.

Racial and ethnic discrimination, income disparities, and other structural barriers continue to keep most Latinas in the United States and Latin America in poverty. Under these conditions, they are constantly searching for ways to survive and thrive emotionally, physically, and economically. The demand for cocaine, primarily from Anglo-Europeans in the United States and Europe, has given Latin American communities that have historically grown coca leaf for local consumption, an additional way to support themselves and their families. The incorporation of such families into the global market, however, has put them at the center of the United States–spearheaded international war on drugs. The fact that coca leaf has been used in multiple ways by indigenous peoples in Latin America for thousands of years without any known negative side effects (Laserna 1997), and that the chemical precursors needed to produce cocaine are generally imported into Latin American nations from the United States and Europe (Rossi 1996), have been conveniently ignored by drug-war policies.

The demand for illegal drugs has also given many Latinas the hope that they can generate enough income to escape their dire economic circumstances. In reality, though some Latinas involved in drug-related enterprises may fare a bit better financially than those not so involved, the minor role the women play in such transactions does not allow them to permanently escape poverty and leaves them open to being arrested and imprisoned for long periods of time.

At the same time, Latinas in the United States and Latin America who are addicted to drugs have been denied adequate access to drug recovery programs by local, state, and federal governments that continually target them for arrest and incarceration and interfere with their chances of recovering from addiction. Ironically, the same elites allow drug kingpins and others working within law enforcement and other government agencies to freely participate in illegal drug enterprises.

Although education and drug treatment have been recognized as the most effective means to reduce the demand for illegal drugs (U.S. Office of National Drug Control Policy 1997), and there has been a recent tendency among some states in the United States to make sentencing and correction reforms (King and Mauer 2002), governing elites throughout the United States and Latin America continue to insist on pursuing policies that emphasize repression and imprisonment. Focusing on demand would require governments to spend more money on education and treatment programs rather than on law enforcement and military solutions (Dunn 1996). The fact that the latter options have been the preferred ones clearly demonstrates that the ultimate goal is not to reduce the demand for illegal drugs but to pursue social agendas that only serve to maintain the subordination of those already oppressed.

NOTES

1. The term "Latinas(os)" includes Chicanas(os). Also, as used here, Latin America refers to the nineteen Spanish-speaking countries located in South and Central America and the Spanish-speaking Caribbean.

2. See Agreda et al. 1996; Azaola and Yacamán 1996; Bloom 1996; CANY 1992; CANY 1999; de Achá 1996; de Achá 1998; del Olmo 1998; Díaz-Cotto 2004; Díaz-Cotto 2006; Human Rights Watch 1995a; Human Rights Watch 1997a; Human Rights Watch 2000; Mann 1995. African Americans continue to make up the majority of those incarcerated nationally. See also Collins 1997; Flateau 1996; Johnson 2003; Lusane 1991; Sudbury 2002; Sudbury 2004.

3. The combination of increasing imprisonment rates and decreasing crime rates, and the ways in which public and private agencies profit from prison construction and prison labor, has led prisoners' rights advocates to speak of the "prison industrial complex" (Critical Resistance Publications Collective 2000; Flateau 1996; Gilmore 1998; Unión del Barrio 1995).

4. See Bagley 1996; Castillo and Harmon 1994; Centro de Documentación e Información–Bolivia 1994; Federal News Service 1992; Kolts 1992; Levine and Kavanau-Levine 1994; Mollen Commission 1994; Reuter 1998; Rossi 1996; U.S. House of Representatives 1984.

5. Drug-related and mandatory sentencing laws include Second Felony Offender Laws, New York's Rockefeller Drug Laws (CANY 1992), Violent Felony Offender Laws, changes in Consecutive Sentence Provisions (Human Rights Watch 1997a; NYSDOCS 1986a), California's Three Strikes Law (Bloom et al. 1994), and Truth-in-Sentencing Laws. These laws were complemented by the 1994 Federal Crime Control Act. By 1994, all fifty states had passed at least one such law (Beckett and Sasson 2000, 176).

6. In 1994, 82 percent of Latinas, seventy-one percent of African American women, and 41 percent of white women imprisoned in New York were committed for drug offenses (Human Rights Watch 1997a, 14).

7. United States federal agencies involved in the war on drugs have included: the Department of Defense; Drug Enforcement Agency; the agency formerly known as the Immigration and Naturalization Service; the Central Intelligence Agency; the

Federal Bureau of Investigation; Customs Service; Federal Aviation Administration; Bureau of Alcohol, Tobacco, and Firearms; Department of Justice Criminal Division; and representatives from the U.S. State and Treasury Departments (Bagley 1996).

8. Cells cost between US$100 and US$400. The monthly rental fee was US$4 to US$30 (AIN 1997, 34).

9. At the time of the Andean Information Network study, male prisoners earned an average of US$36 per month, not including the government stipend. Women prisoners earned only US$5.50 (AIN 1997, 35).

Works Cited

Agreda, Evelin R., Norma Rodríguez, and Alex Contreras. 1996. *Mujeres cocaleras: marchando por una vida sin violencia*. Cochabamba, Bolivia: Comité Coordinador de las Cinco Federaciones del Trópico de Cochabamba.

Alonso, Carlos, ed. 1997. *Guerra antidrogas, democracia, derechos humanos, y militarización en América Latina*. Ciudad de Guatemala, Guatemala: CEDIB, Transnational Institute, y Inforpress Centroamericana.

Ambos, K. 1996. A comparison of sentencing and execution of penalties. In *European Conference on Drug Couriers*, ed. CEP. Zurich: CEP.

Amnesty International. 1998. *United States of America, human rights concerns in the border region with Mexico*. Located at: http://web.amnesty.org/library/Index/engAMR510031998.

Andean Information Network, ed. 1996. *The weight of Law 1008*. Cochabamba, Bolivia: AIN.

———, ed. 1997. *Children of Law 1008*. Cochabamba, Bolivia: AIN.

Atkins, Andy. 1998. The economic and political impact of the drug trade and drug control policies in Bolivia. In *Latin America and the multinational drug trade*, ed. Elizabeth Joyce and Carlos Malamud. New York: St. Martin's Press.

Azaola, Elena, and Cristina José Yacamán. 1996. *Las mujeres olvidadas: Un estudio sobre la situación actual de las cárceles de mujeres en la República Mexicana*. México, D.F., México: Comisión Nacional de Derechos Humanos y el Colegio de México.

Bagley, Bruce M., ed. 1996. *Drug trafficking in the Americas: An annotated bibliography*. Coral Gables, FL: North South Center Press.

Beckett, Katherine, and Theodore Sasson. 2000. *The politics of injustice: Crime and punishment in America*. Thousand Oaks, CA: Pine Forge.

Bloom, Barbara. 1996. Triple jeopardy: Race, class, and gender in women's imprisonment. PhD diss., University of California–Riverside.

Bloom, Barbara, Meda Chesney-Lind, and Barbara Owen. 1994. *Women in California prisons: Hidden victims of the war on drugs*. San Francisco: Center on Juvenile and Criminal Justice.

California Department of Corrections (CDC). 2000. *California prisoners and parolees, 2000 summary statistics*. Sacramento, CA: Department of Corrections, Administrative Services Division.

———. 2005. *Prison census data: Table 3*. Sacramento, CA: Department of Corrections, Offender Information Services Branch.

Castillo, Celerino, III, and Dave Harmon. 1994. *Powderburns: Cocaine, Contras, and the drug war*. Oakville, Ontario: Mosaic.

Centro de Documentación e Información–Bolivia. 1994. *DEA y soberanía en Bolivia: Cronología 1986–1994*. Cochabamba, Bolivia: CEDIB.

Collins, Catherine Fisher. 1997. *The imprisonment of African American women: Causes, conditions, and future implications.* Jefferson, NC: McFarland.

Correctional Association of New York. 1992. *Injustice will be done: Women drug couriers and the Rockefeller Drug Laws.*

———. 1999. *Mandatory injustice: Case histories of women convicted under New York State's Rockefeller Drug Laws.*

Critical Resistance Publications Collective. 2000. Critical resistance to the prison industrial complex. *Journal of Social Justice* 27, 3 (special issue).

de Achá, Gloria Rose Marie. 1996. *Violaciones a los derechos humanos civiles durante la investigación policial en casos detenidos bajo la Ley 1008.* Cochabamba, Bolivia: RRAI, CEDIB.

———. 1998. Características de las mujeres carcelarias en Bolivia. In *Criminalidad y criminalización de la mujer en la región andina,* ed. Rosa del Olmo. Caracas, Venezuela: Nueva Sociedad.

del Olmo, Rosa, ed. 1998. *Criminalidad y criminalización de la mujer en la región andina.* Caracas, Venezuela: Nueva Sociedad.

Díaz-Cotto, Juanita. 1996. *Gender, ethnicity, and the state: Latina and Latino prison politics.* Albany: State University of New York Press.

———. 2000. The criminal justice system and its impact on Latinas(os) in the United States. *The Justice Professional* 13, 1.

———. 2004. Latinas and the war on drugs in the U.S., Latin America, and Europe. In *Global lockdown: Race, gender, and the prison industrial complex,* ed. Julia Sudbury. New York: Routledge.

———. 2006. *Chicana lives and criminal justice: Voices from el barrio.* Austin: University of Texas Press, forthcoming.

Dorado, María Cristina. 1998. Mujeres latinoamericanas en Europa: El caso de Colombia. In *Criminalidad y criminalización de la mujer en la región andina.*

Dorn, Nicholas, Jorgen Jepsen, and Ernesto Savona. 1996. *European drug policies and enforcement.* London: Macmillan.

Dunn, Timothy. 1996. *The militarization of the U.S.–Mexico border, 1978–1992: Low-intensity conflict doctrine comes home.* Austin: University of Texas Press.

Federal News Service. 1992. *Drug money laundering.* U.S. Congress, Senate Governmental Committee, Permanent Investigations Subcommittee Hearing, February 27.

Flateau, John. 1996. *The prison industrial complex: Race, crime, and justice in New York.* Brooklyn, NY: Medgar Evers College, Dubois Bunche Center for Public Policy.

Gabel, Katherine, and Denise Johnston, eds. 1995. *Children of incarcerated parents.* New York: Lexington Books.

Gilmore, Ruth Wilson. 1998. From military Keynesianism to post-Keynesian militarism: Finance capital, land, labor, and opposition in the rising California prison state. PhD diss., State University of New Jersey–Rutgers.

Green, Penny. 1996. *Drug couriers: A new perspective.* London: Quartet Books.

Harrison, Paige, and Allen J. Beck. 2003. *Prison and jail inmates in 2002.* Washington, DC: Bureau of Justice Statistics.

———. 2004. *Prisoners in 2003.* Washington, DC: Bureau of Justice Statistics.

———. 2005. *Prisoners at midyear 2004.* Washington, DC: Bureau of Justice Statistics.

Henriques, Zelma W. 1982. *Imprisoned mothers and their children: A descriptive and analytical study.* Lanham, MD: University Press of America.

Human Rights Watch. 1995a. *Bolivia: Human rights violations and the war on drugs.* New York: HRW.

————. 1995b. *Crossing the line: Human rights abuses along the U.S. border with Mexico persist amid climate of impunity*. New York: HRW.

————. 1996. *All too familiar: Sexual abuse of women in U.S. state prisons*. New York: HRW Women's Rights Project.

————. 1997a. *Cruel and usual: Disproportionate sentences for New York drug offenders*. New York: HRW.

————. 1997b. *Slipping through the crack: Unaccompanied children detained by the U.S. Immigration and Naturalization Service*. Los Angeles: HRW Children's Rights Project.

————. 2000. *Punishment and prejudice: Racial disparities in the war on drugs*. New York: HRW.

Isikoff, Michael. 1991. Study: White students more likely to use drugs. *Washington Post*, February 25.

Jacobson, Michael. 2005. *Downsizing prisons: How to reduce crime and end mass incarceration*. New York: New York University Press.

Jelsma, Martin, and Theo Ronken, eds. 1998. *Democracias bajo fuego: Drogas y poder en América Latina*. Uruguay: TNI, Ediciones Brecha, Acción Andina.

Johnson, Paula C. 2003. *Inner lives: Voices of African American women in prison*. New York: New York University Press.

King, Ryan S., and Marc Mauer. 2002. State sentencing and corrections policy in an era of fiscal restraint. Washington, DC: The Sentencing Project.

Kolts, James G. 1992. The Los Angeles County Sheriff's Department: A report. Los Angeles: Board of Supervisors.

Laserna, Roberto, ed. 1993. *Economía política de las Drogas: Lecturas latinoamericanas*. Cochabamba, Bolivia: CERES-CLACSO.

————, ed. 1997. *Twenty (mis)conceptions on coca and cocaine*. La Paz, Bolivia: Clave Consultores.

Leone, Richard C., and Greg Anrig Jr., eds. 2003. *The war on our freedoms: Civil liberties and the age of freedom*. New York: Public Affairs.

Levine, Michael, and Laura Kavanau-Levine. 1993. *The big white lie*. New York: Thunder's Mouth Press.

Lichtblau, Eric. 2000. U.S. crime decrease sets record. *Press and Sun-Bulletin*, May 8.

————. 2003. U.S. uses terror law to pursue crimes from drugs to swindling. *New York Times*, September 28.

Lusane, Clarence. 1991. *Pipe dream blues: Racism and the war on drugs*. Boston, MA: South End Press.

Maguire, Kathleen, and A. L. Pastore, eds. 2005. *Sourcebook of criminal justice statistics, 2003*. Available at: http://www.albany.edu/sourcebook.

Mann, Coramae Richey. 1995. Women of color and the criminal justice system. In *The criminal justice system and women: Offenders, victims, and workers*, 2nd edition, ed. Barbara Raffel Price and Natalie J. Sokoloff. New York: McGraw-Hill.

Mauer, Mark, and Tracy Huling. 1995. *Young black Americans and the criminal justice system: Five years later*. Washington, DC: The Sentencing Project.

Meddis, Sam Vincent. 1989. Whites, not blacks, at the core of the drug crisis. *USA Today*: December 20.

Mollen Commission. 1994. *Mollen Commission report*. New York City, July 7.

New York State Department of Correctional Services. Division of Program Planning, Research, and Evaluation.1986a. *Characteristics of female inmates held under custody, 1975–1985*. Albany, NY: New York State Department of Correctional Services.

————. 1986b. *Selected characteristics of the department's Hispanic inmate population*. Albany, NY: New York State Department of Correctional Services.

————. 2001. *2000–2001 crime and justice annual report*. Albany, NY: New York State Department of Correctional Services.

————. 2002. *Men and women under custody: 1987–2001*. Albany, NY: New York State Department of Correctional Services.

Pettiway, Leon E. 1987. Participation in crime partnerships by female drug users: The effects of domestic arrangements, drug use, and criminal involvement. *Criminology* 25, 3.

Pinto Quintanilla, Juan Carlos. 1999. *Cárceles y familia: La experiencia penal de San Sebastian en Cochabamba*. Cochabamba, Bolivia: terre des hommes.

Reuter, Peter. 1998. Foreign demand for Latin American drugs: The USA and Europe. In *Latin America and the multinational drug trade*.

Ross, Luana. 1998. *Inventing the savage: The social construction of Native American criminality*. Austin: University of Texas Press.

Rossi, Adriana. 1996. *Narcotráfico y amazonía ecuatoriana*. Buenos Aires, Argentina: Kohen and Asociados International.

The Sentencing Project. 2003. *New inmate population figures demonstrate need*.

Sudbury, Julia. 2002. "If I die here, least I'll be free": Black women "mules" and the transnational prison industrial complex, *Harvard Journal of African American Public Policy*, viii.

————, ed. 2004. *Global lockdown: Race, gender, and the prison industrial complex*. New York: Routledge.

Unión del Barrio. 1995. The political economy of prisons in occupied America. ¡*La Verdad!* October–December.

United Nations. 1977. *Single Convention on Narcotic Drugs*. New York: U.N.

————. 1987. *The United Nations and drug abuse control*. New York: U.N.

————. 1989. *Body of Principles for the Protection of All Persons under any Form of Detention or Imprisonment*. New York: U.N.

————. 1991. *U.N. Convention against the Illicit Traffic of Narcotics*. New York: U.N.

United Press International (UPI). 1992. Mexican border police abuse illegal immigrants, report says. February 24.

United States Department of Commerce. 2001. *The Hispanic population: Census 2000 brief*: Table 2, p. 4. Washington: U.S. Census Bureau. May.

United States Department of Justice. Bureau of Justice Statistics. 2001. *Prisoners in 2000*. Washington: U.S. Department of Justice.

United States Congress. Committee on Armed Services. 1990. *The Andean drug strategy and the role of the U.S. military*, Washington, DC: House Committee on Armed Services, 101st Cong., 1st Sess.

————. Committee on the Judiciary. 1984. *Police Misconduct*. Hearings before the Subcommittee on Criminal Justice, 98th Cong., 1st Sess. Washington, DC.

U.S. Office of National Drug Control Policy. 1997. *The National Drug Control Strategy, 1997*. Washington, DC: The White House Executive Office of the President.

Watterson, Kathryn. 1996. *Women in prison: Inside the concrete womb*, rev. edition. Boston, MA: Northeastern University Press.

Chapter 12

Tough Men, Tough Prisons, Tough Times

The Globalization of Supermaximum Secure Prisons

Vivien Miller

In May 2004, the publication of photographs showing U.S. military personnel threatening and humiliating detainees at Abu Ghraib prison near Baghdad provoked widespread international condemnation. The iconic image of a hooded male prisoner standing on a box, arms outstretched and with electrical wires connected to his arms and genitals, symbolized the sexual degradation and humiliation of both the individual prisoner and the collective Iraqi nation. The images exhibited also a stark disregard for the rule of law and bore disturbing similarities to torture practices associated with the ousted regime of Saddam Hussein. The Bush administration's approach to prosecuting the war on terror, including the need for "productive" interrogations, critics argued, had created a climate where contempt for the rules and unchecked abuse flourished.

Zillah Eisenstein describes Abu Ghraib as "hyper-imperialist/masculinity run amok." Yet such "obscene practices of human degradation" did not originate with the war on terror; they were already embedded in domestic prisons in the United States and practices on inmates in, for example, solitary or supersecure confinement (Eisenstein 2004, 3; Human Rights Watch 2000). As *New York Times* columnist Bob Herbert concludes in his op-ed piece describing incidents of sexual humiliation at Dooly State Prison in Georgia (in 1996), "the treatment of detainees in Iraq was far from an aberration. They too were treated like animals, which was simply a logical extension of the way we treat prisoners here at home" (Herbert 2004).

Acknowledgment that such actions do not stem solely from post–September 11 security concerns and the war on terror enables us to view the confinement of suspected terrorists and "enemy combatants" through a wider criminological lens of punishment, one that appreciates the dynamics of race and gender in contemporary U.S. penal policy. To explore these issues, this chapter focuses on the connections between the treatment of prisoners in those military prisons in Iraq, Afghanistan, and Cuba that have been set up offshore as part of the war on terror, and practices in and justifications for supermaximum secure prisons in the United States. Starting with the historical development and contemporary application of supermaximum secure confinement in the United States, specifically in Florida, the chapter turns to the U.S. naval base at Guantánamo Bay, Cuba, where up to six hundred foreign nationals have been incarcerated without trial. These domestic and offshore penal establishments are underpinned by, and reinforcing of, a particular racialized ideal of masculinity.

ON THE ORIGINS OF SUPERMAX

All prison regimes and correctional institutions have struggled with, and continue to search for, the most effective and humane means of coping with and disciplining difficult, violent, and incorrigible prisoners. Earlier reliance on corporal punishment gave way in the nineteenth and twentieth centuries to a series of practices that sought to create subordinate and obedient inmates, practices including: solitary confinement and the withholding of food, the breaking of prisoners' sentences into successively less restrictive and punitive parts to inculcate good habits, and rewards for good behavior, such as "good time" or "gain time" laws. As is well documented, Western societies in the eighteenth and nineteenth centuries saw a shift away from physical punishment to the body, and from punishment as public spectacle, to "sentences defined in terms of labor and time" served away from the public gaze (McGowan 1998). Penal reformers at the time urged the adoption of solitary confinement as an alternative to flogging for *all* prisoners, not just the most difficult, "to frustrate vice and promote virtue among prisoners" (McGowan 1998, 77; Emsley 1996, 273). By isolating the individual, it was thought, one encouraged prisoners to reflect on their deeds and clear their consciences in a penal regime based on the severity and certainty of punishment.

Severity and certainty of punishment governed also the first super-secure federal prison, opened on Alcatraz Island in San Francisco Bay in July 1934. Alcatraz was a small disciplinary unit for the most dangerous, escape-prone, and troublesome federal prisoners, who had been transferred from state and other federal institutions (Johnston 1949). It was intended as a "powerful symbol of the consequences for serious criminal conduct," rather than only a means of controlling prison troublemakers. Incapacitation and isolation rather than rehabilitation dominated, until the prison closed in 1963 and was replaced by the federal prison at Marion, Illinois (Ward and Werlich 2003, 55–56).

The origin of the modern supermaximum security prison is usually dated to the lockdown at Marion in October 1983 that followed a week of violence in which prisoners were attacked, and two prison officers killed by inmates, on the same day. A decade previously, in 1973, many states had begun transferring difficult prisoners to a 435-bed "control unit" at Marion that was designed to provide "long-term, highly controlled segregation for inmates with records of serious violence" (King 1999, 163). In 1983, Marion was awarded the previously unheard-of security rating of Level 6, and became a model for managing violent and seriously disruptive prisoners, who were often linked to white supremacist or racially exclusive gangs. In one fell swoop, the U.S. penal system opted for concentration while the prison authorities in other countries, such as Great Britain, continued to disperse high-security-risk prisoners in comparatively small numbers throughout a number of maximum-security prisons, as they had since the late 1960s (King 1999; see Liebling 2002).

Nearly 2 percent of the United States prison population, or some twenty thousand prisoners, are housed in supermaximum security facilities or units (Human Rights Watch 2000). These days, in at least thirty-six states and the federal prison system, the most difficult inmates are removed from general prison populations to one of approximately sixty extended-confinement facilities known as "supermax" prisons, "control unit" prisons, or "close management facilities." Examples include California's Pelican Bay Security Housing Unit (SHU), opened in 1989, Indiana's Maximum Control Complex at Westville, Kentucky's High Security Unit for Women at Lexington, and the federal administrative "maximum" (ADX) prison at Florence, Colorado. Such facilities serve not to contain those who have committed the most heinous crimes, but rather to control potentially disruptive inmates. Individuals are sent to them usually by prison panels or bureaucrats because of their behavior elsewhere in the penal system, rather than on the basis of the crimes for which they were convicted in a court of law.

Although supermax prisons typically are justified by a belief that the removal and isolation of the most violent, assaultive, and escape-prone inmates from the main body of less disruptive prisoners will result in a more efficient and safer penal system, it is clear that certain individuals—namely those who are male and either African American or Latino—tend to be considered disruptive or dangerous more often than others. There is, after all, no freestanding supermax facility for women, although some women are held in high-security control units. Similarly, William Chambliss found that on one particular day in 1993, 98 percent of the "supermax" inmates confined in supermaximum detention in Baltimore were African American (see Chambliss' study quoted in Miller 1997, 227). Data from the SHU at Pelican Bay from the 1990s showed similarly disproportionate numbers of Latino and African American men in supermaximum detention, guarded by predominately white corrections officers (Weinstein and Cummins 1996, 314).

Supermaximum secure facilities differ from other maximum-security prisons in their extreme isolation of prisoners, their reduced environmental stimuli, their negligible recreational, vocational, or educational opportunities, and their extraordinary levels of electronic surveillance and control. Supermax prisoners typically spend twenty-three hours of each day in solitary cells. Depending on their behavior, they may be entitled to three showers per week, one short phone call per month, limited noncontact family visits. They are always shackled and handcuffed when moved from their cells. They may not visit the central library, if one exists, and they will receive only limited educational and religious services, and, usually, no job training at all. Research in Indiana showed that such conditions undermined prisoner-guard relations and were "conducive to custodial abuse." Verbal confrontations escalated to physical assaults, and hostilities became personalized (Human Rights Watch 1997, 27–28). In such extreme contexts, the temptation and provocation to use excessive force against prisoners who have threatened or assaulted staff members can become a real problem (Human Rights Watch 2000; Ward and Werlich 2003). This is illustrated by events that occurred in Florida at the end of the twentieth century.

DOMESTIC CONFINEMENT: SUPERMAX IN FLORIDA

Florida's more than 82,000 inmates are housed in 131 prisons with thirty thousand employees. The number of inmates on "close management" in Florida is reported to have more than tripled during the late 1990s, from 1,009 in mid-1995 to 3,176 in mid-1999 (Smith 1999). The most violent and troublesome prisoners are sent to maximum solitary confinement units at the Florida State Prison (FSP) at Starke or other state maximum-security facilities. For example, they may be housed in X-Wing at Starke, in one of thirty windowless cells measuring nine feet by seven feet, complete with metal bed and thin mattress, a stainless steel sink and toilet, or in B-Wing at Union C.I., which has ninety-six similarly dimly lit and heat-stifling cells. As one journalist notes, "X Wing or X-Ray Wing as it is officially called, is the end of the line for prisoners who refuse to follow the rules. Criticized by human rights activists as a form of cruel and unusual punishment, it is at the end of a vast hallway separated by numerous sliding, locked gates" (Becker 1999a). Inmates have no access to television, few possessions, little exercise, and infrequent showers. There are also strip cells to underline that an inmate has no right to privacy.

Corrections officers in contemporary Florida can use waist chains, legirons, and, on medical orders, a four-point restraint to tie a prisoner to the bed. They can also incapacitate inmates through the use of electrical devices (Becker and Freedberg 1999a). Now renamed Q-Wing, this wing has video cameras and pepper spray to add to the methods of surveillance and control: "No proponent of tough prisons need worry about conditions on 'Q Wing,' the darkest corner of Florida's most notorious prison" (Tobin 2002; Smith 2002). However, Florida inmates described close management "as nothing short of hell," and recounted "a constant struggle to keep their minds clear, and amid perpetual boredom, a never-ending build-up of anger. Some say they bide their time plotting revenge" (Smith 1999).

On July 17, 1999, Florida State Prison inmate Frank Valdes died in X-Wing from a beating by prison guards. Thirty-six-year-old Valdes was a career criminal. At the time of his death, he was under capital sentence for murdering a Palm Beach County corrections officer during an escape attempt in 1987, and had been on X-Wing for several months, where he was threatening to report physical abuse and medical neglect of prisoners to news media. The circumstances of his death demonstrate the damaging interplay of race and gender that occurs in the extreme conditions of supermaximum secure detention.

An altercation between Valdes and a prison officer took place on July 16. The officer returned the next day to inform Valdes he was writing up a disciplinary report for threatening him the day before; Valdes responded with racial abuse—"Fuck you, nigger"—and threatened to kill the guard (Smith and Morgan 1999). A "cell-extraction" team of five guards returned to forcibly remove Valdes from his cell. Guards admitted that they struggled with Valdes, but denied using excessive force. Valdes was taken to the prison infirmary, where no serious injuries were reported. He returned to his cell and died that afternoon. Correctional officers claimed most of Valdes' injuries had been "self-inflicted." They claimed Valdes began climbing the cell bars, then repeatedly threw himself on the concrete floor of his cell, and banged his head against his steel bed. Autopsy reports showed that Valdes' injuries—twenty-two broken ribs, a broken nose, broken sternum, fractured left clavicle, the jaw broken in two places, other disfiguring wounds to the face, and a shoe or boot print on his stomach—were more consistent with a beating (Smith and Becker 1999; Becker 1999b; Boedy 2000).

A state criminal investigation began immediately, followed by a federal civil rights investigation, but it would take prosecutors many months to penetrate the wall of official silence of the "good ol' boy" network of guards. The *St. Petersburg Times* launched a probe into state prison conditions in general and close confinement conditions in particular. As several guards broke ranks, and as prisoners were interviewed, it became apparent that, amid a culture where officials ignored some guards' overzealous conduct and punished whistle blowers, some corrections officers used excessive and unprovoked violence to remind inmates who was in charge.

Stories emerged of a number of male guards admitting a willingness to administer harsh physical punishments to unruly prisoners, especially African American men. Racism against African American officers was also said to be rampant, practiced by both inmates and fellow corrections officers. A clique of white guards at one institution was alleged to wear knotted key chains to signify they were prepared to cover up improper use of force. Others engaged in sexually inappropriate conduct toward female prisoners, at other facilities. Inmates reported their fear of the "catchdog" or enforcer "who could be relied upon to rough up inmates who were out of line—inmates who[m,] in prison lingo,'showed their butts' by acting up or complaining about their civil rights" (Becker 1999b; Smith 2001). Some allegations by prisoners were dismissed as untrue. Complaints of inmates being choked, kneed, punched in shower cells or strip cells after they were restrained, and denied medical treatment, however, were not found groundless.

Conditions of employment for correctional officers also were scrutinized, and resulted in calls from many quarters for greater professionalism through better training, more stringent education requirements, and improved pay (at the time, less than $25,000 for some ranks) to counter a prison culture grown too tolerant of brutality and violence. Further, one in six corrections officers at FSP were found to have arrest and/or criminal records, ranging from drunken driving to battery to manslaughter, often dating from after they were hired—raising additional questions about on-the-job stress and official hiring and appraisal procedures (Becker, Smith, and Freedberg 1999).

The Valdes case highlighted further the incidence of prison violence. Auditors noted in 2000 that inmate-on-inmate batteries had increased 39 percent over the previous year, and inmate-on-prison staff batteries had increased by 7 percent. They questioned whether longer sentences, more determinate sentences, fewer opportunities for early release, and less incentive to behave, coupled with shortages of work and of education programs, were to blame (Oppel 2000). Newspaper reports painted a picture of rampant violence and unmanageable inmates who routinely punched, stabbed, threw feces, and spat at guards. Guards responded with verbal and sometimes physical aggression (Becker and Freedberg 1999a; 1999b).

Although the FSP warden had declared that prolonged solitary confinement was rarely used, in a December 1999 exposé of Florida's use of "near-perpetual lockdown" or "close management" and its impact on long-term or life-term prisoners, journalist Adam C. Smith found some had been in close confinement for up to twelve years. For example, twenty-nine-year-old Frank Lowry, an inmate at Santa Rosa C. I. serving a twelve-year term for armed robbery, had spent all but twenty-one days since 1995 alone "in a roughly 60-square-foot cell." Many correctional officers welcomed concentration as providing safer prisons for prison officers and inmates, but there remained ongoing concerns as to the psychological and physical effects of this type of confinement on inmates, many destined eventually to reenter free society. Lowry wrote to Smith, "I've seen guys slice their wrist, their arms, and their necks. I've seen guys bite chunks out of their arms trying to sever the main veins.

I know guys who would swallow bed springs, tooth brushes, strips of Coke cans, nails, razor blades, pens, pencils—anything that would puncture their insides just to get away from the CM cells" (Smith 1999).

In theory, the segregation of dangerous inmates from the general prison population should produce safer prisons, and the tough supermax conditions should deter other prisoners from violent or disruptive behavior. However, in his analysis of current practice, criminologist Roy King argues that the "use of super-max custody [in the U.S.] has become at best a pre-emptive strategy that is almost certainly disproportionate in scale to the problems faced and at worst a routine and cynical perversion of penological principles" (King 1999, 163). Moreover, the retreat from rehabilitation that super-max embodies at its most extreme has exacerbated class, race, and gender antagonisms, and increased the volatility of prisons (Sabo, Krupers, London 2001). Thus, in its review of two supermaximum security prisons in Indiana in the mid-1990s, Human Rights Watch warned, "Without guidance and control by principled authorities, supermaximum security prisons can become as lawless as the prisoners they confine" (Human Rights Watch 1997, 3).

Men, manhood, and masculinity in prisons are constructed around domination and aggression, and are always vulnerable to loss. Physical assault and sexual violence are embedded in prisoner hierarchies in which violent men are located at the top and feminized males at the bottom (Man and Cronan 2001, 130–131). Elite males in prison range from administrators to guards to gang leaders to prison toughs. The prison code therefore contains a number of commandments: suffer in silence, never admit fear, do not snitch, do not act gay, do not help the authorities, do not trust anyone, always be ready to fight, and always be prepared to kill. Disciplinary problems increase as men "need to maintain a tough image so they can avoid victimization on the yard. Prison magnifies male competition and violence, and the hyper masculine posturing continues even after a prisoner is placed in solitary confinement" (Krupers 2001, 193). Further, prison conduct and cultures are often tied directly to racial affiliation, where "the predatory culture of the street, centered on hypermasculinist notions of honor, toughness, and coolness has entered into and transfixed the social structure and culture of jails and prisons" (Wacquant 2001, 110). Escalating racial and ethnic tensions, rampant overcrowding, and increased inmate frustrations and belligerence justify increased administrative deployment of lockdowns, searches, and solitary confinement. Thus, the supermax merely magnifies the problems of prison violence, rather than offering a constructive solution.

In spite of the identification of the endemic and institutional nature of problems in the Florida system and elsewhere, and in apparent willful disregard for their enormous social and economic costs, new supermaximum facilities continue to be established throughout the United States. Public indifference, judicial reluctance to interfere in correctional policies, and a political climate that encourages elected officials to demand more punitive forms of punishment have fueled supermax expansion. Thus, "[p]rolonged segregation that previously would have been deemed extraordinary and inconsistent with concepts of dignity, humanity, and decency has become a corrections staple" (Human Rights Watch 2000, 2).

Recently, a new overseas market for these institutions has emerged. The commencement of the so-called war on terror accelerated the establishment by the U.S. military of super-high-security facilities around the world. There are significant differences between the function and internal regimes of military-run prisons and civilian or domestic prisons, yet there are also many similarities. Those military prisons set up as part of the war on terror, such as Guantánamo Bay, Cuba, have adopted many of the architectural designs and the management practices associated with supermaximum secure facilities in the domestic U.S. penal system.

THE GLOBAL U.S. PENAL ARCHIPELAGO?

In January 2002, the U.S. government established a special military prison at the American naval base at Guantánamo Bay to house detainees from the war in Afghanistan (the prison had previously been used to hold Haitian and Cuban refugees intercepted on the high seas). Described by Amnesty International as an "American gulag in the Caribbean" (Amnesty International 2005), the detention center is made up of a number of distinct buildings and facilities holding specific populations. It is a complex institution that is unaccountable to the U.S. courts or public and, in the main, inaccessible to anyone other than members of the International Red Cross and military lawyers for the confined. Much of what is known about the conditions at Guantánamo comes from reports by FBI agents who witnessed detainee abuse and from the statements of former detainees (see Human Rights Watch 2004; 2005; Rose 2004). These witness accounts suggest striking parallels with the U.S. domestic practice of supermaximum security.[1]

Camp X-Ray, the first, makeshift prison camp at Guantánamo Bay, consisted of tiny cages open to the intense Caribbean sun and lacking in privacy. Prisoners were forbidden to speak to each other. Early photographs from the camp, authorized for publication across the world, showed inmates clad in orange boiler suits, with blacked-out goggles over their eyes and masks over their mouths and noses, manacled, and kneeling in submission in their individual cages or transported around the camp lying prostrate on, and shackled to, trolleys. The pictures caused international outrage and brought allegations of torture (Amnesty International 2005; Human Rights Watch 2005).

Inmates at Guantánamo Bay were transferred in April 2002 to the purpose-built prison camp, Camp Delta. Here, they were confined in wire-mesh cells measuring six feet eight inches by eight feet for over twenty-three hours per day, and allowed very limited, solitary exercise three times a week. Arc lights burned into the cells through the night, and armed snipers occupied the watch-towers to ensure that the detainees could be viewed at all times and that per-manent surveillance was not impeded. Prisoners being transferred to the interrogation units were chained at the ankles, waist, and hands, and guards held each man's arms as he walked (Human Rights Watch 2004; 2005; Harris and Wazir 2002).

The prison camp was designed principally for interrogation rather than for detention, but as inmates remained there for months, then years, the dis-tinctions between unlimited interrogation and indefinite detention became increasingly blurred. As of January 2005, some 550 people (including at least three who were minors when taken into custody) were being held as "enemy combatants" at Guantánamo, though only four faced charges. The interroga-tion techniques utilized included stripping prisoners naked, covering them with hoods, depriving them of sleep and light, and other forms of sensory depriva-tion. They were officially termed "not quite torture, but as close as you can get" or "torture lite" (Dyer 2003). Several other countries employ such tech-niques, which are not legal under the U.N. Convention against Torture and Other Cruel, Inhuman, or Degrading Treatment or Punishment, but, as Amanda Ripley observed, "since [U.S.] military and government agencies operating abroad function with fewer legal constraints, they take more risks" (Ripley 2004, 43). Guerrilla fighters and hardened terrorists were undoubtedly harder to manipulate than ordinary domestic offenders, but it is also the case that the Geneva Conventions have routinely and deliberately been overlooked in the wake of 9/11.

Details about life inside the camp, the treatment of prisoners, and interro-gation and punishment regimes emerged in 2004 following the release of some of the "low value" detainees, who have alleged months and years of ill-treatment and often abusive interrogations. One former detainee described the manner in which he was transferred from his cellblock to an interrogation booth. He recalled his hands being shackled to a body belt with another set of chains attached to his ankles, severely restricting his leg movement. He was then left to lie on the interrogation booth floor. His request to visit the bathroom was denied, and he was forced to urinate in the corner of the interrogation booth. His interrogator used a mop to cover the inmate in his own urine while racially abusing him (Mubanga and Rose 2005, 4; see also Human Rights Watch 2004; Amnesty International 2005).

This account was very similar to a joint statement issued by two other for-mer detainees in which they described how they were chained to the floor for hours and seated on plastic chairs that could be easily hosed down when pris-oners urinated during the course of interrogations. They complained also of "short shackling," where they were forced to squat without a chair with their hands chained between their legs and to the floor. Air conditioning was turned up, strobe lighting and loud music were played to inflict further discomfort, and dogs were used to frighten detainees (Human Rights Watch 2004, 14).

Minor violations of camp rules could result in punishment from an "Instant Reaction Force" riot squad. Inmates found guilty of infractions could be subject to "CI [comfort item] loss," where books, cups, and board games were removed. The "BI [basic item] loss" punishment meant the inmate's "thin mattress, trousers, shirts, towel, blanket, and flip-flops were all taken away, leaving him naked except for boxer shorts in an empty metal box." In the punishment "Quebec block," blankets were removed between 6 A.M. and 11 P.M., and no communication with other prisoners was allowed. Guards could also reward or reprove prisoners by housing them with prisoners who spoke the same language or transferring them to detention blocks where prisoners spoke unfamiliar or different languages (Mubanga and Rose 2005). Some prisoners were sent to Camp Echo, the supermaximum security part of Guantánamo Bay, for protesting their detention by spitting, fighting, and throwing feces at guards.

Those who spent long periods of confinement there were reported to have developed severe mental health problems (Mubanga and Rose 2005, 5). Their reactions mirror those in the domestic U.S. prison system, where prolonged social isolation can exacerbate and create severe mental health problems among inmates. Inmates in supermaximum security may suffer from depression, acute anxiety, uncontrollable rage, claustrophobia, hallucinations, and loss of concentration and memory (Human Rights Watch 1997; 2000).

In early 2002, the Red Cross began to voice its concerns over the mental and physical deterioration of the Guantánamo detainees in the indefinite and isolating carceral regime. Prisoners had responded to the conditions of their confinement by engaging in hunger strikes, incidences of self-harm, and a reported twenty-eight suicide attempts, and officials noted some inmates developed significant psychological problems (Dodd and White 2004). For example, a March 2002 account reported that more than one hundred prisoners at Camp X-Ray had gone on hunger strike after guards removed a prisoner's turban during a prayer session (Campbell 2002). In 2005 media reports emerged indicating that such behavior had become endemic and military medics were force-feeding numerous individuals, in defiance, once again, of international law (Rose 2006).

International criticism of the regime at Guantánamo Bay focused both on the treatment accorded the detainees and the physical conditions of their confinement and on the wider issue of human rights. For example, Amnesty International asserts that all those currently held in Guantánamo are arbitrarily and unlawfully detained (Amnesty International 2005, 4). From 2002, an indefinite sentence of preventative detention in a penal colony was viewed as

the appropriate means of dealing with dangerous foreign criminals and terrorists. Prisoners were held without formal charges, not told of the evidence
against them, and questioned by U.S. interrogators without legal restriction,
ostensibly because they were hardened terrorists linked to violence, but also to
provide information about other suspected terrorists.[2] As human rights lawyer
Clive Stafford-Smith observed, "The steps the U.S. is taking are extreme, and the
rule of law seems to be the first casualty in the war on terrorism" (Stafford-
Smith 2002).

In April 2002, Amnesty International sent a sixty-two-page memorandum
to the U.S. government listing complaints over the treatment of detainees in
Cuba (and Afghanistan), and over "its failure to respect fundamental international human rights standards" (Amnesty International 2005; Engel 2002). The
Bush administration responded by arguing that the Geneva Convention did
not cover conditions at the camp because the inmates were "enemy combatants" rather than "prisoners of war." Kate Allen, director of Amnesty International U.K., noted, "This has been disastrous human rights public relations for
a country that has regularly promoted itself as a 'beacon' for democracy, justice, and the rule of law" (Allen 2004). Judicial criticism mounted in late 2003.
For example, Lord Steyn, a senior law lord in Britain, in November 2003
delivered a scathing attack on the treatment of detainees by the U.S. government and its military and civilian courts, branding this treatment "a monstrous
failure of justice." Others were keen to remark that Britain had also detained
indefinitely without charge suspected terrorists, at Belmarsh and Woodhill high-
security prisons. The Muslim Council of Britain, for example, had termed
Belmarsh Prison, in southeast London, Britain's own "mini Guantánamo Bay"
(Webster and Ford 2005; Verkaik and Brown 2004).[3]

Amnesty International issued another report on May 13, 2005, castigating
the U.S. administration for "jettison[ing] basic human rights protections for
detainees" and keeping detainees in legal limbo. Although some hoped that
the release of several inmates from Camp Delta in late 2004 and early 2005
might signify the beginning of the end of the current regime, at the time of
writing Guantánamo Bay remains in full operation. It has been reported that
the Pentagon has been exploring the legality and practicality of constructing
a smaller permanent prison to house those detainees it considers too dangerous to release. Another option, however, would be to construct prisons in the
detainees' countries of origin so they could be confined on home soil. This
further extension of the "American archipelago of international prisons" would,
it is charged, allow the U.S. government to "minimize scrutiny of its interrogation techniques" (Watson 2005; Editorial 2005). Indeed, as ongoing accusa-
tions about secret offshore CIA prisons suggest, supermaximum security has
already become a template for the export of U.S. prison regimes overseas.

Evidence that the interrogation techniques used at Guantánamo Bay and Abu Ghraib had been exported from the U.S. domestic prison system emerged as specific individuals came under press and official scrutiny. In Abu Ghraib alone, one of the army reservists convicted of abusing Iraqi prisoners, Charles Graner, was a corrections officer at a Pennsylvania supermaximum security prison in his civilian life, and had previously received several reprimands for mistreating U.S. inmates (Buncombe 2005; Baxter 2005; Watson 2005). Similarly, O. Lane McCotter, appointed by Secretary of Defense Donald Rumsfeld to oversee the development of the new Iraqi corrections system, was formerly a prison administrator in Texas, New Mexico, and Utah. Observers noted that the abuse and humiliation at Abu Ghraib were "eerily similar" to the video and written evidence of bound and naked Utah prisoners in the former isolation chamber at Utah's Point of the Mountain Prison (Burton 2004).[4]

CONCLUSION: THE UNITED STATES AS PENAL HEGEMON

In 1910 Winston Churchill famously admonished the British House of Commons, "The mood and temper of the public in regard to the treatment of crime and criminals is one of the most unfailing tests of the civilization of any country." Should the supermax Camp Delta and Abu Ghraib therefore be regarded as measures of contemporary U.S. civilization? One journalist declared, "It may not amount to torture, but the cramped metal cages baking in tropical heat in the U.S. base in Guantánamo Bay seemed to belong to another, more brutal era. This is a sort of Caribbean gulag, and without doubt the scene before us would raise concern if it was being run by any other country" (Borger 2002).

The abuses that have taken place in Florida, Cuba, Iraq, and elsewhere underline how easily concentration and supermaximum security lead to inhumanity and degradation. However, in an age when many Americans believe they are experiencing high domestic crime rates, together with global threats from terrorism, public sensitivity is inevitably limited. In the United States, "getting tough" on criminals has occurred hand in hand with a hardening of attitudes and implementation of punitive policies toward welfare recipients, immigrants, and other politically unpopular and marginalized groups (see Flavin, Calavita, Bosworth, and Sanchez, this volume). The shift from welfarism to conservative neoliberalism has given rise to new conceptualizations of "dangerousness" and dangerous populations that, in turn, has led to an ever-increasing penal population and to the construction of supermaximum secure facilities (see Mauer 1999; 2001).

It is unclear, in other words, whether events at Guantánamo Bay and in Abu Ghraib will have an impact on public attitudes toward the treatment of domestic offenders or prevent prisoners from being abused or killed in circumstances similar to those surrounding Frank Valdes in Florida. As Bob Herbert observes, "Very few Americans have raised their voices in opposition to our shameful prison policies. And I'm convinced that's primarily because the inmates are viewed as less than human" (Herbert 2004). Prisoner abuse—whether occurring domestically in prisons throughout the United States, or at Abu Ghraib and Guantánamo Bay—not only encourages the objectification and abuse of people we believe are of lesser value than ourselves, but it can become "normal" or "natural" so that it goes unnoticed and unchallenged, unless public opinion is sufficiently roused (Tarrant 2004, 16). Without the photographic evidence of the objectification and abuses in Cuba and Iraq, it is unclear whether the public would have raised their voices in protest. Frank Valdes and the other men in domestic supermax prisons are unsympathetic characters, largely out of sight and out of mind.

The U.S. domestic prison has come to be viewed as an uncivilized institution, "a site of misrule and disorder rather than civility and rehabilitation; as a site whose conditions even the prison authorities themselves were increasingly prepared to recognize were beyond the boundaries of what was culturally tolerable in a supposedly civilized society" (Pratt 1998, 509). The prison is seen as the site of riots, sexual violence and murder, and other disturbances, and prisoners as irredeemably bad people, often predators or superpredators who pose an incontrovertible risk to the public. These images took hold at precisely the same time that contemporary prison populations became overwhelmingly African American and Latino. Further, the predominance of non-whites and the fusion of prison and ghetto cultures helped perpetuate popular (but historically grounded) associations of blackness with criminality and violence (Wacquant 2001, 117). A permanently heightened fear of crime inevitably lowered thresholds of sensitivity and embarrassment, while a permanently heightened fear of international terrorism has had a similar effect on the treatment of prisoners abroad. The humiliation, degradation, and brutalization of prisoners thus have acquired "legitimacy" in select circumstances.

The putative function of supermaximum security prisons is to deter bad behavior and ensure greater safety for all prisoners, but the realities of such confinement (such as the total isolation, sensory deprivation, technological monitoring and surveillance) and the impact on inmates (including exacerbated racial and ethnic tensions, increased mental health problems, increased sense of injustice, and resentment among volatile prisoners) promises the opposite. Increased use of "prisons within prisons" leads to human rights abuses and violations of international standards on the treatment of prisoners. At the very least, the application of such confinement increases the distance between staff and prisoners, reveals the fragility of custodial concepts such as safety and respect, and engenders an almost complete lack of empathy among staff;

at worst, the conditions degrade and brutalize staff as they are complicit in or witness to abuses and violations. Still, supermaximum detention is a management tool that requires no emotional or economic investment in the rehabilitation of the individual inmate, and has obvious benefits for cash-strapped, overcrowded, and potentially unmanageable prison systems both in the United States and abroad. The "global prison economy" enables the United States to exercise "an enormous influence over the development of the style of state punishment throughout the world," already evident in Turkey and South Africa, for example (Davis 2003, 101–102); the war on terror allows the United States to stretch that influence even further.

NOTES

1. The prison also seems to pioneer techniques later used elsewhere in the "war on terror." In 2003, for example, Lt. Gen. Sanchez laid out specific interrogation techniques for use by coalition forces in Iraq that were modeled on those used against detainees at Guantánamo Bay (Sanchez 2003). These strategies, eventually employed for instance at Abu Ghraib, included sleep "management," the inducement of fear at two levels of severity, loud music and sensory agitation, "stress positions," and the use of canine units to exploit the detainees' fears of dogs.

2. On June 29, 2004, the U.S. Supreme Court used a 1789 law to rule that detainees at Guantánamo Bay could challenge their detention in U.S. courts and could sue over alleged international human rights abuses. The prison was no longer a legal black hole beyond the reach of the domestic courts. At the same time, the Pentagon announced the establishment of the first, five-member, U.S. military tribunals since World War II, to try four Guantánamo suspects for conspiracy to commit war crimes and other offenses (Lewis 2004).

3. In December 2004, eight foreign terror suspects were held in Belmarsh and Woodhill Prisons, two in Broadmoor, and one under house arrest.

4. An advocate of the use of total restraint chairs and boards to immobilize scores of dangerous or mentally ill inmates, McCotter resigned from his Utah position in 1997 after a mentally ill prisoner died after spending sixteen hours nude in a restraint chair. In 2001, the Department of Justice opened an investigation into civil rights abuses at Management & Training Corporation, McCotter's current employer (Burton 2004).

WORKS CITED

Allen, Kate. 2004. Guantánamo Bay: Two years too many. *The Guardian*, January 11.

Amnesty International. 2005. *Guantánamo and beyond: The continuing pursuit of unchecked executive power*. New York: Amnesty International.

Baxter, Sarah. 2005. Deadlier face of torture emerges, 10-year sentence for Abu Ghraib guard. *The Sunday Times*, January 16.

Becker, Jo. 1999a. State prisons open door of X wing to the media. *St. Petersburg Times*, August 19.

———. 1999b. Guard: Bosses backed abuse. *St. Petersburg Times*, December 30.

Becker, Jo, and Sydney P. Freedberg. 1999a. Full investigations of inmate abuse reports are rare. *St. Petersburg Times*, August 7.

———. 1999b. A second place for troublemakers. *St. Petersburg Times*, August 7.

Becker, Jo, Adam C. Smith, and Sydney P. Freedberg. 1999. Crimes often don't cost guards their jobs. *St. Petersburg Times*, August 29.

Boedy, Matt. 2000. Fearful guards describe beating. *St. Petersburg Times*, February 18, 1B.

Borger, Julian. 2002. In a sniper's sights: Life in Camp X-Ray. *The Guardian*, January 25.

Buncombe, Andrew. 2005. U.S. soldier found guilty of abusing prisoners at Abu Ghraib. *The Independent*, January 15.

Burton, Greg. 2004. Utahans who rebuilt prison are in hot seat. *Salt Lake Tribune*, May 16.

Campbell, Duncan. 2002. Hunger strike at Camp X-Ray. *The Guardian*, March 1.

Davis, Angela Y. 2003. *Are prisons obsolete?* New York: Seven Stories Press.

Dodd, Vikram, and Michael White. 2004. No rights, no charges, no lawyers . . . life in the Cuban camp beyond the law. *The Guardian*, February 20.

Dyer, Clare. 2003. Law lord castigates U.S. justice. *The Guardian*, November 26.

Editorial. 2005. There can be no ambivalence over the torture and abuse of prisoners. *The Independent*, January 15.

Eisenstein, Zillah. 2004. Sexual humiliation, gender confusion, and the horrors at Abu Ghraib. Located at: http://www.selvesandothers.org/view1034.html.

Emsley, Clive. 1996. *Crime and society in England, 1750–1900*, 2nd edition. London: Longman.

Engel, Matthew. 2002. Amnesty sends U.S. dossier of complaints over Afghanistan detainees. *The Guardian*, April 15.

Harris, Paul, and Burhan Wazir. 2002. Distant voices tell of life for Britons caged in Camp Delta. *The Guardian*, November 3.

Herbert, Bob. 2004. America's Abu Ghraibs. *New York Times*, May 31.

Human Rights Watch 1997. *Cold storage: Supermaximum security confinement in Indiana.* Available at: http://www.hrw.org/reports/1997/usind/.

———. 2000. *Out of sight: Supermaximum security confinement in the United States.* Vol. 12, 1. February. Available at: http://www.hrw.org/reports/2000/super-max/.

———. 2004. *Guantánamo: Detainee accounts.* October. Available at: http://hrw.org/backgrounder/usa/gitm01004/.

———. 2005. *Guantánamo: Three years of lawlessness.* January 11. Available at: http://hrw.org/english/docs/2005/01/11/usdom9990_txt.htm.

Johnston, James A. 1949. *Alcatraz Island prison, and the men who live there.* New York: Charles Scribner's Sons.

King, Roy D. 1999. The rise and rise of super-max: An American solution in search of a problem? *Punishment and Society* 1: 163–186.

Krupers, Terry A. 2001. Men's health in men's prisons. In *Prison masculinities*, ed. Don Sabo, Terry A. Krupers, and Willie London. Philadelphia, PA: Temple University Press.

Lewis, Neil. 2004. Military tribunal begins for terror suspects. *New York Times*, August 24.

Liebling, Alison. 2002. A "liberal regime within a secure perimeter"?: Dispersal prisons and penal practice in the late twentieth century. In *Ideology, crime, and criminal justice: A symposium in honour of Sir Leon Radzinowicz*, ed. Anthony Bottoms and Michael Tonry. Cohampton, UK: Willan Publishing.

Man, Christopher D., and John P. Cronan. 2001. Forecasting sexual abuse in prison: The prison subculture of masculinity as a backdrop for "deliberate indifference," *Journal of Criminal Law and Criminology* 92: 127–185.

Mauer, Marc. 1999. *Race to incarcerate*, New York: The New Press.

———. 2001. The causes and consequences of prison growth in the United States. *Punishment and Society* 3, 1: 9–20.

McGowan, Randall. 1998. The well-ordered prison: England, 1780–1865. In *The Oxford history of the prison: The practice of punishment in Western society*, ed. Norval Morris and David J. Rothman. Oxford: Oxford University Press.

Miller, Jerome G. 1997. *Search and destroy: African American males in the criminal justice system*. Cambridge: Cambridge University Press.

Mubanga, Martin, and David Rose. 2005. How I entered the hellish world of Guantánamo Bay. *The Observer*, February 6.

Oppel, Shelby. 2000. Auditors hammer prison system. *St. Petersburg Times*, December 22.

Pratt, John. 1998. Towards the "decivilizing" of punishment? *Social and Legal Studies* 7: 487–515.

Ripley, Amanda. 2004. The rules of interrogation: It's a military business, but some methods work better than others. *Time*, May 17.

Rose, David. 2004. *Guantánamo: America's war on human rights*. London: Faber and Faber.

———. 2006. Scandal of force-fed prisoners. *The Observer*, January 8.

Sabo, Don, Terry A. Krupers, and Willie London. 2001. Gender and the politics of punishment. In *Prison masculinities*. Ed. Don Sabo, Terry A. Krupers, and Willie London. Philadelphia, PA: Temple University Press.

Sanchez, Ricardo S. 2003. *CJTF-7 interrogation and counter-resistance policy*. Available at: http://www.aclu.org/SafeandFree/SafeandFree.cfm?ID=17851&c=206#FileAtach.

Smith, Adam C. 1999. Life in lockdown. *St. Petersburg Times*, December 5.

———. 2001. Guards charge racism, retaliation. *St. Petersburg Times*, April 18.

———. 2002. Critics say prison abuse now comes in a spray can. *St. Petersburg Times*, February 17.

Smith, Adam C., and Jo Becker. 1999. Autopsy shows inmate died from beating. *St. Petersburg Times*, July 29.

Smith, Adam C., and Lucy Morgan. 1999. Inmate's death leads to one arrest. *St. Petersburg Times*, November 4.

Stafford-Smith, Clive. 2002. No justice in Guantánamo Bay. *The Observer*, December 1.

Tarrant, Shira. 2004. Who's accountable for the abuse at Abu Ghraib? *Off Our Backs*, September–October.

Tobin, Thomas C. 2002. Jurors walk in doomed inmate's footsteps. *St. Petersburg Times*, January 26.

Verkaik, Robert, and Colin Brown. 2004. Belmarsh: A new affront to justice. *The Independent*, December 18.

Wacquant, Loic. 2001. Deadly symbiosis: When ghetto and prison meet and mesh. *Punishment and Society* 3: 95–134.

Ward, David A., and Thomas G. Werlich. 2003. Alcatraz and Marion: Evaluating supermaximum custody. *Punishment and Society* 5, 1: 53–75.

Watson, Roland. 2005. Laughing torturer of Abu Ghraib. *The Times*, January 12.

Webster, Philip, and Richard Ford. 2005. Terrorist suspects to be kept under house arrest as state powers grow. *The Times*, January 27.

Weinstein, Corey, and Eric Cummins. 1996. The crime of punishment: Pelican Bay maximum security prison. In *Criminal injustice: Confronting the prison crisis*, ed. Elihu Rosenblatt. Boston, MA: South End Press.

Humanizing Difference

TOWARD A NEW PENALITY

Jeanne Flavin and Mary Bosworth

If it takes a gulag to maintain a winner-takes-all society,
then it is society that must be changed rather than the
prison expanded.

—Jock Young, *The Exclusive Society* (1999)

AS THE CHAPTERS in this collection have shown, various
notions of race and gender have been written into practices and ideas of punishment. Dehumanizing processes that previously legitimated slavery, colonialism, and racist immigration legislation today justify a penal system that targets certain communities and individuals more harshly than others. It is not just crime control strategies that are marked by deeply racialized and sexist assumptions, however, but also strategies pertaining to welfare, immigration, and reproductive rights. Incarceration has a profound impact on entire communities, on the struggle for decent wages and working conditions, and on access to healthcare, education, and housing. Strategies of punishment such as sentencing and incarceration are both upheld by and themselves reinforce these diffuse relations of social control. In such a way, racial, ethnic, and gender differences come to be regulated.

If prejudice and inequality are inscribed in the nation's culture, history, and way of thinking, what is to be done? Is there any hope for change, or are we left with an irredeemable system? Where should reform begin? Although we cannot hope to answer all of the questions that the essays in this collection have raised, in this conclusion we aim to map some steps forward. In the process, we suggest a number of ways to address the entrenched problems of racism and sexism in the U.S. system of punishment.

Toward a Politics of Recognition

If we are to make any meaningful change to such an inequitable system, we must start by documenting our shared values and attributes. We have a tendency, for instance, to treat persons convicted of crimes as individuals separate and distinct from their families and friends, rather than as participants in a social network where—even in the most damaged families and neighborhoods—people help each other out (Maruna 2001; Petersilia 2003; Flavin and Rosenthal 2003). This approach has led to gaps in our scholarship and policies that exacerbate the problem (Flavin 2004). Within families, for example, women act as advisors, advocates, mediators, and financial managers; yet most discussions of the impact of incarceration on women (both within and without prisons) focus on mothers' ties to young children or women's relationships with husbands or boyfriends, rather than recognizing the range of roles women occupy in family and society. As a result, few services are available to support women in their attempts to "hold down the home front" while they cope with a family member's involvement in the criminal justice system.

We must also identify less dehumanizing and debilitating responses to crime. Some practices, already common in Scandinavia, such as lowering the mortality rate among people who inject drugs by providing them with clean injection equipment, and distributing naloxonoe to heroin users for peer administration in the case of overdose face significant public resistance in the United States yet are worth pursuing. Others require virtually no effort at all, such as discouraging the use of pejorative terms like "convicts," "inmates," "crack babies," and "addicts."[1] One obvious place to start is by abolishing the death penalty, a brutalizing practice that sends a message that some lives are more valuable than others. Racial inequalities in capital sentencing are legion, with those convicted of killing whites far more likely than others to be sentenced to death. The death penalty also contributes to a culture of punishment that distinguishes the United States and helps legitimate a broader policy of mass imprisonment (Bedau 1998; Banner 2002; Zimring 2003).

We should try to make our current penal institutions more humane, while also revisiting the penalties inflicted on people after they have served their sentence.[2] Evidence suggests that improvements can be made through enabling prisoners to practice self-governance. For example, the women incarcerated at Bedford Hills Correctional Facility in New York State have been instrumental in implementing a nationally recognized program that permits women who give birth while in prison to keep their infants with them for up to a year. They have also participated in a long-term study of the impact of college programs both within prison and after release (Fine et al. 2002). Prisoners' meaningful participation in the development and implementation of programming can ensure that programs are culturally competent and more responsive to their needs. It also provides a means of recognizing prisoners' value to society, which, in turn, challenges the legitimacy of the harsh treatment many face upon release. When we deny people convicted of felonies a chance at receiving financial aid to attend college, threaten to evict people from public housing should a friend or family member convicted for a drug offense visit them, strip away felons' voting rights, fail to enforce legislation prohibiting discrimination against people convicted of crimes, bar people with criminal records from working in occupations that have no connections to their crimes, we create a climate where the person's debt to society is never paid (Mauer and Chesney-Lind 2002). We are, in effect, permanently disenfranchising an entire class of people and jeopardizing their survival (Christie 2004).

It is not just criminal justice policy that needs addressing, but also criminology and the administration of the criminal justice system. At minimum, we need to include more women and minority men as scholars, administrators, policymakers, and legislators. On a superficial level, "descriptive" representation of women and minority men helps to ensure that the system appears to reflect the will of "we, the people." Even more important than symbolic reasons, however, are the substantive ones. We need to bring more diverse experiences and insights to our understanding of justice and punishment. Admittedly, as we have learned from the abuses of power and human rights violations at Abu Ghraib, Guantánamo Bay, and in prisons across the United States, the presence of women and minority men in and of itself does not guarantee that human rights will be respected. But as it is, when an entire field or occupation has privileged white male nativist norms, we must seriously question whether the issues deemed fundamental to our understanding of punishment include those important for people who are not white, male, or born in the United States. We need to overcome our biases and imagine new ways of viewing race and punishment. This is a task for everyone.

Researchers and advocates need to seek out more firsthand accounts from those we punish, as well as from their families, friends, neighbors, and communities. Narrative, especially when placed in social and historical contexts, not only adds texture and detail, but also is a particularly effective way of reminding us of the bonds we share. Such an approach may assist those behind bars, by providing an outlet for their voices and a practical recognition of their existence (Bosworth et al. 2005; Santos 2003; Ross and Richards 2003).

Criminologists should not be afraid to speak out. For too long, the discipline has been compromised by its practical and financial association with the criminal justice system (Hillyard et al. 2004). Now is the time for public intellectuals to share their knowledge and research with the public (Jacobson 2005).

Finally, we should make and evaluate our social policies (including those related to justice and punishment) on the basis of how they will impact the most vulnerable and powerless members of our society.[3] Taken to its natural conclusion, such a shift would replace responses to crime that are based on the assumption that offenders are solely a "burden" or "drain" on society with approaches that would provide opportunities to advance offenders' (and thus society's) moral, cultural, and economic growth. In this pursuit, we must forge a joint politics of recognition and redistribution (Fraser and Honneth 2003). As criminologist Jock Young observes (1999, 59), "the late modern world celebrates diversity and *difference*, which it readily absorbs and sanitizes; what it cannot abide is difficult people and *dangerous* classes, which it seeks to build the most elaborate defenses against." Ideas of dangerousness, as this collection has demonstrated, depend on notions of race and gender. They are also driven by economics. Those who society fears the most, and thus who are the most vulnerable, are, and always have been, the poor. Reforming aspects of the labor market would, in other words, reduce the prison population by providing greater numbers of people with legitimate economic options in their communities (Beckett and Western 1999; Parenti 1999).

TRANSCENDING BORDERS

A profound lack of imagination defines the U.S. system of punishment. Much can be learned by considering other countries' responses to crime and injustice, particularly those that recognize that incarceration should be a punishment of last resort rather than the default response it often is today. Elsewhere, in Europe, Japan, and Australia, for example, there is greater reliance on noncustodial sanctions such as community service, electronic monitoring, day fines, and mediation. Average prison sentences are also considerably shorter.

Some jurisdictions, like Canada, have tried to tackle the race and gender inequalities within their women's prison system. Although the impact of policy changes has been mixed (Hannah-Moffat 1995; Shaw 1996), the involvement of feminist and indigenous groups in designing programming and institutions suggests that there is at least some room for progressive intervention in the day-to-day management of penal institutions.

In Europe, most countries pursue harm-reduction policies, rather than punishment, in their fight against drugs. Providing people addicted to drugs with treatment on demand and medical information when they are ready to quit is not only cheaper and more humane than incarcerating them, but it may be a more effective response to the problem of substance use. Consider, too, that at least two dozen countries and territories (including Australia, Canada, England, and France, as well as Iran, Indonesia, Kyrgystan, and Macedonia) have methadone programs in prisons (Catania 2005; EMCDDA 2000; Gerlach 2002). Germany, Kyrgystan, Spain, and Switzerland also offer needle exchange programs. Meanwhile, in the United States, only a handful of jails (and no prisons) make methadone available.

Restorative justice is another way of addressing crime that is being successfully pursued in a variety of countries, including Australia, New Zealand, and

Canada (Daly 2003). Approaches based on restorative justice seek to repair the harm crime causes to individuals, communities, and relationships, and to hold offenders accountable for the harms they have caused. According to Kathleen Daly, one of the key proponents of this approach, restorative justice and mediation may be particularly useful for highly gendered crimes like sexual assault (Daly 2002). Unlike traditional courtroom settings, mediation conferencing minimizes further trauma to the victim, while holding the offender accountable. Such a response to crime has also been successful with indigenous communities.

Finally, truth and reconciliation commissions offer another way of holding individuals (including officials) accountable, to resolve historical injustices, and to heal communities marred by racial discord. They have been used with varying degrees of success around the world, most notably in South Africa, Bosnia, and South America (Avruch and Vejarano 2001). The first such commission was sworn in the United States in May 2004 in Greensboro, North Carolina. The city of Greensboro had paid a civil judgment to settle the 1979 incident in which members of the Ku Klux Klan and the American Nazi Party publicly killed five people and wounded ten others who had gathered for a march for racial and social justice. Members of the Ku Klux Klan, Nazis, and the Greensboro Police Department also were found jointly liable in one of the deaths. The city had never apologized or publicly acknowledged any wrongdoing, which led to lingering distrust and anger. Although it is too soon to tell how effective community reconciliation commissions will be in the United States, they may offer a mechanism for calling attention to past wrongs while providing a way to move forward.

Approaching punishment in a comparative and international manner has many implications for criminology and its cognate disciplines. It can propel scholars across not only national boundaries, but disciplinary ones as well, to appreciate for instance the contributions of public health to our understanding not only of substance abuse, but also of woman battering, gun violence, and youth violence. The comparative approach also requires a conceptual and historical appreciation of punishment, as each nation's penal problems emerge from its history and culture. Although everywhere prisons are characterized by an overrepresentation of minorities, for example, who those minority communities are, the crimes for which they are punished, and the ways they are treated varies. Looking across borders sheds light both on U.S. particularism and on its shared problems.

CONCLUSION

At the time of this writing, the United States is engaged in a "war on terror" in Iraq and Afghanistan that has raised deeply troubling questions about the future of penal policies here and elsewhere. Practices that have become commonplace, including the detention of hundreds of people without charge, the lack of legal representation and fairness in judicial proceedings, brutal and inhumane conditions of confinement, and the abuse of detainees, compromise us all. Political leaders in the highest positions have been found to lie about the presence of weapons of mass destruction, and have engaged in cover-ups. The racial profiling of the Muslim community that began after 9/11 continues. An entire generation of young men and women continues to be cast under suspicion. Civil liberties and respect for human rights are under siege (Benhabib 2004). These large-scale abuses of power call to mind historic wrongs such as slavery, the Trail of Tears and other Indian removal campaigns, the internment of Japanese and Japanese-Americans during World War II, and involuntary sterilization programs.

At the same time, on a domestic level, some legislators and their constituencies across the United States have started to challenge some of the harshest punitive policies, particularly those associated with the war on drugs. While historically there has been a lack of public support for anything that does not purport to "get tough" on crime, the situation is changing. Declining crime rates have lessened public concern over street violence, and people have begun to articulate greater interest in issues such as education, the economy, and health care (Tonry 2004, Jacobson 2005). In response to the high costs of maintaining the criminal justice system, legislators have been prompted to reexamine some of the most stringent laws, such as those imposing mandatory minimum sentences and forbidding early parole. There is vocal, and increasingly effective, criticism in New York State, for example, of the mandatory minimum drug laws known as the Rockefeller Laws. In 2000 California made drug treatment, rather than prison, mandatory for first- and second-time drug offenders. Communities in Oregon and California once again have called for a consideration of legalizing medical marijuana.

These developments may signal the beginning of a reversal in a decades-long trend toward more punitive anti-crime measures (Jacobson 2005). The challenge remains, however, as how best to ensure progressive public sentiments are reflected in legislation and policy, particularly in an era when many of our political leaders are not concerned about the public holding them accountable for their actions, and where there is an apparent willingness to demonize entire groups of people, including immigrants, people who use drugs, women on welfare, and those charged with or convicted of a crime. As at other times, none of these policies would be possible without some collusion from the broader society (Bauman, 1989). For as long as they continue, we are all fellow travelers down this path of injustice. As this conclusion has argued, there are many alternative routes we could tread. The question then remains, solely, which one shall each of us take?

NOTES

1. For example, the term "addict" is often used broadly (and incorrectly) to refer to anyone who uses drugs, regardless of whether or not dependent on them.

2. Although there are undoubtedly pitfalls in tinkering with the criminal justice system as we risk merely making it more palatable through cosmetic changes, the level of misery that many people endure behind bars require scholars, activists and practitioners to work together for pragmatic solutions while always also trying to change the reliance of the US on incarceration in general (Davis 2003; Jacobson 2005).

3. The idea of a "preferential option for the poor" has been articulated by the United States Catholic Bishops, for instance in their statement, "The quality of the national discussion about our economic future will affect the poor most of all, in this country and throughout the world. The life and dignity of millions of men, women, and children hang in the balance. Decisions must be judged in light of what they do for the poor, what they do to the poor, and what they enable the poor to do for themselves. The fundamental moral criterion for all economic decisions, policies, and institutions is this: They must be at the service of all people, especially the poor" (U.S. Catholic Bishops 1986, 24).

Works Cited

Avruch, Kevin, and Beatriz Vejarano. 2001. Truth and reconciliation commissions: A review essay and annotated bibliography. *Social Justice* 2, 1–2: 47–108.

Banner, Stuart. 2002. *The death penalty, an American history*. Cambridge, MA: Harvard University Press.

Bauman, Zygmunt. 1989. *Modernity and the Holocaust*. Cambridge: Polity Press.

Beckett, Katherine, and Bruce Western. 1999. How unregulated is the U.S. labor market? The penal system as a labor market institution. *American Journal of Sociology* 104: 1030–1060.

Bedau, Hugo. 1998. *The death penalty in America*. New York: Oxford University Press.

Benhabib, Seyla. 2004. The rights of others : Aliens, residents, and citizens (The Seeley Lectures). Cambridge: Cambridge University Press.

Bosworth, Mary, Debi Campbell, Bonita Demby, Seth Ferranti, and Michael Santos. 2005. Doing prison research. *Qualitative Inquiry* 11: 249–264.

Catania, Holly. 2005. Project director, International Center for Advancement of Addiction Treatment, Baron Edmond de Rothschild Chemical Dependency Institute of Beth Israel Center. Personal email communication, June 24, 2005.

Christie, Nils. 2004. *A suitable amount of crime*. New York: Routledge.

Daly, Kathleen. 2002. Sexual assault and restorative justice. In Heather Strang and John Braithwaite, eds., *Restorative justice and family violence*, 62–88. Cambridge: Cambridge University Press.

———. 2003. Mind the gap: Restorative justice in theory and practice. In Andrew von Hirsch, Julian Roberts, Anthony E. Bottoms, Kent Roach, and Mara Schiff, eds., *Restorative justice and criminal justice: Competing or reconcilable paradigms?* 219–236. Oxford: Hart Publishing.

Davis, Angela. 2003. *Are prisons obsolete?* New York: Open Media Series.

European Monitoring Centre for Drugs and Drug Addiction (EMCDDA). 2000. *Reviewing current practice in drug-substitution treatment in the European Union*. Lisbon, Portugal: EMCDDA.

Fine, Michelle, et al. 2002. Changing minds: The impact of college on a maximum secure prison. The Graduate Center of the City University of New York and Women in Prison at Bedford Hills Correctional Facility.

Flavin, Jeanne. 2004. Giving family members their due. *TPCI Review*, March. Cambridge, MA: National Institute of Corrections.

Flavin, Jeanne, and David Rosenthal. 2003. La Bodega de la Familia: Supporting parolees' reintegration within a family context. *Fordham Urban Law Journal* 30, 5: 1603–1620.

Fraser, Nancy, and Axel Honneth. 2003. *Redistribution or recognition? A political-philosophical exchange*. London: Verso.

Gerlach, Ralf. 2002. Drug-substitution treatment in Germany: A critical overview of its history, legislation, and current practice. *Journal of Drug Issues*.

Hannah-Moffat, Kelly. 1995. Feminine fortresses: women-centered prisons? *Prison Journal* 75, 2: 135–164.

Hillyard, Paddy, Joe Sim, Steve Tombs, and Dave Whyte. 2004. Leaving a "stain upon the silence": Contemporary criminology and the politics of dissent. *British Journal of Criminology* 44, 3: 369–390

Jacobson, Michael. 2005. *Downsizing prisons: How to reduce crime and end mass incarceration*. New York: New York University Press.

Maruna, Shadd. 2001. *Making good: How ex-convicts reform and rebuild their lives*. Washington, DC: American Psychological Association.

Mauer, Marc, and Meda Chesney-Lind, eds. 2002. *Invisible punishment: The collateral consequences of mass imprisonment*. New York: The Free Press.

Parenti, Christian. 1999. *Lockdown American: Police and prisons in an age of crisis*. New York: Verso.

Petersilia, Joan. 2003. *When prisoners come home*. New York: Oxford University Press.

Ross, Jeffrey Ian, and Stephen C. Richards, eds. 2003. *Convict criminology*. Belmont, CA: Wadsworth Publishing.

Santos, Michael. 2003. *About prison*. Belmont, CA: Wadsworth Publishing.

Shaw, Margaret. 1996. Is there a feminist future for women's prisons? In Roger Matthews and Peter Francis, eds., *Prisons 2000: An international perspective on the current state and future of imprisonment*. London: Macmillan.

Tonry, Michael. 2004. *Thinking about crime: Sense and sensibility in American penal culture*. New York: Oxford University Press.

United States Catholic Bishops (USCB). 1986. Economic justice for all: Catholic social teaching and the U.S. economy. Washington, DC: USCB.

Young, Jock. 1999. *The exclusive society*. London: Sage.

Zimring, Franklin E. 2003. *The contradictions of American capital punishment*. New York: Oxford University Press.

Notes on Contributors

CYNDI BANKS is associate professor in the Department of Criminal Justice at Northern Arizona University. She has published five books and numerous articles and chapters in the areas of cultural criminology, indigenous imprisonment, criminal justice ethics, gender and incarceration, gender and work in the criminal justice system in developing countries, and punishment in the United States. She has extensive experience working in juvenile justice, child rights, and alternative sentencing in Papua New Guinea and Bangladesh, and is currently on sabbatical in Iraq working on justice integration and human rights issues.

MARK BEEMAN is professor of sociology at Northern Arizona University. His research interests include race and ethnic relations, macrosociology, development, and comparative sociology. He has written on affirmative action, stereotyping, structural adjustments, and the media.

MARY BOSWORTH is University Lecturer in Criminology and Fellow of St. Cross College at the University of Oxford. She has published widely on imprisonment, with a particular focus on gender. She is currently working on a comparative study of immigration detention in the United Kingdom and the United States. Her new book, *Explaining U.S. Imprisonment*, is due out in 2007.

KITTY CALAVITA is professor of criminology, law, and society at the University of California, Irvine. Her research interests include migration and law, citizenship, race and racism, and legal decision making. Her most recent book is *Immigrants at the Margins: Law, Race, and Exclusion in Southern Europe* (Cambridge University Press, 2005).

GEETA CHOWDHRY is the director of ethnic studies and professor of political science at Northern Arizona University (NAU). She is the coeditor of *Power, Postcolonialism, and International Relations: Reading Race, Gender, and Class* (Routledge, 2002). Her most recent articles include: "Child Labor in a Postcolonial World," in Geoffrey Underhill and Richard Stubbs, eds., *Political*

Economy and the Changing Global Order (Oxford, 2005); and, with Mark Beeman and Karmen Todd, "Educating Students about Affirmative Action: An Analysis of Sociology Texts," in Barbara Scott, Joya Misra, and Marcia Segal, eds., *Race, Gender, and Class in Sociology: Towards an Inclusive Curriculum* (ASA 2003).

JUANITA DÍAZ-COTTO is associate professor of sociology, women's studies, and Latin American and Caribbean studies at the State University of New York at Binghamton. She is the author of *Gender, Ethnicity, and the State: Latina and Latino Prison Politics* (1996) and of *Chicana Lives and Criminal Justice: Voices from El Barrio* (2006). She is also editor (under the pseudonym Juanita Ramos) of *Compañeras: Latina Lesbians (An Anthology)*, 3rd ed. (Lesbianas Latinoamericas, 2004). Her website is www.juanitadiazcotto.com.

JEANNE FLAVIN is associate professor of sociology at Fordham University. She is coauthor of the book *Class, Race, Gender, and Crime: Social Realities of Justice in America* (Rowmand & Littlefield, 2006). Her publications reflect her interest in promoting more humane responses to people (including pregnant women) who use drugs and people infected with HIV. Presently, she is writing a book for New York University Press about the criminal justice system's regulation of women's reproductive rights.

JAMES W. MESSERSCHMIDT is professor of sociology in the criminology department at the University of Southern Maine. He is the author of numerous articles, chapters, and books on gender and crime, including *Capitalism, Patriarchy, and Crime, Masculinities and Crime, Crime as Structured Action, Nine Lives,* and most recently, *Flesh and Blood* (Lowman and Littlefield, 2004). Currently, he is working on three research projects involving: the sex-gender distinction and criminological theory; the gendered body and interpersonal violence; and global masculinities, political crimes, and the state.

VIVIEN MILLER is principal lecturer in American studies and history at Middlesex University, North London. She is the author of *Crime, Sexual Violence, and Clemency: Florida's Pardon Board and Penal System in the Progressive Era* (University Press of Florida, 2000) and of several articles including "'The Last Vestige of Institutionalized Sexism'? Paternalism, Equal Rights, and the Death Penalty in Twentieth- and Twenty-First-Century Sunbelt America: The Case for Florida," which appeared in the *Journal of American Studies* (2004).

LISA E. SANCHEZ is assistant professor in the department of ethnic studies at the University of California, San Diego. Her research interests include transnational and global studies, gender, race, ethnicity and the law, sexuality and culture. She is currently completing a book manuscript on women's negotiation of the sex trade in Oregon.

Leslie Smith graduated from Fordham University, earning a masters degree in sociology. She previously worked in human rights advocacy in the United States and the former Yugoslavia. She currently resides in the Bronx.

Zoe Spencer received her PhD in sociology from Howard University in May 2005. Her areas of specialization are race, class, and gender inequality and urban sociology, with an emphasis on African American women. She is currently on faculty in the department of social and behavioral sciences at Cheyney University of Pennsylvania.

Martin G. Urbina is associate professor of criminal justice at the University of Wisconsin–Milwaukee. Dr. Urbina's research interests include Latinos and Latinas and the U.S. legal system, juvenile delinquency and the juvenile justice system, capital punishment, women in prison, and law and society. His recent publications have examined the nature and motive of punishment. Professor Urbina was awarded a Certificate of Recognition for Outstanding Teaching in 1999.

Michael Welch is professor in the criminal justice program at Rutgers University, New Brunswick, N. J. He is author of several books including *Scapegoats of September 11th: Hate Crimes and State Crimes in the War on Terror* (Rutgers University Press, 2006), *Ironies of Imprisonment* (Sage, 2005), and *Detained: Immigration Laws and the Expanding I.N.S. Jail Complex* (Temple University Press, 2002). Welch is a visiting fellow at the Centre for the Study of Human Rights, London School of Economics. He invites you to visit his website: www.professormichaelwelch.com.

Vernetta D. Young is associate professor of administration of justice in the department of sociology and anthropology at Howard University. Dr. Young has taught at American University and at the University of Maryland at College Park. She completed her PhD in criminal justice at the State University of New York at Albany. She is coeditor of *African American Classics in Criminology and Criminal Justice* (Sage, 2001) and coauthor of *Women behind Bars: Gender and Race in U.S. Prisons* (Lynne Reiner, 2005). Her areas of research interest include race, gender, and crime; the history of juvenile justice; and victimization.

INDEX

abortion, 95, 101–103, 111n5
Abu Ghraib prison, 176, 178, 200, 211, 218
adoption, 106–107
adultery, 67–69, 72, 74, 92n4
Afghanistan, 176–179, 201, 207, 210
Africans, African, Americans, 49, 51, 54, 66, 77, 101, 105, 121, 173, 175, 179, 186, 202, 204, 212, in colonial period 13, 15, 20–27, 66; in Reconstruction 77–94
Agamben, Giorgio, 167, 169
agency, 8, 24, 92n8, 98
Alaska, 32–48
American Civil Liberties Union (ACLU), 101, 143, 144, 160
Amnesty International, 55, 159, 207, 209–210
Antebellum period, 18–24, 65–76
Arabs, Arab, Americans, 145, 150, 157, 158, 160, 179, 180, 182, 221
Asians, Asian, Americans, 118, 121–122, 125, 127–128, 130, 140, 179
assimilation, 6, 37–38, 40, 42, 45, 57, 121, 123, 125
asylum, asylum, seekers, 135, 141–143

Bhabha, Homi, 135, 144
Black codes, 25, 28, 73, 92n9, 168
Bolivia, 189–193
border control, 50, 52, 54–56, 126, 136, 151. *See also* borders
borders, 126, 136–138. *See also* border control
Bracero Program, 118, 125–127

California, 51, 52, 54, 55, 127, 128, 138, 142, 145, 157, 171, 175, 181, 185, 186, 201, 202, 221
capitalism, 7–9, 14–15, 16–17, 40, 118–119, 170
castration, 21, 24, 84, 85, 86–91
Cesaire, Aimé, 18
children, 23, 25, 27, 32, 35, 36, 39–40, 42, 95–111, 118, 128, 142, 187–188, 189, 191, 192, 194. *See also* family
child welfare system, 105–109
Chinese Exclusion Law, 1882–118, 121, 122, 128
citizens, citizenship, 22, 32, 51, 52, 55–57, 81–83, 126–129, 134–135, 138, 140, 143, 152, 169, 170, 180, 181, 187
Civil War, 25, 26, 28, 65, 68, 121, 129
Class, 13, 19, 28n4, 41, 43, 58n3, 58n5, 66–67, 72, 74, 78–79, 99, 100–101, 110, 119
Colombia, 54, 58n2, 193
colonial law, 18, 21–24, 27–28, 66, 80
Colonialism, 2–4, 13, theories of, 14–16, 43–44, 50; examples of, 17, 32–48, 49–61, 65, 66
contraception, 100–101, 102–103, 110, 192
convict leasing, 26–28, 73
Constitution, 24–25, 28, 81, 82, 101, 103, 129, 143–144
corporal punishment, 22–23, 27, 70–72, 153, 154, 158, 201
crime, 21–24, 25–27, 41–42, 45–46n5, 66–69, 73–74, 80–81, 141, 152, 170–171, 185; fear of, 57–58, 124–125, 151, 160, 168, 170–176, 212